Pipe Dream Blues

Racism and the War on

Drugs

by Clarence Lusane

with a contribution by Dennis Desmond

SOUTH END PRESS BOSTON, MA

Any properly footnoted quotation of up to 500 sequential words may be used without permission so long as the total number of words quoted does not exceed 2,000. For longer quotations or for a greater number of total words, authors should write to South End Press for permission.

Design and layout by the South End Press collective
Cover by Cheryl Hanna
Printed in the U.S.A.

Library of Congress Cataloging-in-Publication Data

Lusane, Clarence, 1953-
  Pipe dream blues : racism and the war on drugs / Clarence Lusane
with contributed chapters by Dennis Desmond.

    p. cm.
  Includes bibliographical references and index.
  ISBN 0-89608-411-6 : $30.00. – ISBN 0-89608-410-8 (pbk.)
  1. Narcotics, Control of–United States. 2. Discrimination in criminal
justice administration–United States. 3. United States–Race relations.
I. Desmond, Dennis, 1952-   . II. Title.
HV5825.L88 1990   90-27575
363.4'5'0973–dc20   CIP

South End Press / 116 Saint Botolph Street / Boston, MA 02115

99 98 97 96 95 94 93 92   3 4 5 6 7 8 9

To Karen whose support and criticism are the wings on which I fly; and to Dooney Wilson, whom I've never met, but whose life and struggle must be significant to us all.

Clarence Lusane

To family and friends; and all those striving to overcome their chemical dependency in the search for a more productive life.

Dennis Desmond

Acknowledgments

No book is an island. Many hands and minds contributed to the development and completion of this book. First, it is important to acknowledge the people who can't be acknowledged by name. The nature of this study meant discussions and interviews with individuals, including law enforcement officials, drug traffickers, drug users, journalists, and government employees, who, for a variety of reasons, want to and should remain anonymous. For most of these individuals, they took a great deal of personal and career risks to provide us invaluable information. This book would not have been possible without their aid.

Special thanks to those who read and commented on various versions of the manuscript. This includes Karen Bass, Chris Booker, Carol Page, and Margaret Summers. Their feedback and criticisms were priceless in shaping and writing the book. A thousand thanks!

Also, special thanks to those who not only took the time to share their views and experiences, but furnished important information and materials, much of it confidential or difficult to locate. This includes Abu el-Zarabi; Peter Andreas, the Institute of Policy Studies; Dana Austin, Director of Environment, Community Development and Race Program, the Panos Institute; Marcellus Boston, Senior Counselor, the Washington Area Council on Alcoholism and Drug Abuse (WACADA); Peter Brewton, Reporter, *Houston Post;* Richard Broughton, Northern Virginia Crack Task Force, Metropolitan Washington Region, Drug Enforcement Agency; Josephine Butler; Acie Byrd; Mary Cassal, National Outreach Director, Christic Institute; Jo Ann Kawell; Ron Clark, Executive Director, Rap, Inc.; Tom Clifford; Imani Countess, the Washington Office on Africa; the office of former Congressman George Crockett (D-MI); Judy Crockett, Legislative Representative, the Washington office of the American Civil Liberties Union; Jackie Davidson; Joe Davidson, Reporter, *Wall Street Journal;* members of the Public Safety Transition Team of Mayor Sharon Pratt Dixon of Washington; Konrad Ege, Reporter, *National Reporter;* staff of former Congressman Walter E. Fauntroy (D-DC); Daniel Fiedler, Executive Director, National Organization for the Reform of Marijuana Laws (NORML); Don Foster, News Director, *WPFW*; Catherine Hargrove, Director of the Inter-Agency Youth Project, Washington Office of Criminal Justice Plans and Analysis; Cedric Hendricks, President, Washington Correctional Foundation; Joe Hicks, Assistant Director of Communication, Los Angeles office of the ACLU; Earl Ofari Hutchinson; Maurice Jackson; Katherine McFate, the Joint Center for Political and Economic Studies; Gregory T. Moore, Executive Director, Citizenship Education Fund; Clare Mundell, Coordinator, *The Drug Bulletin*, Washington Office of Criminal Justice Plans and Analysis; Ibrahim Mummer; Gaston Neal, Alcohol and Drug Abuse Services Administration (ADASA); Gregory Porter, NORML; Jamin Raskin; Kim Rattley, American Friends Service Committee; Steve Rickman, former Director of the Statistical Analysis Center, Washington Office of Criminal Justice Plans and Analysis; Kweisi Rollins, ADASA; Sam Smith, Publisher, *The Progressive Review;* Jeanne Tapscott, AIDS Program Coordination Office, Washington, D.C., city government; Carl Taylor, Michigan State University; Leroy Thrope, Citizens Organized Patrol Efforts of Greater Washington, D.C. (COPE); Napoleon Turner, Public Health Analyst, ADASA; Joseph Wright, Executive Director, WACADA; Dr. Elsie Scott, former Executive Director, National Organization of Black Law Enforcement Executives (NOBLE); staff at the Washingtonian Room, Martin Luther King, Jr., Library, Washington, D.C.; Judge Reggie Walton, Office of National Drug Control Policy; Frank Watkins, National Rainbow Coalition.

Cheryl Hanna, a gifted and committed artist and a dear friend, conceived and designed the cover—the stunning "front door" to the book. Despite tremendous time constraints, Cheryl's artistry more than rose to the occasion.

Thanks to Leta L. Holley for her hard work and dedication in indexing the book.

Finally, South End Press must be acknowledged and thanked for their faith that this book would be completed. South End is publishing some of the best progressive books in the country and providing important avenues for courageous new voices in these changing and difficult times. The South End staff provided bountiful encouragement and critical suggestions along the way. In particular, deepest gratitude and love to Tanya McKinnon and Loie Hayes for their ever-ready support.

Table of Contents

Part III
A Different Path

Part I

Dope vs. Hope:
The Politics of Drugs

INTRODUCTION

"Pipe Dream Blues" is a blues song written in 1924 that tells the story of one woman's battle with drug addiction. The story takes places in an opium den in the Chinatown section of a city. No matter how hard she tries, she always ends up with a hot pipe filled with opium in her hand at the end of the day. Her dreams of wealth, fame, and happiness disappear daily in the opium smoke. At the end of the song, despite her addiction, she continues to hope for the best.

The dreams of thousands of African Americans are rapidly going up in smoke. The twisted curls of smoke emanating from pipes filled with crack, heroin, PCP, ice, and other deadly substances symbolize the blurred nightmares that are strangling community after community. While Blacks and other people of color in the United States comprise less than 15 percent of all drug users, the damage and havoc caused by substance abuse and by the destructive impact of the federal government's drug war is felt much more deeply in those communities. An FBI study notes the fact that while Blacks represent only 12 percent of all illegal drug users, Blacks are 41 percent of all those arrested on cocaine and heroin charges.[1]

From the jungles of Bolivia to the high plains of Laos, from the dingy and rank basements of the inner cities and rural United States to the executive suites of the largest U.S. corporations, from the White House and beyond, the drug crisis has linked tens of millions across the globe.

The national and international illegal drug crisis is both rooted in and the expression of deeply troubled economic, political, and social relations. As this crisis of race, class, and global politics unfolds, the battle against illegal drugs has taken on a character not unlike the religious crusades of medieval Europe.

The U.S. government's "war on drugs," at best, obscures all of these relationships and, at worst, perpetuates them. The potential long-term harm of the drug war is not that it won't end illegal and deadly drug

3

trafficking and abuse. The real danger is that it will mask the brutal social realities that must be addressed if suffering and destruction caused by the drug crisis is to stop.

The government, in engaging its drug war at home and abroad, has aimed its weapons overwhelmingly at people of color. Despite the fact that Whites are the majority of users and traffickers, Blacks, Latinos, and third world people are suffering the worst excesses of a program that violates civil rights, human rights, and national sovereignty.

At the same time, there is an urgent need to address the harm caused by the explosion of drug trafficking and abuse, particularly in communities of color. The drug crisis and its underlying causes are very real indeed. As the National Urban League wrote in *The State of Black America 1989,* "Substance abuse is the single major leading social, economic, and health problem confronting the African-American community."[2]

The economic and political policies of the United States, particularly during Ronald Reagan's Presidency, fettered the opportunities for advancement for millions around the world and in the United States. Reagan was determined to halt the development of progressive governments in Nicaragua and Grenada with anti-communist, pro-militarist foreign policy initiatives. His program was funded by the shift of federal dollars from sorely needed social programs to the military budget and, perhaps more disastrous, by massive, unprecedented deficit spending.

The U.S. government uses the drug war to obscure the collusion of U.S. intelligence agencies with major international trafficking networks. In the past, anti-communist foreign policy aims have served as justification for the CIA and other agencies to knowingly allow traffickers to import illegal drugs into the United States. One critical question that has been conspicuously avoided by the Bush administration and the media monopolies is: "Has the CIA escalated the drug crisis in the United States by assisting the efforts of known drug traffickers?"

The end of the Cold War has meant a shift in foreign policy rhetoric. The new international enemy of humankind has been transformed from a communist to a drug dealer/terrorist or "narco-terrorist." Although new enemy images are being created, the ends have remained the same. Opening up and protecting markets for U.S. corporations and waging low-intensity/high-death military and political campaigns against third world liberation movements continue to be the *real* reasons for U.S. intervention abroad. This is perhaps nowhere as clear as in the Persian Gulf conflict. What Iraq did to Kuwait in 1990 with tanks and guns, the United States is doing to the rest of the world with dollars, computers, and mass media (along with tanks and guns).

In this milieu of economic destruction, public corruption, ideological dogmatism, international aggression, and shameless discrimination, it's easy to see why social disintegration is escalating. Concern for values of community that only a few years ago would have prevented or limited the invasion of drugs into many Black, Latino, and poor neighborhoods has been increasingly replaced by survival-driven individualism and materialism.

Rather than initiate a desperately needed "Marshall Plan" to eliminate poverty, the Bush administration has continued to escalate the U.S. war on "drugs." Bush's declaration of war on users and dealers threatens their civil liberties and has had virtually no impact on the roots of the drug problem, either internationally or domestically. Mass waves of police actions against street sales into inner city communities have moved drug markets indoors. Drug sales and use in the suites and board rooms of America's large and small corporations have remained effectively untouched. The decline in casual use has been matched by a larger and more intractable addiction population disproportionately located in communities of color.

Linking Drugs and Racism

Our motivation for writing this book was personal and political. Like many other people we know, Dennis and I have lost (and are losing) family members and friends due to drug addiction, the violence associated with drug trafficking, or AIDS contracted through intravenous drug use. We have also seen relatives and friends go to jail and have the fabric of their lives destroyed as illegal drugs have taken over their lives. Finally, we have watched with frustration and anger as legal drugs, particularly tobacco and alcohol, have also slowly killed our loved ones.

This book is an effort to put into an historic and political context the relationship between drugs and racism. Drug trafficking and abuse has crossed all class, race, gender, and national boundaries and is a society-wide and global problem. But this is a problem with a distinct racial edge. What is cast as a "problem" in the White community is, in fact, a *crisis* in communities of color. The survival and healthy development of a whole generation of Black youth and community is at stake. A pivotal step in grasping the breadth and depth of the problem, and solutions to it, is understanding illegal and legal drugs in the African American community within a specific historic context.

Our aim, however, is to do more than just set the historic record straight. The most important goal of this book is to empower the reader with the data and analysis in order to intellectually and politically strengthen the work of those struggling to end the harm of the drug crisis in our nation and our world.

Many valuable and well-researched critiques and studies of federal anti-drug policies have been done, such as Alfred McCoy's *The Politics of Heroin in Southeast Asia* and Edward Jay Epstein's *Agency of Fear*. However, little attention has been given to the systemic racism that has historically characterized all U.S. federal anti-drug wars, including the current one. In the political atmosphere of the 1990s, where law enforcement has been given priority over prevention and treatment, there has not been much popular focus on the link between the past and current administration's social and economic policies and the escalation of the drug problem.

Although the principal focus of this book is on the role that illegal drugs play in communities of color, exposing the link between legal and illegal drug harm is also an important concern. Legal narcotics, such as alcohol, tobacco, and prescription drugs, kill many times more people and arguably reap more harm in the long run than do all the illegal drugs combined. Many legal prescription drugs are as dangerous and addictive as heroin or cocaine. These sanctioned drugs have an especially destructive effect in the African American, Latino, and Native American communities. To describe drug abuse as a health crisis in communities of color, one must certainly include these drugs.

The leadership required to move beyond the current situation has yet to emerge. Neither traditional nor "official" leadership in communities of color has demonstrated a vision or strategy capable of resolving the current crisis. While some progressives have developed a critical and important analysis in terms of the drug situation, few have roots in low-income communities of color or have organic links with community leaders and activists who are actively engaged in anti-drug work.

There is a critical need for a revitalized and clear-headed anti-racist movement that anchors a broader mass movement for social change. The long-term goals of these movements can be nothing less than the national and international redistribution of wealth from the rich to the poor and the expansion and institutionalization of political democracy. The fall of communist regimes in Eastern Europe does not invalidate socialist aims of peace, justice, and equality. Capitalism in the United States and elsewhere has yet to demonstrate that it can achieve these goals.

Washington, D.C.: A "Test Case" for Drug Policies

In elucidating the goals of the book, the District of Columbia becomes a compelling case study of the way drugs and racism are linked. Washington is important because it was selected by drug czar William Bennett as the "test case" for the administration's drug policies. The dramatic arrest and trial on drug charges of Mayor Marion Barry provides a gold mine of insights into the political complexities and contradictions facing the Black community in the present period. The lessons to be drawn from the nation's capital, given the drug epidemic and dramatic political changes, are rich and possibly prophetic. Crime, racism, AIDS, and poverty, issues confronting the Black community and other communities, are highlighted and concentrated in the political battles and drug epidemic crisis being played out in Washington, D.C.

Washington is unique in that it is severely handicapped in its efforts to abate the District's drug and violence epidemics (and the roots of those epidemics) as long as it is denied self-determination and full democratic rights for its citizens, i.e., statehood. The District's battle with Congress and the White House over statehood, in a real sense, echoes the fights of local jurisdictions and other nations for fairness, justice, and genuine democracy.

By studying the drug crisis in the District and efforts to address it by the community, city leaders, and Congress, we discovered valuable political strategies and anti-drug methods that need to be shared. Many of the progressive and useful approaches to treatment, law enforcement, and anti-drug education being carried out or proposed in the District can be duplicated in other areas. The administration's drug war has been woefully negligent in promoting and facilitating this type of national exchange.

For many in Congress, the granting of statehood to the District is partially conditioned by the perception and the reality that city leaders are doing their best to eradicate the city's drug and violence problems. In the Eighties, the drug-driven violence and the foibles of former Mayor Barry gave statehood foes handy weapons and excuses for denying District citizens self-determination, although many would not support statehood for the District no matter what.

With Barry no longer a justification for rejecting statehood and more jurisdictions acknowledging the failures of the federal drug war, the true political agendas of the District's enemies become clearer. The coming period will expose the real reason they oppose statehood for the District: as former Congressman Walter Fauntroy has said, the city is "too Black, too liberal, too urban, and too Democratic."

This book is written principally for people across the country and around the world who are attempting to answer the questions that the drug and political predicaments facing people of color and workers the world over have given rise to. We hope that the facts and analysis presented in this book provide an important step in this process. This book is also written for progressive activists and thinkers across the country who too often have been peripheral to many of the debates and struggles concerning the anti-drug campaigns. Beyond the hype and hysteria of the Reagan and Bush administrations, progressives must face the fact that there is indeed an illegal drug trafficking and drug abuse epidemic, particularly in racially and economically underprivileged and low-income communities.

Some experts, such as drug historian Dr. David Musto, have argued with some degree of accuracy that drug use has risen and fallen throughout this century and that no matter what, the current crisis will soon abate. A crucial point that is missed, however, is that long after the drug crisis story moves to the back pages, the problem will remain. Communities of color and poor communities will still suffer more harshly from these conditions unless every effort possible is made now to eradicate them.

This book developed from extensive research, dozens of interviews with experts and activists from every perspective on the drug and political issues discussed here, and the authors' own observations and participation in these processes. Critical input and recommendations from those whose daily lives are consumed in fighting to end the mayhem and damage of the drug problem has been graciously welcomed, although, of course, the authors take ultimate responsibility for the views and analysis developed herein.

The book is divided into three parts. In the first part, Chapters One through Six, the racial aspects of the national and international drug crisis are analyzed and critiqued. Provocative questions and issues thus far ignored by the administration are raised and explored in detail.

Chapter One establishes the parameters through which the drug crisis is viewed, that is, the present politics of race in the United States. Chapter Two traces the historic interplay of federal anti-drug campaigns and racism. Each period demonstrates how these campaigns have used racist tactics and ruses against African Americans, Latinos, Asian Americans, and Native Americans to advance conservative programs while failing miserably in the goal of eliminating drug trafficking or abuse. Chapter Three looks at the impact that the drug crisis is having on women and children, and, in particular, the disturbing increase in attacks on the rights of women through the vehicle of the drug war. Chapter Four focuses on the Bush administration's so-called war on drugs, the excesses of that war, and how and why the war is being lost. Chapter Five sorts through the complex and tangled maze of illegal and legal drug profits, and who really is benefiting from trade in illegal drugs and who is not. Chapter Six details the international side of the drug crisis and how U.S. foreign policy, overt and covert, has been central to its development.

Part Two provides a specific focus on the District of Columbia. The struggle to address the drug crisis in the city serves as a case study. The battle for statehood is placed within this framework and provides important background and insight into the complicated drug battles being waged in the city and against the intrusion of the administration's drug war.

Chapter Seven provides a brief look at the recent history of race and class relations in Washington, D.C., paying particular attention to the relationship between the battle for statehood and the city's drug crisis. Chapters Eight and Nine trace the historic development of drug trafficking and drug abuse in Washington. Chapter Eight looks at the development of illegal drug trafficking and abuse in the city from the beginning of World War II up to the current period. In Chapter Nine, the contemporary crisis is discussed in detail, with a focus on the economic and social roots of the problem in the city. The political economy of the drug trade in the District of Columbia is analyzed, as well as effective and progressive anti-drug programs that are being carried out by District citizens and the city's relationship to the federal anti-drug plans.

In Part Three, which consists only of Chapter Ten, a number of recommendations and suggestions that address the drug trafficking and abuse crisis in the nation and internationally are put forth. These suggestions and proposals, from national and international experts and activists, are intended to fuel a more honest and fruitful community discussion than has existed up to now. These conclusions serve as the beginning of a discussion rather than an end.

Clarence Lusane wrote Chapters 1 through 6, 8, and 10; Dennis Desmond wrote Chapters 7 and 9.

Chapter 1

BLACK TO THE FUTURE
The Continuing Dilemma of Racial Politics

Hide nothing from the masses of our people. Tell no lies. Expose lies whenever they are told. Mask no difficulties, mistakes, failures. Claim no easy victories.

—Amilcar Cabral
Slain leader of the African Party for the Independence
of Guinea and Cape Verde, Guinea-Bissau

"How did we get into this situation?" the Black community commonly asks itself. As the hurricane-like force of the drug epidemic and the abuses of the drug war ravage the Black community, they signal a more acute and deadly social crisis: the poverty-driven marginalization and elimination of the Black poor.

The battle over drug policy, despite administration denials, is being waged on a terrain fraught with racial conflict. The disproportionate impact of the drug crisis on people of color has raised old questions about just how much progress has been achieved by Blacks and other people of color in the United States.

Meanwhile, in spite of the best efforts and most militant rhetoric of today's Black leadership, the deterioration of the Black community continues at breakneck speed. By every index available, Black America is crashing. The Black community is suffering record rates of homicide, infant mortality, school dropout, AIDS infection, hunger, and homelessness. More than anything, the economy of the Black community is in a shambles. Even the briefest glimpse of poverty in the United States, which disproportionately impacts the Black community, is thoroughly heartbreaking.

The Black infant mortality rate is twice that of Whites, and, at the other end, Black life expectancy is falling. Between the cradle and the grave, things do not get much better. Black unemployment continues to be twice that of Whites, and a White high school dropout will have a better chance of finding work than a Black college graduate.

According to the Census Bureau, about half of the poor heads-of-household work. Yet, at a 1990 minimum wage of only $3.80, even if an individual who headed up a family of four worked full-time, they could have an income that was $4,188 below the official poverty line. Even with the April 1991 rise in minimum wage to $4.25, that same family will fall $3,252 short.[1]

Nearly forty million people live under the official poverty level, which is a mortifying $7,704 for a family of two, $9,435 for a family of three and $12,092 for a family of four. The situation is even worse than the numbers indicate, because the income for the average poor family of four is $4,851 below the poverty line and for women-headed households, $5,206. Twenty percent of America's children struggle to live under the poverty line, but many lose that struggle—an estimated 10,000 children die every year due to poverty.[2]

Although two-thirds of America's poor are White, four out of every nine Blacks are living in poverty. Poverty rates for the African American community are the highest in the nation at about 31.6 percent, nearly two and one-half times the national level in 1989. Half of the Black children born in America are born poor. More than 56 percent of families headed by single Black women are in deep poverty. For Latina women in the same situation, the figure is 59 percent.[3]

These statistics have been depressingly consistent for more than a decade. The real-life impact of these numbers has meant a life of denial of basic material and social needs for millions, along with the intense rejection and stifling alienation that accompanies poverty. At this level of deprivation, as one study points out, "serious family needs—such as food, clothing, medicine, early learning assistance, and housing—are not being met."[4]

Conservatives have argued that poverty figures are overstated, because food stamps should be seen as income and also because the figures include students. They offer little evidence that most students are supported primarily by their parents. Instead, we argue that these figures don't reveal the true extent of poverty. The crucial gauge used to determine who is poor, the "official poverty line," is fundamentally flawed. Eligibility for food stamps, Medicaid, Head Start, and other programs is set by the poverty line. The official poverty line was established in 1967. This line is based on the costs of a minimally adequate diet in 1963.[5]

Mollie Orshansky, a Social Security Administration researcher who did the original work to develop the poverty line, observed that a typical family spent a third of its budget on food. Calculating the cost of a basic "food basket," Orshansky then multiplied this dollar amount by three and came up with what is now taken as the poverty threshold. These vastly outdated thresholds are adjusted yearly for inflation.

The punch line is that if the poverty line was adjusted even to match the standard of living provided by the cost of food in 1967, not to mention the cost in 1991, the number of people "officially" living in poverty would nearly double. Under new poverty-line thresholds suggested by Patricia Ruggles, the author of *Drawing the Line: Alternative Poverty Measures and Their Implications for Public Policy,* the poverty rate increases from 13.5 percent to 24.1 percent.[6] Among other things, these new thresholds take into consideration the fact that housing, not food, takes up a large part of a family's budget.

Other communities of color are facing similar economic problems. The Latino community, projected to be the largest community of color in the United States in the coming years, replicates many of the deadly social statistics found among Blacks.

The drug crisis of the late Eighties and Nineties did not fall from the sky. Its roots were in the growth of poverty throughout the United States, particularly in communities of color. Its political roots are in two developments in the Eighties that will continue to have profound and long-term economic and social impact: the empowerment of the Reagan/Bush right with silent complicity by the Democrats and the wholesale abandonment of the Black poor by a small but visible Black leadership.

Is There a Conspiracy?

The flood of illegal narcotics into the Black community has led more than a few to speculate that a "conspiracy" exists to destroy the African American community through drugs. Many believe that either a section of the government or a group of White racists is carrying out a plan of Black genocide via drugs. Ample historic evidence points to a correlation between high levels of Black activism followed by the increased presence of illegal drugs in the Black community. Most notably, as the Civil Rights and Black Power movements of the Sixties gained momentum and after the urban rebellions in the major cities, more illegal drugs entered the Black community than at any other time in history. Prior to today's crisis, the greatest amount of heroin use in Black American history occurred between 1965 and 1970.

Whether or not there is a conspiracy, Black people's need for money and consequent desire for psychological escape, exacerbated by the alienating and inequitable environment of poor communities, go a long way in explaining the drug crisis. That this situation would be exploited by those within and without these communities is not only a logical response under the capitalist system, but a rational one. The structures and institutional mechanisms of capitalism, and the systemic levers of racism accompanying it, are in themselves explanation enough.

Capitalist power determines not only who has jobs and who doesn't, but also what type of job and where. The lack of a viable economic life in the Black community is the result of a conscious decision to locate businesses, industries, and services elsewhere. The structure of the national economy is similarly controlled to the degree that people of color are disproportionately channelled into the lowest paying and most back-breaking jobs. Further, economic underdevelopment takes place in the social context of (de facto) segregated schools, political disempowerment, and a racist cultural milieu.

The fact is that judges, politicians, police officers, the CIA, and other authorities, as well as organized racists, *are* involved in drug trafficking, money laundering, or payoffs. It's virtually impossible, in fact, to have the magnitude of drugs that flow into the Black community without official and semi-official complicity. Federal narcotics agents have been charged and arrested on numerous occasions for such crimes.

The Black community has been the market of choice for drug traffickers. While traffickers do not discriminate in whom they sell to, they, like all astute capitalists, chase the easiest profit to be gained with the least risk. Again, we do not have to identify a conspiracy. Pure and simple profit is enough motivation.

To believe that drug trafficking and abuse in the Black community is primarily the result of a conspiracy not only dismisses the social and economic roots of the problem but tends to lead to despair, cynicism, fatalism, and political paralysis. Conspiracies imply that mysterious and unknown forces are at work. This has often been the case, as in the Atlanta Black child murders of 1979-81. Very few in the Black community are satisfied that the "real" killer of those children has been brought to justice. From the days of slavery to Emmitt Till to the Atlanta youth, the unsolved murders of Blacks have bred a deep distrust of official inquiries that failed to investigate or acknowledge the racial character of these homicides.

However, many of the forces at work to penetrate and undermine the Black community are too well known. Capitalism's drive for profit at any cost, human or otherwise, means that the poor and powerless are vulnerable to every form of exploitation available. Ultimately, we need to expose and end the racist mechanisms of the economic and political system.

The Three R's: Reaganism, Reaganomics, and Racism

In the late Seventies, the conservative challenge to domestic and foreign policy began to take hold. Conservative spokespeople on a variety of issues, from anti-Sovietism to anti-abortion, found new life and energy. At the center of this revitalized political movement was the attack on working people and people of color. Republican Party and right-wing think tanks began to propagate the message that for all intents and purposes racism was no longer a serious factor in U.S. public life.

This view bullied its way into public policy with the election of Ronald Reagan in 1980. It was not, however, limited to just a fringe wing of the Republican Party. Mass defections of Whites from the Democratic Party indicated that a significant number of Whites believed that the gains and battles of the Sixties and Seventies in effect had eliminated racism from the American reality. Most Whites believed that Black faces in high places meant that racism was dead.

A poll by the National Opinion Research Center at the University of Chicago, conducted between February and April 1990, found that most Whites still harbor extremely negative and racist views about Blacks, Latinos, and Asians. In the poll, 62 percent of Whites said they believe Blacks are more likely than Whites to be lazy, 51 percent believe that Blacks are not patriotic, 53 percent believe Blacks are less intelligent than Whites, and 78 percent said they believe Blacks would rather live off welfare. Similar views were held of Latinos and Asians. Seventy-four percent of Whites felt that Latinos prefer welfare and 56 percent thought Latinos were lazy. Asians were seen as less patriotic by 55 percent of Whites and less intelligent by 36 percent.[7]

Reagan's view that racism had disappeared neatly fit into his political objective of "getting government off the backs of the American people." In fact, what he really meant was to lift all regulations on corporations. Money spent on unnecessary social programs and overly strict government regulations, the Reagan backers argued, were the reasons that the U.S. economy was faltering. If America was to be economically strong again, they continued, the rich must be allowed to develop in whatever way they saw fit, unburdened by labor unions, health regulations, and affirmative action programs.

Right-wing ideologues, such as Defense Secretary Caspar Weinberger, Attorney General Edwin Meese III, Office of Management and Budget Director David Stockman, Secretary of HUD Samuel Pierce, and CIA Director William J. Casey, were brought in to carry out conser-

vative policies, which they did with vicious enthusiasm, gross incompe-
tence, and, in too many instances, blatant corruption. Under Reagan's
men, environmental safeguards, workplace health and safety standards,
banking regulations, and other hard-won protections were thrown out.
At the same time, they also shifted billions of dollars from badly needed
social programs to the military.

As the savings & loan and HUD scandals of the early Eighties
demonstrated, Reagan's watchdogs pillaged and raped the nation, relentlessly carrying out a program of racialized austerity, anti-commu-
nism, and generalized assault on working people. As detailed in Chapter
Five, these scandals were linked to the drug crisis in that they served
as vehicles for money laundering, covers for organized crime figures
who dealt in illegal narcotics, and funding resources for CIA-backed
rebels who trafficked in cocaine and heroin.

Meanwhile, the inner cities were left to decay. As factories and
other businesses folded, the tax base of cities declined, and employees
at city service agencies found themselves unable to serve those most in
need. Worse, the demand for low-skilled Black labor, which had been
the base for building nearly every major city in the United States,
virtually disappeared. Low-skilled and unskilled jobs were lost by the
tens of thousands in cities and towns across the country. In Los Angeles,
more than 80,000 low-skilled industrial jobs in auto assembly, tires, and
similar occupations were lost.[8]

Reagan slashed billions from social programs that had a direct and
immediate impact on the health, education, housing, and employment
opportunities of poor people and people of color.[9] By the middle of
Reagan's second term, his Medicaid cuts meant an 18 percent drop in
the number of poor individuals who were eligible for coverage, from 64
percent in the mid-1970s to 46 percent in 1986. After eight years of
Reagan's housing cuts, the homeless population grew from about
500,000 in 1980 to more than two million by 1990. Reaganomics meant
that close to 200 rural health community hospitals closed between 1981
and 1990.[10]

Meanwhile, Reagan's support for non-democratic governments
abroad in South Korea, the Philippines, Haiti, Turkey, Chile, and many
other nations mirrored increasingly anti-democratic sentiments at
home. As Reagan happily built on the military budget of $1.9 trillion, the
consequences of domestic government priorities destroyed the hopes
of millions of people. For people of color, this was only the beginning.
Overt racial violence and incidents surged in the Reagan years. From
the rise of skinhead racists to the gestures and actions of Ronald Reagan

himself, public acts of racial violence and racism saw a revitalization in the Eighties.

According to a report that reviewed the incidence of hate crimes in the Eighties issued by the Klanwatch Project of the Southern Poverty Law Center, at least 230 organized hate groups—including the Ku Klux Klan, skinheads, Nazis, and other White supremacist groups—operated throughout the United States. The report, titled *Hate Violence and White Supremacy,* documents dozens of hate crimes from the past decade. This includes eleven murders, sixty cross-burnings, and nearly 100 documented shootings and assaults taking place in forty states and the District of Columbia. While the visibility of the KKK has declined, according to the report, many other groups are growing in numbers and influence.[11]

Reagan's veto of a sanctions bill against South Africa, his eight-year snubbing of the Congressional Black Caucus, and many other actions either on his part or on the part of his administration were a central aspect of America's resurgent racism in the Eighties that only widened the divide between Whites and Blacks. Moreover, his visit and wreath-laying at the gravesites of Nazi soldiers in Bitburg, Germany, placed the nation's anti-Semitism and racism in an international spotlight. The U.S. invasion of Grenada in 1983, resulting in civilian deaths, further demonstrated that the lives of third world people meant little to the administration. From South Africa to Latin America, and from the Middle East to Asia, this government consistently set out to destroy people of color.

Ironically, in this context, a number of Black conservative apologists gained prominence—at least in the media. Through their work in the Reagan administration and with right-wing think tanks, these Black apologists enjoyed a new visibility.

The late Clarence Pendleton, an anti-civil rights Black Reaganite, was installed as chairperson of the Civil Rights Commission, formed by Congress via the Civil Rights Act of 1957 to research and make recommendations regarding civil rights policies. In the past, the CRC had produced many timely and relevant studies that detailed the civil rights and human rights advances and setbacks faced by people of color, women, and other locked-out sectors of U.S. society. In a number of legal cases involving civil and voting rights violations, those studies had been instrumental in advancing civil rights through public policy.

With the installation of Pendleton, Linda Chavez, and other arch-conservatives, the mission and character of the CRC changed dramatically. Since Reagan could not abolish the CRC, he believed that civil rights was a dead issue and did the next best thing: he stacked the

Commission with conservative ideologues who paralyzed it. Under Pendleton's rule, the CRC reversed itself on key civil rights questions such as affirmative action and busing, and focused instead on garbled issues such as discrimination against White males. The ideological battles among the commissioners and between Congress and the President effectively diminished, and continues to diminish, the work of the CRC.

Other Black conservatives achieved fleeting fame by challenging civil rights leaders and other Black elected officials. Often disguising their perspective as a class-oriented analysis cast in support of the Black "underclass," right-wing Blacks argued that poor Blacks were dependent on government-financed social programs and too easily acquiesced to dysfunctional behavior by Black leadership—and thus caused their own oppression and suffering.

These views were voiced strongly by Black conservatives Thomas Sowell (author of *Civil Rights: Rhetoric or Reality*) and Walter Williams (author of *State Against Blacks*). But perhaps the most misleading book was libertarian sociologist William Julius Wilson's *The Declining Significance of Race*. Wilson argued that the internal pathologies of the Black community accounted for the current plight of the Black poor, while moral rebirth, self-sufficiency, and expanding the fruits of capitalism to Blacks were the key to freedom.

The racist legacy of the Reagan era will surely take years to overcome.

The momentary triumph of conservative policy makers in the Eighties brought material deterioration in the lives of millions of people, a group consisting disproportionately of people of color, and—significantly—a less-than-democratic climate in which these people could struggle for redress. The government's positive role of addressing the social problems of poverty and drug abuse had, for all intents and purposes, been seriously eroded.

A Crisis of Vision, Strategy, and Leadership

The African American community in the 1990s faces a decisive crisis of vision and strategy. Modern capitalism depends on the rhetoric of democracy while reinforcing, in the strongest possible measures, the reality of economic inequity. The rise of Reaganism in the Eighties and the accompanying racist theories and policies pulverize all hopes for the steady advance of racial tolerance and progress, illusions that permeated the U.S. body politic in the Sixties and Seventies. In the 1990s, to reverse the rightward turn in American politics, the Black community needs a new strategic thrust and organizational capability. If drugs, homelessness, hunger, and the other social horrors that have decimated African-American communities across America are to be over-come, a new road must be taken.

The ascendancy of conservative public policy parallels the decline of traditional Black leadership. In the 1950s and 1960s, the nation's rapid and large economic growth meant that the social programs demanded by Black leaders could be granted. Indeed, to isolate the more radical sectors of the Black community, White power structures put moderate Black leaders in the position of seemingly delivering the "goods." Thus, Black leadership was still subject to the whims of White power and the fluctuations of the economy.

Detroit is an example of this phenomenon. The urban rebellions of 1966, 1967, and 1968 forced the city's White power structure to accept the rise of a Black mayor, Coleman Young, and to create social pro-grams. Job-training programs and community-based social services, all administered by Blacks, were established by a new alliance between White corporate power brokers and moderate Black elected officials. Then, the near collapse of the U.S. auto industry in the late 1970s signalled the end of corporate handouts to the city and started Detroit on its apparently endless economic decline. Concessions to Blacks won in the late Sixties were lost.

In Black communities across the nation, economic and social decay resulted from the inability of Black leadership to win concessions from government and corporate sources.

For the roughly twenty years between 1955 and 1975, the Civil Rights and Black Power movements gave strategic clarity and direction to the Black community. Each movement, with its overwhelming pleth-ora of organizations and leaders, had a clear set of goals, objectives, and tactics. Millions of ordinary Black workers, students, and youth partic-ipated in these struggles.

A critical goal of the Civil Rights movement was the end of *de jure* Jim Crow segregation. As far as many leaders were concerned, that moment was achieved with the passage of the Civil Rights Act of 1964 and the Voting Rights Act of 1965. However, the victory was a double-edged sword. The movement, with its principal base in the South, went into a state of political confusion at that point, as characterized by Dr. Martin L. King, Jr., in his book *Where Do We Go From Here: Chaos or Community?*

For many of the middle-class and ideologically moderate leaders of the movement, the end of legal segregation meant tremendous personal opportunities as elected officials, members of corporate boards, or well-paid administrators of social programs. This view was challenged by King and others, as well as those in the Black Power movement. King also saw the need to principally tackle issues that affected poor and powerless people through mass mobilization and non-violent protest. He also sought to link international issues to the Black freedom struggle. He criticized the U.S. war against the Vietnamese. A number of Black leaders broke with King during this period, such as Roy Wilkins of the NAACP, while others reluctantly stood by King until he was killed, rarely reaching agreement with him on goals, strategy, and program.

The Black Power movement sought, and to a great deal achieved, its goals of Black representation in local, state, and federal politics and the establishment of Black political institutions. In the urban enclaves of the Northeast, Midwest, and West Coast, city after city elected Blacks as mayors, council members, school board representatives, and congresspeople. At the same time, local Black institutions, from schools to co-ops to small businesses, began to establish themselves. Black nationalists, progressive and conservative, saw sweeping changes in every major city and even in many smaller cities in the nation.

By 1975, however, a retrogression was evident. The majority of the political gains and new economic opportunities realized by the movement had gone to a small sector of the Black middle class. True enough, a number of positive developments benefitted the Black masses: reform of local racist police departments, access to avenues of elected power, funding for community-based programs, job training, educational opportunities through government grants, affirmative action, and desegregated housing and social facilities. But by the mid- to late Seventies, economic and social advances ground to a halt.

Under President Jimmy Carter, critical federal programs such as housing and food stamps suffered cuts. Similar economic austerity initiatives were being taken at the local level. Some Black civil rights leaders, including Ralph Abernathy and Hosea Williams, felt so betrayed by Carter that they supported Reagan in 1980 when he ran for President. Other leaders, such as Coretta Scott King, felt the need to support Carter although he had clearly not lived up to the promises of increased support for programs for poor people.

Other communities of color in the United States have, more or less, followed a similar pattern of political development. Important distinctions exist between the Black community and other communities of color in terms of goals and issues such as immigrants' rights and language barriers, but overall the social crisis facing these communities was strikingly similar. Leaders of color were frequently ineffective in creating an alternative political program.

As the 1980s unfolded, the most critical development affecting the Black community was the inability of Black leadership to establish a vision of progressive social change. No sector of Black leadership developed a strategy, a program, or an organizational apparatus that won wide acceptance from the Black masses. The momentum won by the electrifying victory of Mayor Harold Washington in Chicago and the insurgent presidential candidacy of Rev. Jesse Jackson were offset by the rapid decline of life in urban and rural Black America.

Many political leaders seemed to be caught off guard at the swiftness and brutality of the conservative attack on civil rights and poor people. Their reliance on the Democratic Party quickly became problematic as Reagan's budget cuts were easily passed by the Democratic-dominated Congress.

As a result, in the late Eighties political ideology took a back seat to practical achievements. If a nationalist group or the Guardian Angels could remove drug dealers from the neighborhood, fine. If a particular Black candidate promised to deliver and was clearly the lesser of so many evils, fine. The pragmatism of the Black community is real and highly understandable. Within the Black community, the lack of a vision and the capacity to implement that vision boiled down to a struggle for survival, neighborhood by neighborhood, family by family, individual by individual.

At the core of a new vision for Black America in the 1990s must be an all-sided development strategy and class (as well as racial) equality. The concrete issues facing Black poor people, both working and non-working, must be addressed immediately, strategically, and with long-term vision both inside and outside of the electoral arena. Paramount in the coming period is Black unity with other people of color and with other poor communities in the United States and internationally.

Contrary to common belief, the Black nationalist community has not resisted unity with other people of color and poor Whites. Many nationalists have called and worked for unity across the color line in recognition of the "we are in the same boat" situation facing Latinos, Asians, Native Americans, Arab Americans, and others. Many of the major civil rights organizations, which have focused almost exclusively on Black rights, have done little to bridge the gap between the different communities of color. With more resources and influence than comparable organizations among Latinos, Asians, or Native Americans, these organizations could play a key role in furthering the rights and advancement of these sectors of U.S. society. More often than not, however, the civil rights groups have secured an exclusive niche.

None of this is to deny the real differences that exist between the Black community and other communities of color. The Black community's battles with Asian store owners in New York and Washington, D.C., for example, is rooted in genuine issues of economic inequality and racism. Although in some of these circumstances class and race are often linked, there is little denying that some Asian store owners have expressed racist views in defending their exploitation of the Black community. The Japanese in the late Eighties and early Nineties, due to increased economic power in relation to the U.S., became openly complicit with American White supremacy when a high-ranking Japanese official publicly denigrated African American community and identity. This affront fueled feelings of prejudice and animosity on the part of African Americans who find themselves unable to compete with the success of Japanese capitalists and immigrants in the American economy.

The demands of the Civil Rights and Black Power movements retain their legitimacy precisely because the broad masses of Blacks are still disenfranchised. The Black middle class, often espousing conservative politics on a wide range of issues, benefitted most from the gains of both movements. On issues such as increased taxes, low-income housing, public education, and criminal justice, wide gaps exist between the wealthy minority and poor majority within the Black community.

The stark conditions facing most Blacks in the 1990s provide a convenient opening for the propagation of political agendas that worked in the past, although they need to reflect the lessons learned in that period. The struggle for civil rights is critical for the entire Black community and many other sectors of U.S. society. However, some Blacks have been hurt more than others by the conservative agenda.

Black Youth: Attacked, Abandoned, Angry, and Addicted

While drug trafficking and abuse have transcended all social, economic, and racial lines, its most sinister effects are on poor and working-class Black and Latino youth. The proliferation of hard-drug use in these communities plays the dual role of social control and economic delusion. A drugged-out community, pacified, subdued, and bent on self-destruction, is not likely to rise up against the White corporate power structure. The youth of those communities, who are most likely to rebel, are at the center of the drug epidemic and the government-sponsored drug war.

As the drug and violence crisis of the inner cities has grown, mostly Black and Latino youth have become the scapegoats of politicians and law enforcement officials, who hide their heads in the sand, unable to see the desperate reality that these youth face. Rendered more economically marginal and politically voiceless daily, these youth have been abandoned by Black leadership. For the most part, Black leaders at many levels—elected, civil rights, nationalist, or progressive—have lost contact with Black youth.

Many Whites believe that most young Blacks are violent and prone to crime. Studies show, however, that the proportion of crime and violence committed by young Blacks and that committed by young Whites is similar. A National Youth Survey of youth aged eleven to seventeen, conducted between 1976 and 1980, concluded that, with the exception of 1976, there were "no significant race differences" in violent or serious offenses between White and Black youth.[12]

What accounts for the perception of Black youths as prone to crime is the pervasive racial bias—facilitated by media sensationalism—in arrest, prosecution, and imprisonment. One study indicates that when White and Black teenagers commit the same crime, the police and the courts are seven times more likely to charge Black teenagers with a felony, and to convict and jail them.[13] The rate of incarceration for teens is forty-four to one for Blacks versus Whites.[14]

If arrest records are the barometer by which to measure violent crime, Blacks commit aggravated assault at a rate three times that of Whites. On the other hand, if victim surveys are the barometer, the rate is virtually identical: 32 in 1,000 for Blacks and 31 in 1,000 for Whites.[15]

This discriminatory and institutionalized pattern of legal assault has resulted in nearly 25 percent of all young Black males being either on parole, on probation, or incarcerated compared to 6 percent of young White males.[16]

The rate for youths held in short-term detention has increased by 15 percent in the last decade. However, for Whites the increase was only 1 percent, while for youth of color it was 30 percent. Between 1985 and 1986, the number of White youth referred to court for drug law violations dropped by 6 percent. For youth of color, the referral rate *increased* by 42 percent.[17]

The creative resistance of Black youth to these harsh inequities is sharply captured in popular-culture forms such as rap music. From the brutal and bitter (and intolerably sexist) music of Two Live Crew and NWA (Niggers With Attitude) to the uplifting and struggle-oriented songs of Stetatsonics and Public Enemy, Black youth have made it clear that they understand the identity of the problem.

Their response is generally positive and reflects a fighting spirit that has disappeared among many Black adults. Youth are giving new life to political activism, resulting in the popularity of Malcolm X, militant support for the freedom struggle in South Africa, and a willingness to challenge authority, both Black and White. Black students have taken over Black campuses, especially Howard University and Fisk College, demanding a more responsive and relevant education from Black administrators and trustees.

The lure of the drug culture is most troubling. Government reports and local data indicate that only a very small percentage of Black youth is actually involved in drug trafficking and drug use. Young Blacks are less likely to use legal and illegal drugs, specifically alcohol, than their White counterparts. One study found that while only 39 percent of White youth between the ages of twelve and seventeen had never used alcohol, among Black youth the number was 60 percent. The same study found that only 24 percent of young Blacks had ever tried drugs of any kind compared to 31 percent for young Whites.[18]

Nevertheless, the violence and negative health-related aspects of the drug *culture* impacts a significant proportion of Black youth, especially poor Black youth. Unsafe and frequent sexual activity related to drug use, for example, is spreading AIDS and other sexually transmitted diseases.

Violence is endemic to the drug subculture. Dress, language, music, and social relations reflect a need to assert power in a situation designed to make youths, particularly Black youths, powerless.

The growing homicide rate among young Black men is higher in some cities than the casualty rate among soldiers during the war in Vietnam. One of every 1,000 young Black males is murdered, and homicide is the reason for more than 40 percent of deaths for Black males between the ages of fifteen and twenty-four. A young Black male is six times more likely to be murdered than a young Black female, nine times more than a young White male, and twenty-six times more than a young White female. Black men in Harlem have less chance of reaching the age of sixty-five than men in Bangladesh.[19]

The drug epidemic—and the government's repressive response to it—threatens to eliminate an entire generation of Black youth. Even as this book is being written, hundreds of Black youth are being killed around the nation while thousands more are being arrested and put on a life path of institutionalization and rejection. Yet, many elected officials and national leaders fail to recognize the urgency of this issue.

As we unfold the saga of the drug crisis, we hope to unmask the historic imperatives, social relations, and political issues that challenge the African American community—*and the entire nation*—in this last decade of the twentieth century. The future of Black America depends on how we resolve the current crisis.

Chapter 2

RACISM AND THE DRUG CRISIS

...around the country, politicians, public officials, and even many police officers and judges say, the nation's war on drugs has in effect become a war on Black people.

—Ron Harris, journalist[1]

While the facts show that the majority of drug users and drug profiteers are White, the nation and the world are bombarded with images of young Black males who are handcuffed, lying on the ground dead, or herded behind prison walls—all due to trafficking or abuse of illegal drugs. The racist myth is that most inner-city, young Black males are gun-toting, crack-smoking criminals-in-waiting. From the days of slavery to the trumped-up cases of the Scottsboro boys and the Wilmington Ten, to the death by a White mob of Yusef Hawkins in New York, the very presence of young Black males is seen as a threat to White society. This perspective, repeated in countless ways, is an objective truth for many schoolteachers, judges, police officers, politicians, and journalists.

Although the incidence of trafficking and drug abuse is relatively the same for Blacks and Whites, their resources and political capacity to confront the problem differ. Inner-city and poor communities, disproportionately people of color, are locked into a cycle of poverty, illegal drug trafficking and abuse, and increased poverty.

The question of political power becomes essential because illegal drugs have such a powerful economic and social impact in these communities. Efforts to address problems, such as Black-on-Black crime and AIDS, are shaped by the political perspectives of those who seek to address them. While observers from either end of the political spectrum would agree that Black-on-Black crime, of which the current drug crisis is the most representative expression, is one of the most serious issues facing African Americans, few would agree on its causes, impact, and resolution.

Conservatives, both Black and White, argue that a moral revival is needed to reestablish the kinds of values that would prohibit drugs in the Black community. From their perspective, primary concern for the victim necessitates more prisons in which to house drug dealers who prey on the Black community. Many conservatives argue that crime causes poverty. Businesses are hesitant to locate in high-crime areas, they argue, and residents in these areas are intimidated from participating in crime-fighting, community-building projects. Leading conservative voices from Thomas Sowell to Robert Woodson have stated that Black civil rights leaders benefit from the perpetuation of poverty and, therefore, intend to do very little to eliminate it.

At first glance, this line of reasoning may seem compelling and attractive. Surely, the values of community and charity have disappeared in many of our neighborhoods, Black and White. Individuals must take responsibility for their actions, as conservatives demand, and all the racism in the world does not excuse the brutal gunning down of a sixty-five-year-old grandmother in order to get money to buy drugs, or the rape of a fifteen-year-old junior high school student by a drug dealer seeking payment. But for conservative thinkers, jail and "just say no" slogans are adequate and appropriate responses to the danger posed by drug traffickers and drug users.

Their answers are inadequate to resolving a situation that in many sectors of the Black community has developed over generations: the culture and material reality of poverty. The reproduction of self-destructive behavior was neither sudden nor benign. After years of facing brutality, conscious divide-and-conquer political tactics, and marginalization into depressed communities, Black Americans have developed a conditioned response. For every strong individual who has risen above those conditions, many more did not and could not. While many have chosen not to sell or abuse drugs, too often drug dealing is the only means of economic or mental survival.

While it is difficult to pinpoint why a particular individual abuses drugs, many addiction experts target a low level of self-esteem as a critical factor. In recent history, intellectuals such as Karl Marx and Richard Wright have noted that the crushing impact of poverty leads to alienation and low self-esteem. Consequently, when a whole community faces this condition, in an atmosphere that promotes identity through material consumption, social deterioration becomes inevitable. Alienation shatters the spirit and destroys the ability to love oneself and others. The escalation of violence and the devaluation of life is rooted in the isolation and nihilism symptomatic of our consumer society.

Former California assemblywoman and activist Maxine Waters, now a member of Congress, speaks to the conservatives' flawed analysis. She writes,

In the face of this horror story, we have the rationalizations of police and national officials that the "disintegration of the family" or "lack of values" are responsible for what is the colossal failure of local and federal officials to wage an effective war against drugs—one in which the strategy of prevention would be clearly defined and underwritten by the necessary resources in money and man- and womanpower and coordinated with respected community activists capable of contributing to the detection and apprehension of those who prey on the community from within and without.[2]

With an amazing blindness, conservatives of all colors dismiss a long history of denial of opportunity and resources to the poor sectors of the Black community. They refuse to acknowledge that whole generations are being victimized by systemic factors. They have abandoned hope that the loss of so many young Black males to drugs and violence is preventable.

Beverly Coleman-Miller, special assistant to the Commissioner of Public Health in Washington, D.C., dramatically points out that in the District of Columbia, a young Black male is dying every sixteen-to-twenty hours.[3] Such figures are socially determined and socially driven. In 1969, the National Commission on the Causes and Prevention of Violence astutely wrote,

> To be young, poor, male; to be undereducated and without means of escape from an oppressive urban environment; to want what society claims is available (but mostly to others); to see around oneself illegitimate and often violent methods being used to achieve material success; and to observe others using these means with impunity—all this is to be burdened with an enormous set of influences that pull many toward crime and delinquency. To be also Black, Puerto Rican or Mexican-American and subject to discrimination adds considerably to the pull.[4]

If we are to rescue the generations of Black and Latino youth and the inner-city poor who are the most trapped in the ravages and destructiveness of the drug lifestyle, we need to first grasp the historic development of drug trafficking and abuse. What has been popularly described as a boom in drug trafficking and abuse in the Black community, as one writer put it, can more rightfully be called an echo of the past.

In the Beginning

In traditional African cultures, as in most of the rest of the world, alcohol use was common. Palm wine was a regular part of the diet, an important part of community and of medical use against measles and dysentery. It was also used as a medium of exchange. Traditions dictated when, where, how, and how much alcohol was consumed. Natural substances, such as kola nuts and guinea corn, were used as intoxicants, but with moderation.[5] In southern Africa, marijuana was used as an intoxicant as well as for other purposes. It was used by women to ease childbirth and as an ingredient in breads and soups. It is speculated that the plant was probably brought to the Mozambique region by Arab traders centuries ago.[6]

The link between deadly drugs and African Americans began in the era of the slave trade. During the seventeenth, eighteenth, and nineteenth centuries, many of the companies that controlled the trafficking of slaves from Africa to the New World, such as the British East India Company, were also the companies that would later come to dominate the world's opium trade.[7]

Large-scale production of sugar led to the development of molasses and rum. Rum became a key part of the triangular slave trade that took ships carrying captured Africans from West Africa to the Caribbean and North America in exchange for raw materials and commodities produced by the colonies that were then taken to Europe, where they were sold for large profits. Rum exports from the Caribbean islands grew from 58,000 gallons in 1721 to more than two million gallons by 1765.[8] The sales from rum accounted for one-quarter of all products sold from the islands. New England rum traders eventually monopolized the trade, however, and by 1770 controlled four-fifths of all exports to Europe and Africa.[9] Rum was traded to Black slave dealers in exchange for the captured Africans. This noxious and ruinous type of trading became so popular that two distilleries were opened at Liverpool just to provide rum to dealers going to Africa.[10] In addition to its value as a commodity, traders often gave rum to Black dealers to get them drunk, making it easier to swindle and cheat them.

Portuguese slave trafficking gave rise to tobacco addiction on the part of Africans on the West Coast. In Guinea, for example, slave traders would sell captured Blacks for as little as six or seven seventy-five-pound rolls of Brazilian tobacco.[11] By the late seventeenth century, addiction was so pervasive that a slave or a farm animal could be traded for as little as a single length of twisted leaf.[12]

Slaves found alcohol easy to obtain or make despite laws forbidding alcohol consumption. Yet African patterns of consumption, marked by moderation, persisted during slavery. According to Eugene D. Genovese in *Roll Jordan Roll: The World the Slaves Made:*

> Slaves maintained relative sobriety, especially when compared to Whites and Indians of the period. Slaves neither often drank to excess nor acted upon their knowledge of the narcotic effects of hemp. Rarely, apart from holiday frolics, at which getting drunk became a test of manhood for the young men, did widespread drunkenness occur among slaves, although it did among masters, overseers, and neighboring poor Whites.[13]

This view contradicts the views propagated by slave owners that drinking was a serious problem among slaves. Researcher Denise Herd writes that "...the rhetoric of slave holders emphasizing the problems of Black drinking must be seen as a function of social and political reality rather than as a reflection of actual conditions. The legal measures prohibiting Blacks from using alcohol were a means of asserting social dominance and an attempt to tighten social control mechanisms in order to preserve the tenuous institution of slavery."[14]

In the seventeenth century, African slaves brought the hemp plant, which produces marijuana, with them to the New World, where it grew wild and plentiful in Jamaica and other countries, including the United States.[15] Hemp was widely used in colonial America to produce many products from paper to clothes to rope. To what extent marijuana was used by slaves is not well documented, but given their knowledge of the plant, it probably was used as an intoxicant at certain ceremonies or rituals.

For more than two centuries, hemp was one of the most important crops in the United States. In 1619, generally noted as the year the African slave trade began in the United States, the Jamestown colony in Virginia passed a law forcing farmers to grow hemp.[16] Both George Washington and Thomas Jefferson cultivated the plant.[17] Hemp was legal tender from 1631 up until the 1800s. A number of areas were so dominated by the plant that they named themselves after it—such as Hempstead, Long Island; Hempstead County, Arkansas; and Hempstead County, Texas.[18]

Although hemp grew all over the South, Kentucky and Missouri were the chief growing areas. Slaves were forced to plant and harvest this valuable product. The buds, roots, stems, seeds, and leaves were all commonly used ingredients in hundreds of medicines that were prescribed for ailments such as asthma, glaucoma, nausea, tumors, epilepsy, back pain, sleep, and stress. Ship sails, ropes, food oils, textiles, paints, and many other products were made from hemp by slaves.[19]

In other parts of the country, natural intoxicants were used by native people mainly, but not solely, for religious and spiritual purposes. For example, indigenous people in the Western hemisphere had used peyote, a hallucinogenic plant, for centuries. The use of peyote and other plants came under attack with the introduction of alcohol.

Guns, diseases, and alcohol were used by White colonialists in the war to conquer Indian lands. Just as tobacco and opium addiction were used against the Africans and Chinese, respectively, alcoholism was introduced among Indians, and became a problem among the poorer and nomadic tribes. Researchers believe that while alcoholism among Indians was not initially genetic, heredity was a key factor in their susceptibility to addiction. Indians produced less of the enzymes that break down alcohol and, therefore, were more susceptible to alcoholism.[20]

In the mid-1800s, the biggest drug problem facing the American population was opiate addiction. Due to the wide dissemination of opium derivatives including laudanum, morphine, codeine, and other drugs as medicine, many people became "medical" addicts. During the Civil War, for example, many of the injured soldiers who were injected with morphine to ease pain became addicted. This addiction became so widespread that it became known as the "Soldier's Illness."[21]

The medical profession used opium, morphine, and codeine in its medicines as painkillers and relaxers. In the era before non-addictive painkillers such as aspirin and bufferins, opiates were the only relief available and were broadly distributed to the ill and infirm, especially the elderly. In addition, many older, middle-class White women who could afford prescribed medicine became addicts. It did not take long before many thousands of addicts were created. One out of every 400 people in the United States was addicted to opium derivatives. It was estimated that about 250,000 people were addicted to opiates by 1900.[22]

In the nineteenth century, in the years following slavery, few references to Black drug use can be found. There certainly was no evidence of disproportionate use or of significant abuse among Blacks.

Surveys and studies done at the end of the last century concluded that most opiate users (morphine, heroin, etc.) came from the middle and upper classes. An 1885 Iowa study stated that the majority of opiate users "are to be found among the educated and most honored and useful members of society." In 1889, a survey of druggists and physicians reached the same conclusion. Both druggists and physicians reported that the middle and upper classes comprised the overwhelming bulk of their customers and patients.

During this period, users also tended to be middle-aged or older. An 1880 Chicago study reported that the average age for male opium users was 41.4 years of age and for women 39.4 years. The Chicago study also concluded that female users outnumbered male users three to one. The 1885 Iowa study reached a similar conclusion with its estimate that women were 63.8 percent of all opiate users.[23]

In the 1850s, when many Chinese came to the United States in response to the gold rush in California, there was little record of opium use. A significant amount of this first wave of Chinese came from the merchant class and engaged in commerce. By 1852, Chinese immigrants had investments of more than two million dollars in California. The growing wealth of Chinese small businesses and manufacturing enterprises threatened White businesses. A second wave of Chinese came to the United States in the 1860s and 1870s to work on the railroads. Some Chinese were even brought to Mississippi to work in the rice fields to displace Black sharecroppers. As the economic downturn of the mid-1870s grew worse and wages fell, White laborers began to see Chinese laborers as competition for scarce jobs. It was in this period that opium use began. It was mainly the poor Chinese who smoked opium, and its use was encouraged by the Chinese merchant class. As the small merchants began to suffer from the economic recession of the 1870s, they turned to prostitution, gambling, and drugs as critical sources of income.[24]

It did not take long for racial prejudice against the Chinese to arise and for their drug use to become a target. A number of racist laws were passed, including the Chinese Exclusion Act of 1882. In 1887, the federal government outlawed opium importation and smoking among Chinese Americans, although White citizens had no such restrictions.[25]

England had its own opiate abuse problem. In England, opium use affected all classes, but especially the impoverished working class crowded into cities. Karl Marx wrote in *Capital* about the horrific rate of death of working-class children—26,000 per 100,000 in 1861—partially due to the habits of parents of "dosing with opiates" their ill children.[26]

At the turn of the twentieth century, opiate addiction in the United States was to some degree fueled by the domestic production of opium. Opium was legally and abundantly grown in the United States in the eighteenth and nineteenth centuries. At least ten states cultivated the crop, including Vermont, Connecticut, California, Arizona, Virginia, Tennessee, South Carolina, Georgia, Florida, and Louisiana.[27]

Along with the morphine and opium addicts, there was an increasing number of cocaine users. Its use for illicit and pleasurable purposes was small and initially restricted to lower-class White males and Chinese immigrants. Cocaine use expanded dramatically as cocaine found its way into many commercial products.[28]

According to drug historian Dr. David Musto, pure cocaine was first taken from the coca plant by Austrian chemist Albert Niemann in 1860.[29] U.S. physicians, and Dr. Sigmund Freud, at first thought that cocaine could be used to cure morphine and alcohol addiction. The medical profession and astute commercial interests saw the financial potential of capitalizing on cocaine's energy-enhancing properties.

In the late 1800s, pharmaceutical companies, many of which have grown to become some of the large corporations of today, became involved in the importation and dispensation of cocaine and its by-products; these included Squibb, Merck, and Parke Davis. Merck sold Sigmund Freud his first gram of cocaine for $1.27. Rather than just rely on unknown importers, the Parke Davis company sent botanist Dr. H. H. Rusby to Bolivia to purchase coca leaves directly. Rusby is credited with first coming up with the idea of refining the cocaine at its source and then shipping the more portable product to the United States. He later wrote a book, *Jungle Memories,* on his experiences.[30]

Unconstrained by any regulations, salesmen sold cocaine door-to-door. It was often distributed free by employers to their workers to give them a productivity boost. The American Hay Fever Association made cocaine its official remedy due to the product's ability to drain the sinuses. By 1885, cocaine-based products were being sold as cigarettes, inhalants, crystals, tablets, ointments, sprays, teas, and liquor. Coca wines and soft drinks containing cocaine appeared, such as the legendary Coca-Cola and other soft drink brands with provocative names such as Rocco Cola, Koca Nola, Nerv Ola, and Dope.[31]

Coca-Cola originally contained not only cocaine, but an extract of the African kola nut that also had intoxicating properties. By the time of the 1906 Pure Food and Drug Act, Coca-Cola was being made from decocainized coca leaves; that is, the cocaine alkaloid was removed.[32]

As the importation of opium, morphine, and cocaine increased, and their distribution within the country expanded, harmful addictions to these drugs became too obvious to ignore. By 1900, the first mass anti-drug campaign was in full swing. The major targets of the first anti-drug campaign were rural White males, the largest group of addicts and users; immigrant groups, in particular Chinese opium smokers; and, as the campaign grew, southern Blacks. The first federal anti-drug law, passed on February 14, 1902, was somewhat bewildering, but indicative of things to come. The law made it a punishable offense to supply opium for non-medical purposes to any aboriginal native of any Pacific island lying between the 20-degree north and 40-degree south latitude, and between 120-degree east and 120-degree west longitude. The law, however, only applied to islands "not in the possession of any civilized power, revealing that addiction was not the lawmakers' only motivation."[33] It wasn't long, though, before the anti-drug campaigns started in earnest.

The American Pharmaceutical Association, pharmacist organizations, and drug companies at first fought any effort at regulation and reform. When it became clear that regulation of drugs was inevitable, these groups successfully sought to shape the new laws. After much fighting, a compromise was reached and, in May 1906, Congress passed the District of Columbia Pharmacy Act, the first federal drug control law.

In June 1906, Congress passed the Pure Food and Drug Act, requiring manufacturers to list addictive drugs contained in their products. The law was apparently successful, for within a few years sales of those products dropped by one-third.[34]

Within a few years, Washington, D.C. would become the center of both the national and international war against opium. In 1909, President Theodore Roosevelt appointed Washington, D.C.-based physician Dr. Hamilton Wright to lead a commission to an international conference on stopping the opium trade in Asia. The administration's political goal was to increase the U.S. influence in the Far East.

Wright created the strongest anti-drug regulations ever in the United States and earned the title "Father of America's Drug Laws." According to Musto, Wright felt that the United States had to set an example of strident anti-drug laws in order to convince other nations to do the same. In order to accomplish this goal, Wright used two dishonest but successful tactics: he exaggerated addiction figures and played on the racism of Whites.[35] Although the number of opium addicts was shrinking, as was the importation of opiates, Wright used wildly inflated figures to scare Congress and the nation. Most of the older addicts, many of whom were Civil War veterans, were dying, as were the doctors who relied on opiate remedies. Wright suppressed this information.[36]

In 1910, he issued his *Report on the International Opium Commission.* This report was noteworthy not only for its blown-up figures, but also for its racist myths and lies about drug use among Blacks. The document described in horrifying detail the supposed superhuman strength and extreme madness experienced by Blacks on cocaine, and explained that cocaine drove Black men to rape.[37] Rumors circulated at the time went so far as to claim that cocaine made African Americans bullet proof.[38] Contrary to the report, no evidence exists of disproportionate opiate use among Blacks in the nineteenth century or the early part of the twentieth century. In fact, studies done in Florida and Tennessee around the time of World War I found a lower proportion of opiate use for Blacks than for Whites.[39]

Yet, article after article appeared that claimed that Blacks were using cocaine at alarming levels. One article that was written in a medical journal complained about the "disastrous use of cocaine among the negroes and lower class Whites who were snuffing cocaine and lying around in every conceivable state of depravity" in Chattanooga. Another article written in the *New York Times,* titled "Negro Cocaine 'Fiends' Are a New Southern Menace," stated that southern sheriffs had switched from .32-caliber guns to .38-caliber pistols to protect themselves from drug-empowered Blacks. The article was subtitled "Murder and Insanity Increasing Among Lower Class Blacks Because They Have Taken to 'Sniffing' Since Deprived of Whiskey by Prohibition."[40]

In the United States, the concerted effort to paint all addicts as drug-crazed Blacks or Chinese led to the most critical anti-drug legislation in the early part of this century: the Harrison Narcotics Act of 1914. This act was written as a tax law and effectively eliminated the use of morphine, opium, heroin, and other addictive drugs through strict regulation and harsh penalties. Although cocaine is not considered to be in the narcotic family of drugs, it was included in the Act. Physicians tried to get around the law by opening clinics that would dispense opiates in compliance with the Act, but they were shut down by the early Twenties. Armed raids by Treasury agents rapidly discouraged doctors who tried to continue the distribution of opium-based medicines.

Racist fabrications were not limited to the United States. In 1911, the White South African government outlawed marijuana, known as "dagga," in an effort to stop the growing radicalization of Blacks. Dagga was blamed for making Blacks rebel and fight back against racist laws and growing White power. White South Africans continued to allow Black miners to smoke it because Whites believed that it made Black workers more productive. South Africa led the international fight to ban hemp and had direct and significant influence over White political leaders and legislators in the U.S. South.[41]

The racial fears played upon by the anti-drug campaigns worked in harmony with the general wave of racial attacks that were sweeping the country. The legacy of lynching that had seen over 1,000 Black victims by the end of World War I went into high gear after the war.[42] In 1917, thirty-eight Blacks were lynched. By 1918, the number had risen to fifty-eight and a year later, after the war had ended, more than seventy lynchings were recorded. At least ten of the Black men hanged in 1919 were still in uniform.[43] The "Red Summer" of 1919, as writer James Weldon Johnson termed it, became even more deadly for Blacks as the nation experienced twenty-five race riots.[44]

The Ku Klux Klan and other racist groups enjoyed a free hand as J. Edgar Hoover's newly organized FBI focused on eradicating the communist threat. The Klan grew from a small group of racists in the early 1910s to over 100,000 by the early 1920s. In the first year following the end of the war, the Klan made over 200 public appearances in twenty-seven states.[45] To add to the racial fires, the Black community saw an alliance formed between temperance groups and racist organizations such as the Klan. In the past century, temperance organizations had forged ties with abolitionists and been reliable friends to the ex-slaves following the Civil War.[46] In a number of cases, the leadership of the two movements had been identical. However, as attitudes changed and tolerance for drinking grew in the 1910s and 1920s, the movement sought and accepted allies from any quarter.[47]

W.E.B. Dubois wrote about the problems of alcoholism and of prohibition:

> Nothing demonstrates more clearly the limitations of half-baked minds than the present discussion of the United States concerning liquor. We are not, in fact, discussing liquor at all. We are discussing laws. Laws depend for their enforcement upon public opinion. There is no royal road to manners and morals. They cannot be established by an act of Legislature or royal proclamation. They can only by instilled by parental advice, the love of friends and human contact. All other methods have failed and will fail. We are a drunken land and drunken race. Not because of prohibition or the open saloon but because we have ceased to teach temperance to the young.[48]

After World War I, large numbers of Blacks moved to northern cities in search of employment opportunities and to escape the terrorism of southern Whites. Most Blacks, while finding the North to be somewhat more secure, found little opportunity to enter the economic or social mainstream.

The development of a Black underground economy led to the rise of Black bootleggers during the 1920s. This development, in turn, led to a dramatic increase in Black alcohol consumption and related problems. The rate of deaths due to alcohol among Blacks grew every year from 1918 to 1927.[49] Often seen as folk heroes who outfoxed the law and White competitors, Black bootleggers plied the community with rivers of hard liquor.

The war against marijuana after World War I also became a vehicle for attacks on the Black community. Although marijuana had existed in the United States for centuries, it wasn't used primarily as an intoxicant until the early part of this century. One of the first recorded incidents of marijuana smoking occurred in the famous Storyville section of New Orleans, which became a major marijuana-importation and -distribution center.[50] Most of the marijuana came from Mexico, Cuba, the Caribbean, or Texas. From Louisiana, it traveled across the country to other major cities.

Many of the Black, White, and Mexican dockworkers became smokers as shiploads of the weed came into New Orleans. As they moved on, they took as much marijuana as they could carry with them and helped to spread its use across the nation.

At the same time, New Orleans had become the magnet for jazz musicians as the new music form began to grow and develop passionate followers. Both Black and White jazz musicians smoked marijuana and came to enjoy the headiness and pleasure that it gave.

By the mid-1920s, however, a full-scale anti-marijuana campaign was in full swing. In 1925, Louisiana made marijuana possession and use a felony. Many other southern and southwestern states soon followed suit. Blacks and Mexicans became the main targets of this new wave of anti-drug fever.

In 1931, jazz great Louis Armstrong became a victim of this campaign. He was arrested in Los Angeles for marijuana possession and served ten days in jail. He was then released with a six-month suspended sentence. One year earlier he had recorded "Muggles," a song about marijuana.[51]

Black jazz and blues musicians in the Twenties, Thirties, and Forties wrote many songs about drugs. From well-known artists such as Cab Calloway, Bessie Smith, Fletcher Henderson, and Leadbelly to hundreds of unknowns, they joyfully and woefully sang about getting high on "reefer" (marijuana), "dope" (heroin), and "caine" (cocaine). Some of the songs that were recorded include Pipe Dream Blues (1924), Cocaine Habit Blues (1930), Reefer Man (1932), Kickin' the Gong Around (1933), Take a Whiff on Me (1934), Dopey Joe (1938), and Dope Head Blues (1941). One of the most popular packages of cigarette papers used for rolling marijuana cigarettes was called *blanco y negro* (White and Black) and featured a Black saxophonist on the cover.[52]

Hysterical newspaper headlines and radio broadcasts blamed marijuana-intoxicated Blacks and Mexicans for many heinous crimes they claimed were being committed against Whites. According to these stories, similar to earlier ones about cocaine, marijuana gave Blacks superhuman strength and extraordinary and violent sexual desires.[53]

Linking sex, race, and drugs seem to touch the deepest nerves of the American people. The suppression of inter-racial socializing by government decree and racist organizations had been strong since the days of slavery. The fear of miscegenation re-emerged, with rising inter-racial sex and drug use, and drove many Whites to near-hysteria. The proliferation of heroin use, as in the past, found cultural expression in many of the popular pulp novels of the time. Numerous books about White women who were seduced into drugs and sex by men of color were published, including *Marijuana Girl* by N.R. de Mexico (1951), *Narcotic Agent* by Maurice Helbrant (1953), *The Dream Peddlers* by Floyd Miller (1956), *Rock 'N Roll Gal* by Ernie Weatherall (1957), and *The Needle* by Sloan M. Britain (1959). These books sold in the tens of thousands as White and Black Americans continued to be fascinated by the image of inter-racial sex and drug use.

The Hearst newspaper empire was the chief vehicle for the spread of these racial tales. It was the Hearst papers that first popularized the term "marijuana."[54] Few realized until it was too late that the evil marijuana cigarette being attacked in the Hearst papers and by federal authorities was the same hemp plant that had provided so many useful and essential products for decades.

William Randolph Hearst's antagonism toward Mexicans and Blacks was rooted in both his own racist world outlook and in the service of his own greed. He was more than a little upset when Pancho Villa's army seized about 800,000 acres of his land during the Mexican revolution.[55]

Also, hemp's use as a high-quality paper substitute threatened the lumber and newspaper industries controlled by Hearst, especially after the invention of state-of-the-art, affordable hemp stripping machines in the 1930s. The USDA was predicting that hemp would be the number-one crop in America, and even as late as 1938, one year after marijuana was outlawed, *Popular Mechanics* referred to hemp as the $1 billion crop.[56] Hearst, along with the Dupont chemical companies, which had just invented a wood pulp process of their own, formed an alliance to outlaw hemp.[57]

This federal side of this campaign was orchestrated by Harry Jacob Anslinger, who had made his reputation as a hardline law enforcer during prohibition. In 1930, he became director of the Federal Bureau of Narcotics and remained so for the next thirty-two years. Anslinger's agents helped to spread the rumors and tales about the dangers of Black and Mexican drug use.[58] Success came for Anslinger in the Fall of 1937 when the Marijuana Tax Act, which made use and sale of marijuana a felony, became law.[59]

Anslinger's hatred of people of color was legendary. In official memos to his staff, he would refer to a Black person as a "ginger-colored nigger."[60] He testified before a southern-controlled Congress that "coloreds with big lips lured White women with jazz and marijuana."[61] In the 1940s, he ordered files to be kept on all jazz and swing musicians. This included jazz greats such as Duke Ellington, Thelonius Monk, Dizzy Gillespie, Cab Calloway, and Count Basie. Even White performers who were close to Blacks, such as Jackie Gleason, Milton Berle, and Kate Smith, came under his scrutiny.[62]

Anslinger hated the way jazz artists boldly defied social and cultural values he held dear. Inter-racial sex, drug use, and bohemian lifestyles were taboos that directly contradicted the conservative social and political views of Anslinger.

Anslinger became friends with right-wing Wisconsin Senator Joseph McCarthy and participated in the anti-communist witch hunts of the 1950s. Their fierce and frenzied battle against drugs and communists was the height of disingenuousness. Anslinger admits in his autobiography that he had supplied McCarthy with morphine for many years. His ludicrous and hypocritical justification was that he was protecting the junkie senator from communist blackmailers who could exploit his addiction.[63]

The Heroin Surge: Black Power vs. White Powder

The Mafia Dons sit around the table. The room is as dark as the tone of the men who occupy it, and a deadly seriousness pervades the atmosphere. The issue is how to end the battle over whether or not to deal drugs that has lead to internecine war among the "families" and with outsiders. Don Corleone expounds on morals versus profits to be reaped by entering full-scale into the drug trade. He proposes a compromise that everyone agrees on: organized crime will move into drug trafficking, but will only sell to Blacks.

This scene, from *The Godfather*, had its duplicate in real life. Prior to the Forties, illegal use of light drugs (marijuana) and hard drugs (heroin and cocaine) was restricted to a small segment of society, including the African American community. Jazz greats Charlie Parker and Billie Holiday were infamous heroin addicts, but for the most part, hard-core drug abuse was small and isolated. By 1951, however, due to the Mafia's marketing focus, over 100,000 people were addicts in the United States, many of them Black.[64]

Heroin traffic in the Black communities of the East Coast was controlled by New York's big-five Mafia families, in addition to the French-Cuban connection run by Florida-based gangsters: the Joseph Bonanno family, which was the most deeply involved; the Carlo Gambino family; the Vito Genovese family; the Thomas Lucchese family; and the Profaci-Maglioco family.[65] Reportedly, these five families had taken over from the Jewish mob, which up to the Forties had controlled the drug and numbers rackets in Harlem and other Black areas. The Black street name for heroin was "smack," that came from the Yiddish work *shmeck,* meaning "smell."[66]

Jewish dominance over the rackets had begun in the bootlegging days of the 1920s. The legendary Arnold Rothstein, famous for bribing the Chicago White Sox to throw the 1919 World Series, controlled a significant portion of all illegal liquor in New York City. In the early 1930s, Jewish gangster Dutch Schultz took control of most of the illegal activities in Harlem that were being operated by Harlem's scattered Black and Puerto Rican crime figures. He controlled the area up until his death in 1935, after which the Italian mobsters took over.[67]

The decision by the organized crime families to sell hard drugs almost exclusively to the Black community created a heroin addiction crisis of stunning proportions. This crisis was facilitated by the pay-offs to police officials, judges, politicians, and other White power brokers who had little interest in the welfare of the Black community. As addiction grew, burglaries, robberies, and other crimes were being committed as junkies attempted to finance their habit. Although figures were exaggerated to show an increase in drug-related crime, they were sufficiently frightening to convince New York legislators to pass the strongest anti-drug laws in the country. Unlawful possession of a hypodermic needle, for instance, carried a six-month automatic sentence.[68]

Every major city with a substantial Black population suffered a heroin epidemic. The Black nationalist organization, Nation of Islam (NOI), found many of its recruits in the clutches of heroin addiction and grew from a small religious group into one of the major organized forces in the Black community of that period. Malcolm X describes in his autobiography his easy access to heroin, cocaine, and marijuana. Known as Detroit Red, he eventually became a drug dealer in Boston and New York:

> I kept turning over my profit, increasing my supplies, and I sold reefers like a wild man. I scarcely slept; I was wherever musicians congregated. A roll of money was in my pocket.

Every day, I cleared at least fifty or sixty dollars. In those days...this was a fortune to a seventeen-year-old Negro.[69]

Most of NOI's work with drug addicts was done by Muslims who themselves had been junkies. With amazing success, the NOI turned hundreds of addicts into disciplined Muslims and members of the growing nationalist group. The NOI's anti-drug program, as Malcolm X described it, was a six-stage process.[70] Ostensibly, it was not a recruitment program, but those who went through the process were informed that the only way to really stay drug-free was to join the NOI.

In the first stage, as advocated by other treatment programs, the addict first had to admit that he or she was addicted to drugs. Although ex-addicts worked with the individual to take this first step, it often could take months of work. Stage two involved coming to grips with why a Black person in America used drugs in the first place. In the nationalist rhetoric of the NOI, Black drug use was an attempt to escape or blunt the hurt of racism. For the Muslims, this was the critical distinction between their anti-drug work and the work being done by others.

This led to the punch line of stage three, where the addict was told that the only true freedom was to join the NOI and submit to Elijah Muhammad. The addict-candidate would begin the rites of initiation including visits to Muslim establishments and discussions about Islam. In stage four, after association with the NOI and its positive values and strong beliefs, the addict would have accumulated enough self-esteem to begin to believe in himself. This new self-worth provided the strength to go to the next stage.

Finally, in stage five, the addict went through the merciless and brutal process of non-chemical detoxification. Muslim brothers (or in the case of a woman addict, Muslim sisters) helped the addict go "cold turkey."

The sixth stage came full circle when the newly initiated, drug-free brother or sister went out and found another addict, usually an old acquaintance from the drug scene, and began the process of transformation with them.

During this period, a number of Black heroin dealers wrestled away distribution networks from the Italian, Cuban, and Jewish mafias. Prior to this time, if a Black drug dealer wanted to buy some drugs, he had to go through one of organized crime's chosen Black middlemen. In New York, the most infamous dealer was Ellsworth Raymond "Bumpy" Johnson, who was immortalized in the movie *Shaft*. Well-dressed, smooth-talking Bumpy was the most powerful Black underworld figure in New York from the late Forties to the mid-Sixties. Yet he was always beholden to the Italian mobsters who sponsored him.[71]

Some low-level Black dealers operated around the time of the Korean War. Bap Ross was credited with bringing innovative distribution and marketing techniques to street-level dealing. He established a system whereby pushers to whom he distributed would only be told by one of his workers where to pick up the heroin. The heroin package would be hidden in a hallway or behind a radiator by another of Ross's operatives. Although Ross was eventually caught, these techniques demonstrated the creative ways that dealers could avoid the law and minimize risks.[72] Another Black dealer, John Freeman, worked with Joseph Valachi up until the time Valachi was arrested.[73] None of these dealers, however, had any real independent power. That changed with the arrival of Frank Matthews, the first Black drug kingpin of the modern era.

Matthews, born in Durham, North Carolina, in 1944, got involved in numbers running in New York City. Through this work he had come into contact with drug big shot Louis Cirillo, one of the Mafia's biggest distributors on the East Coast.[74] When Matthews decided to go independent in 1967, he was told in no uncertain terms by the Mafia that they would tolerate no competition, especially from a Black man. Undeterred, Matthews made contact with the French connection on his own and installed his network of numbers runners and operatives as his base. Pool halls, candy stores, laundries, and other businesses in New York's Black communities soon became retail outlets for Matthews's heroin. Within a year, he controlled all or a significant amount of distribution in Black communities in every major city in the country, including Philadelphia, Baltimore, Cleveland, Detroit, Cincinnati, Chicago, Kansas City, Las Vegas, and Los Angeles.

Despite threats from the Mafia and the emergence of local rivals, Matthews was never overthrown. Between 1967 and 1971, he grossed over $100 million, making him a multi-millionaire before he was thirty.[75]

Matthews hired hundreds of people and set up operations all over New York to cut and bag heroin and later cocaine. He started a number of innovations that did not exist at other heroin "factories," such as eight-hour shifts and the wearing of surgical masks by workers so that they would not inhale the drugs as they worked. However, these steps were taken more out of a concern for efficiency than for workers' rights.

Matthews even had CIA connections, according to a "Top Secret" Justice Department report written in 1976. According to the report, nine persons indicted for supplying drugs to Matthews had drug importation charges dropped because of their ties to the CIA.[76] In mid-1971, Matthews's heroin supplies from the suffering French connection began to dry up, and he came under more scrutiny from law enforcement agencies. His dealers and his contacts with the Cuban Mafia, some of his key suppliers, started to squeal. He was arrested in Las Vegas on New Year's Day in 1973, his bond set at $5 million.

Matthews was eventually released when the bond was dropped to $325,000, and he returned to New York. By July 1973, Matthews had reportedly converted nearly $20 million in assets into cash. On July 2, 1973, Matthews, a bodyguard, a mistress, and the money vanished and were never found.[77]

Other major Black drug dealers came on the scene following Matthews's disappearance, including his New York successor, the legendary Nicky Barnes, and Los Angeles' so-called "Magnificent 7," the West Coast's first major grouping of Black distributors.[78] Barnes's stature grew even larger than that of Matthews, his mentor, who had taught him the ins and outs of a sophisticated drug operation. As he won well-publicized and numerous acquittals on gun, narcotics, bribery, and murder charges, Barnes's reputation expanded. *The New York Times* dubbed him "Mr. Untouchable."[79] It was not long before Barnes was at the top of the Drug Enforcement Agency's and New York Police Department's target list of key dealers to take down. Barnes proved to be a formidable enemy, however, and, although he was followed and wiretapped, he remained untouched for a number of years. Matthews was one of the first independent big dealers to see the value of laundering drug profits. Barnes followed his example, but his lucky streak came to an end when the White man who washed his money turned out to be an FBI informant. On January 19, 1978, Barnes was found guilty of a 1971 law specifically aimed at big-time criminals who operated "continuing criminal enterprises," and sentenced to life imprisonment and a $125,000 fine.

The Vietnam War created thousands of Black addicts who would eventually become some of the key sources for drugs from Southeast Asia. With roadside access to heroin, opium, and hashish in Vietnam, many Black soldiers became addicts within a few months of their tour of duty. Although there was clear evidence that drug abuse among both combat and support soldiers was growing, the U.S. Armed Forces refused to implement any serious treatment program or make an effort to halt trafficking.[80]

The stress and fears created by war and the racism of the armed services pushed many Black and Latino soldiers to drugs. Black and Latino soldiers served disproportionately on either the front lines or in menial janitorial positions, often under the command of racist officers. Drug use became a way of coping with the dehumanizing treatment they received.

The CIA's collaboration with organized crime and anti-communists guaranteed that the area known as the Golden Triangle, where Laos, Thailand, and Myanmar converge, would become the center of heroin production worldwide, meeting the demand being created back home. (See Chapter Six for more details.) At the height of the French connection, no more than eight tons of heroin a year reached the United States. During the peak of the Vietnam War, more than sixty tons a year of heroin was coming to the United States.[81]

In the early- to mid-Sixties, many of the Black youth gangs, particularly in Los Angeles, Chicago, New York, and Philadelphia, became involved in the Black freedom struggle. In Los Angeles, gangs like the Businessmen, the Gladiators, the Swamp Boys, and the Slausons became the nucleus for many community and political organizations. The Slausons were the base of a Black Panther chapter. Other gangs became involved with Maulana Ron Karenga's United Slaves (US) organization, which rivaled the Black Panthers. The FBI, under the direction of racist J. Edgar Hoover, decided that one effective way to stop the anti-war and Black liberation movements was to go after leaders and activists on drug charges. Numerous activists were set up by narcs and given stiff sentences for the possession of often tiny amounts of marijuana.[82]

The Panthers and other Black radical organizations of the period expressly forbid drug use among their members. In an effort to follow the revolutionary principles exercised by guerrillas in Cuba, Africa, and Vietnam, drug use was seen as counter-revolutionary and destructive to the community. The Panther leadership issued explicit orders that no party member could have in their possession or use any "narcotics or weed" while doing party work.[83] In the Panther lexicon, narcotics were any drugs except marijuana, which was considered benign. Any member found shooting narcotics, meaning heroin, was to be expelled. Orders were also issued against being intoxicated. No member was to have a weapon in their possession while drunk or high. Most Panthers were not addicted to drugs, and anti-drug rules were only rarely enforced.

Similar patterns developed in other ghetto areas. In Chicago, the Blackstone Rangers became an organized, militant force against Mayor Richard Daley and his political machine and for the advancement of Black politics in the city. In the Eighties, under the name El Rukn, they turned back to their old, gang habits of intimidation and petty crime. They eventually became some of Chicago's largest drug traffickers.[84] In the Seventies and Eighties, many (but by no means all) of the Black youth gangs that developed became involved in drug dealing and drug-related violence.

Crack, Crime, and Crisis in the Black Community

> I never ever ran from the Ku Klux Klan and I shouldn't have
> to run from a Black man.
>
> —Kool Moe Dee from the rap song "Self-Destruction"[85]

The destructive impact of illegal narcotics on Blacks, Latinos, and poor people has become murderous. Indeed, whole communities are being destroyed from top to bottom as children take over the role of family breadwinner, mothers become addicts who barter sex for drugs, and drug-addicted, abandoned babies strain already overburdened city hospital services.

Ironically, government solutions to the drug crisis increasingly assume the posture of attacks on the civil and political rights of the Black community. Plans to build more prisons, the barrage of media images portraying young Black males as addicts and criminals, and efforts to physically cordon off entire Black neighborhoods all reek of racism.

In the Black community, the "war on drugs" has raised the question of "war against whom?" One ominous sign of the government's real aim is the Federal Bureau of Prisons' announcement that it plans to build 20,000 new prison cells over the next fifteen years.[86] It is obvious who is expected to fill those jails; at the beginning of the 1990s, African Americans are almost half of the prison population.[87]

The prison population of the United States, partly a result of increased Black incarceration, has nearly doubled in the last ten years. In 1980, there were 329,821 in America's prisons. By 1989, that number had risen to 627,402. In 1980, the rate of prisoners per 1,000 population was 139. By 1988, it had shot up to 256.[88] State after state saw extraordinary growth in incarceration rates.

According to the Washington, D.C.-based Sentencing Project, as of 1990, the United States has the highest incarceration rate in the world (426 per 100,000), which is higher than that of South Africa (333 per 100,000). More than one million U.S. citizens are in jail.[89] The Sentencing Project also released the study that documented that about one in four young Black males in their twenties are either in jail, on parole, or on probation. Only 6 percent of White males in their twenties are in a similar situation, and for Latinos it's about 10 percent.[90] At the same time, only 13 percent of Black youth are in higher education.[91] In Washington, D.C., 16 percent of all Black males under twenty-one will be arrested and charged with selling drugs.[92] By 1994, in Florida, almost half of all

Black men between the ages of eighteen and thirty-four will be incarcerated or placed under court supervision.[93] Even women's prisons, traditionally underpopulated, are overflowing with Black women.

By mainly going after street-level dealers, drug enforcement officers perpetuate the myth that the majority of traffickers and users are people of color. In 1988, however, the FBI and the National Institute for Drug Abuse concluded that Blacks constitute only 12 percent of the nation's drug users.[94] Whites comprise 80 percent of all illegal drug users.[95]

According to the National Institute on Drug Abuse's (NIDA) 1990 figures of the estimated 13 million regular users of illegal drugs, Blacks make up 15 percent, Latinos make up 8 percent, and Whites make up 77 percent.[96] The percentage of drug use is relatively the same for each race. For Blacks, Latinos, and Whites, the figures are 8.6 percent, 6.2 percent, and 6.6 percent, respectively.[97] Even William Bennett recognizes the disparity between myth and fact. He stated that the typical coke user is "White, male, a high-school graduate employed full-time and living in a small metropolitan area or suburb."[98]

Whites are not only the majority of drug users; they are also the most common drug sellers. Contrary to mainstream media images of young Black men spread-eagled on the ground or handcuffed in the latest high-profile drug raid, Whites dominate the drug trafficking industry. Whites also get the lion's share of profits, as they deal narcotics wholesale and behind the security of closed corporate doors.

Although Whites are the majority of drug users, they are not the majority of those convicted for drug use. In 1988, Blacks were 38 percent of those arrested on drug charges. In 1989, that figure grew to 41 percent.[99] In New York, Whites are 47 percent of the clients in state-funded centers, but less than 10 percent of those committed to prison.[100]

The mandatory sentencing laws enacted by Congress and many states in response to citizens' outcry regarding street trafficking and its accompanying violence have resulted in discriminatory arrest and sentencing patterns against Blacks. Since low-level street dealers in urban areas are predominantly Black, they are easier to arrest than the big kingpins, meaning Blacks will go to jail at a greater rate than Whites.

Laws passed by Congress further this bias by giving harsher mandatory sentences for crack cocaine, which is more likely to be found on the Black street dealer, than for cocaine powder. For example, distribution of five grams or more of crack, worth only about $125 on the street, is a five-year mandatory term in prison. In contrast, it would take 500 grams of powder cocaine, worth about $50,000, to receive the same sentence.[101] One gram of crack has roughly become the equivalent of 100 grams of cocaine powder.[102] In response to this blatantly obvious inequity, Seattle federal public defender William Hines stated, "I cannot say with any authority that the law was intended to be racist, but the effect of that law is racist."[103]

Drug laws are also discriminatory at the local level. In Minneapolis, Minnesota, in December 1990, a law was thrown out that gave four years to first-time crack users, but only probation to first-time cocaine powder users. Figures showed that 92 percent of those arrested for crack possession were Black, while 85 percent of those arrested for possessing cocaine powder were White.

The Black community is also victim of the violation of civil liberties due to the Bush Administration's drug war. In Washington, nearly 200 evictions of mostly Black citizens took place on the word of landlords who claimed that these residents were dealing drugs. Although few drugs were found, using warrantless searches, it turns out that most of these tenants were in rent disputes with their landlords.[104]

In numerous Black communities, police departments have launched what are essentially full-scale military assaults. With the logistics of the kind usually reserved for invasions of other nations, police raid Black neighborhoods weekly. Kicked-in doors, ransacked homes, mass arrests, and other brutal tactics are common in these raids. These campaigns have macho-sounding names such as Memphis' Operation Invincible, Los Angeles' Operation Hammer, Chicago's Operation Clean Sweep, Atlanta's Red Dog Squad, and New York's TNT. Not a single White community has been the target of these assaults, although drug use may be of crisis proportions there, too.

Increased police presence in the Black community has meant a general increase in arrests and charges against Blacks. In one Black housing project in Atlanta where drug dealing had become a serious problem, the subsequent police focus on the neighborhood resulted in a disproportionate rise in traffic violations. Although only about 10 percent of Atlanta's residents lived in the project, in the month following the decision by the police to target their community they received more than half of Atlanta's traffic tickets. The same neighborhood was the victim of one-third of the cars towed in the city. Of the 4,800 charges filed against residents in the area, more than 4,300 were either minor traffic charges or misdemeanors.[105] In other cities, citizen groups, civil libertarians, and even law enforcement officials report similar situations. According to David Meyers, assistant director of the Los Angeles County Public Defender's Office, "The number of drunk driving arrests go up. They pick up people they wouldn't otherwise get on petty misdemeanors that are not drug related."[106]

The threat to the civil liberties of Blacks is real. The use of unconstitutional legal tactics echoes centuries of unequal treatment of Blacks by the U.S. justice system. The racist application of the death penalty and inappropriately harsh sentences have historically been challenged by a strong movement for judicial fairness; amendments to the Constitution that have guaranteed equal rights and civil liberty protection were won after hard-fought battles. The American Civil Liberties Union has gotten behind the Black community in a number of instances to stop the erosion of their civil liberties caused by the drug war. In Chicago, the ACLU stopped police raids on Black public housing units after complaints that the Chicago Housing Authority was requiring identification for residents and banning overnight guests.[107] In Boston, the ACLU was involved in a case where Superior Court Judge Cortland Mathers determined that there was an official "search-on-sight" policy against men in the Black communities of Roxbury, Dorchester, and Mattapan.[108] In one incident, a Black man was "accidently" shot by Boston police during one of their street searches.[109] Atlanta citizens in one public housing unit also filed legal suits and raised loud complaints against illegal police tactics. They objected to roadblocks being set up at entrances to their unit and being asked for identification just for being in that neighborhood.

The fight to stop civil liberties abuses against the Black community has been complicated by the fact that many Blacks are willing to relinquish some of those civil liberties in the name of the war against drugs. Many in the Black community who experience the violence much more directly than Whites want relief and are ready to accept brutal law enforcement tactics as a short-term solution.

Chicago's Father George Clements, a national and local anti-drug leader in the Black community, stated unequivocally that he did not care if a few rights were stepped on if it meant ridding the community of drugs. He said, "I'm all for whatever tactics have to be used. If that means they're trampling on civil liberties, so be it. I feel that they're not being strict enough. For me, the bottom line is death."[110]

Drugs and Economic Genocide

The current upsurge in drug trafficking and abuse in the Black community has mainly been driven by a complex web of economic need meeting economic opportunity. It's impossible to grasp the dynamics of the current drug problem without grasping the impact of economic changes on the Black community during the Reagan era. Black males, particularly young ones, have been trapped in a cycle of poverty and unemployment, nothing less than economic genocide. A 1985 Field Foundation study asserts that one-half of all Black men between the ages of sixteen and sixty-five are chronically unemployed.[111] Black youth unemployment has officially hovered around 45 percent or higher for the last decade, and in reality is much higher.[112]

Since 1960, Black youth have suffered the sharpest increases in unemployment and the worst poverty. At least 45 percent of all Black children live in poverty.[113] When Black youths become unemployed, they are unemployed much longer than their White counterparts.[114]

Black family per capita income continues to be a fraction of White income and even has fallen behind the income of Latinos. In 1990, Black family median income was 54 percent of Whites, where it was about thirty years ago. In the mid-1970s, it was 62 percent of Whites.[115] One-third of Black Americans, 9.7 million, lived in poverty in 1990, an increase of 700,000 since 1986. Meanwhile, the poverty level for Whites actually *decreased* between 1986 and 1987 from 11 percent to 10.5 percent.[116] In 1989, 11.9 percent of all Black families earned less than $5,000 annually compared to 6.7 percent in 1976.[117]

The small increase in income among middle-class Blacks is dramatically offset by the growth of poverty in too many Black communities. Indeed, according to an important study done by *Money* magazine in December 1989, racial discrimination continues to prevent the Black middle class from achieving parity with its White counterpart. Among the conclusions drawn by the study were: Blacks earn 10 percent to 26 percent less than Whites with similar educational backgrounds; the median income for Black male college graduates was $26,550 compared to White male college graduates' median income of $35,701; and Black professionals and managers are twice as likely to be unemployed as their counterparts.[118]

Cuts in aid for higher education in the past ten years, under the knife of then-Education Secretary William Bennett, blocked one more avenue out of poverty. In the mid-1970s, when almost twice as much federal grant money for higher education was available to the Black community, the percentage of Black high school graduates who attended college (33.5 percent) was higher than that of Whites (33 percent).[119] Between 1985 and 1990, the impact of Bennett's cuts was a fluctuation in Black college enrollment between 26 percent and 30 percent. Over the same period, White enrollment of high school graduates averaged about 36.6 percent.[120] At the high school level, the drop-out rate for young Blacks is nationally about 25 percent, and is much greater in many urban areas.[121]

During this period, the coca leaf production glut made cocaine plentiful and, therefore, cheaper. A kilogram that sold for $50-60,000 in 1980 goes for as little as $10-12,000 today. The development of crack cocaine, which sells for as little as $2.00 a "rock" in some cities, was the final step in turning cocaine from a faddish drug used predominantly by a small coterie of affluent Whites and some Blacks to a mass product used by hundreds of thousands of people of all races.

Poor Black communities became the ideal market for crack. They provided a ready-made distribution network of existing or easily created street gangs of unemployed youth who could retail crack and other drugs. These communities also had consumers who would purchase the cheap, but potent, product. It's no accident that Los Angeles, Miami, Chicago, and New York, cities that have historically had large Black street gangs, are the major points of drug distribution. In Los Angeles, for example, it's estimated that there are between 80,000 and 100,000 gang members, many of whom deal in drugs.[122]

As a result of the increase in street marketing, the illegal narcotics industry has become a major (perhaps the major) employer of Black youth. Illegal drug trafficking is the major economic activity in many Black and Latino neighborhoods. In the era of Reagan budget cuts, large cash flow into these communities was quite welcome. Due to income derived from drug trafficking, people can buy food, pay rent, and live materially better lives. Black youth can easily make $100 a day or more simply by watching for the police or steering customers in the right direction. A study by the Urban Institute underscores the economic imperative for many young people. The study indicates that more than two-thirds of those who sell drugs don't use drugs.[123]

The Reagan-Bush administrations have made much of the supposed many jobs available to Black youth at fast-food places such as McDonalds. However, McDonalds' low wages and boring work are not an effective alternative to the more lucrative drug trade earnings, and, for those who do choose the fast-food job path, discrimination is a major factor.

A study done in Philadelphia by the Philadelphia Unemployment Project discovered that McDonalds was paying inner-city workers an average of one dollar less per hour than their suburban counterparts: $3.82 versus $4.82. The inner-city workers were overwhelmingly Black and Latino (77 percent) while the suburban workers were majority White (67 percent). In the city's poorer sections, such as North Philadelphia, the gap was even larger.[124]

Chemical Warfare

Blacks are spending between $16 and $20 billion a year on illegal drugs, according to *Ebony*.[125] In every area of Black America, drug abuse is growing. The impact of these developments has been staggering and deadly. The drug epidemic has initiated a wave of violence and a community health crisis of genocidal proportions. One in thirty Black males will be a murder victim.[126] The frequency of accidental murders of citizens caught in the crossfire of drug deals gone sour has demoralized communities across the country.

The drug crisis in the Black community has been labelled by some analysts as "chemical warfare" against Black people. Blacks make up 50 percent of those admitted to emergency rooms for heroin, 55 percent of those for cocaine, and 60 percent of those for PCP.[127] Blacks comprised 31 percent of all people with drug emergencies in 1985 and 25 percent of those in treatment for drugs in 1987.[128]

Heroin use has accelerated the spread of AIDS in the Black community. Heroin addiction, declining prior to the 1980s, has risen again, as many crack addicts also use heroin. It's not just heroin that is spreading AIDS. Many cocaine users are also injecting, and, because the addiction is stronger than that of heroin, users are injecting more frequently, thereby, increasing the chance of becoming infected. Blacks constitute 37 percent of all those who contracted AIDS through needles and 48 percent of those who contracted AIDS through partners who use dirty needles. These patterns of transmission largely explain why Blacks are 27 percent of all people with AIDS, and Black women are 52 percent of all women with AIDS.[129]

Community Dope Busting

In lieu of constructive government action, the Black community has aggressively taken the struggle into its own hands. From Dick Gregory's work in Louisiana to the Muslim Dope Busters in the nation's capital, community-based groups have fought drug dealers on their own turf as well as launched successful education and prevention projects. These groups have also taken the lead in demanding more treatment centers and more local, state, and federal resources.

In the 1980s, Muslim organizations, Black men's groups, and community activists in New York, Detroit, Washington, Atlanta, and other major cities decided to confront street-level dealers and crackhouse operators directly. By aggressively challenging the corner dealer for his turf, these groups caused many pushers to switch rather than fight. Although no particular organization took credit for it, crack houses were burned down in some cities. While some local police authorities decried these endeavors as vigilantism and citizens taking the law into their own hands, most of the residents in those Black communities cheered their work, honored their successes, and wondered aloud why the police had been previously unable to get rid of these dealers.

These displays of courage and action forced other players in the Black community to move. The major civil rights organizations have marshalled their resources and joined in the fight and revamped their work to end drug trafficking and abuse in the African American community. The Urban League, which has historically spoken out against the destructiveness of Black-on-Black crime, in 1989 declared its determination to rid the Black community of drug pushers. Urban League President John Jacob, speaking at the organization's seventy-ninth annual convention, compared the dope dealer with the Ku Klux Klan. He said, "Drugs kill more Blacks than the Klan ever did."[130]

Tilting towards the get-tough banter reminiscent of the Reagan administration, Jacob attempted to prepare the Urban League for a campaign that would take it back to the streets. The anti-drug programs previously run by the Urban League had not been successful in reaching the hard-core addicts or street traffickers. Jacob advocated a program that included closer cooperation with law enforcement agencies, photographing people who openly sold drugs, and support for tougher laws and penalties for drug-related crimes.[131]

The Southern Christian Leadership Conference (SCLC) also started a new anti-drug program. The national program, known as "Wings of Hope," was started on April 18, 1989, and focuses on organizing through the churches.[132] Wings of Hope provides churches and community groups with training in drug prevention through health professionals who are treatment experts. The program also gives training in parental skills and spiritual guidance. Black actor Louis Gossett, Jr., came on board as the national spokesperson for the campaign. The program earned kudos from William Bennett and has been cited by his office as one of the top fifteen community-based, anti-drug programs in the nation.[133] Significantly, SCLC National President Joseph Lowery has not let Bennett's praise mute his criticism of how the federal drug war is being waged. Lowery has been disparaging of Bennett's war on drugs and said that it would not succeed "unless it offers substantial economic assistance to desperate people plagued by the despair of poverty, high unemployment, and homelessness."[134] Rev. Richard Dalton, National Program Director of Wings of Hope, is equally adamant about the need to address the social causes of the drug problem. He sees not only users as victims, but, to some degree, young pushers as well. "Crack dealers are not born, they are made!" he says.[135] The NAACP's *Crisis* magazine has published a number of thought-provoking articles that have called for more of a balance between law enforcement, on the one hand, and decriminalization and treatment on the other.[136]

In order to more effectively unite forces within the African American community against the drug crisis, a number of important national conferences were held in 1989 and 1990 that brought together activists, professionals, and concerned citizens. The largest of these conferences was organized in the Spring of 1989 and 1990 by Rev. Cecil Williams of Glide Memorial Church in San Francisco.[137] The conference was titled "The Black Family/Community and Crack Cocaine: Prevention, Treatment, Recovery—The Death of a Race" and was attended by thousands from around the country. The most important thing to emerge from these meetings was the construction of regional networks where people could share experiences and, when possible, work together in joint projects.

In the written statement welcoming participants to the 1989 conference, Rev. Williams stated, "As an African American, I had not envisioned that we would be involved in yet another era of slavery. Crack cocaine has become the 'master' and we have become 'slaves' of this intensively addictive drug. Our lives are at stake. Our children's lives are at stake."[138] In an earnest and deeply felt call to arms, he went on to say:

> It is at the "bottom" that we are most victimized, and from the bottom we must rise up. Now is the time to call for the Freedom Train. The Freedom Train that freed us once is the train that will free us again. The Conference is the call for us to be the engineers to lead our people to liberation. Prevention, intervention, and recovery are tickets for the train. We must realistically, honestly, actively, and spiritually come together in unity and solidarity to confront the crisis of crack cocaine. We must engage in networking that will ensure our connection, and bring our brothers and sisters back home.[139]

While most African American leaders have been reluctant to embrace radical solutions such as "clean" needle distribution, legalization, and decriminalization, there are a few notable exceptions. Baltimore Mayor and former prosecutor Kurt Schmoke, in a speech before the U.S. Conference of Mayors, called for "a national debate on decriminalization."[140] Schmoke, whose city faces one of the most intractable heroin and crack epidemic problem of any in the nation, says, "I'm convinced that we can't prosecute our way out of this problem. All that we do when we get tough on drugs is inflate the price on the street, and cause more addicts to break into more houses and mug more people."[141]

Former Congressman and judge George Crockett (D-MI) has also spoken out favorably for expanding the discussion about legalization. Crockett, who has a long record of standing strong on progressive issues, believes that legalization could undermine the criminal elements at the root of the violence associated with drug trafficking. He argues further that resources being used against the Black community in the drug war could be put to better use in treatment and prevention programs.[142]

Conclusion

A mass political movement is needed in the Black community. As in the past, we now need Black mass movements, a flowering of organizations and opinions, of ideas and identity, of actions and audacity. But the new conditions and realities of the Nineties must be acknowledged.

Distinct from the past, power—political, economic, social, or cultural—must be delivered to those who toil every day in the service industries, manufacturing sectors, and the public sector of our society. People need to be organized as workers, as communities, and as recipients of the resources of our nation. Homeless unions, tenant organizations, free health-care advocacy groups, and many other underfunded causes should continue to be coordinated and advanced.

The struggle against racism lost much of its focus after the death of King and the end of *de jure* segregation. Too often, the interests of the Black middle class—tax relief, political appointments, higher education opportunities, small-business development—were projected as the immediate interest of all Blacks. But the trickle-down notion that benefits to a few Blacks will eventually accrue to the race as a whole is flawed. Important Black middle-class gains in education, employment, and politics have been offset by cutbacks, increased discrimination against poor people, and the inability to translate political positioning into economic power. In the Nineties, the needs of poor people in the Black community will have more in common with other people of color and poor Whites than with Blacks in the middle class.

At the same time, the institutional and systemic racism that continues in the United States will not only have an impact on African Americans, but on other people of color as well, thereby demanding a unity of interests across racial lines. A rainbow coalition neither hurts Black unity or dilutes the struggle against racism. But that rainbow will only be successful to the degree that it acknowledges and understands the complexities of class and race politics of the current era.

It is not just the potential of Blacks as individuals that is being threatened by the drug crisis. Entire communities are being destabilized as the drug epidemic reaches into every sector of the community. As the next chapter outlines, women who traditionally have not been as caught up in the grips of addiction are becoming addicted in the largest numbers in history. The toll on the Black community is devastating.

Chapter 3

WOMEN, FAMILIES, COMMUNITIES, AND THE DRUG CRISIS

Just as Black family life has always been a barometer of racial and economic injustice and at the same time a means of transcending and surviving those injustices, Black families headed by women reflect the strength and the difficulty of Black life in the 1980s.[1]

—Barbara Ommolade

Though given little attention by the Bush administration, women and their families are being devastated by the drug crisis. Women of color, in particular, are suffering the consequences of addiction as well as the cruel excesses of the drug war.

In all aspects, women are feeling the brunt of the drug crisis and the drug war more harshly than any other sector of society. The impact goes much further than direct physical and psychological injury; entire communities are dissolving as a result of incarceration, addiction, and destabilization, much of which is drug-related. The extended family system that has operated since slavery has been eroded as Black communities find themselves under siege. Poor people are being forced out of inner-city neighborhoods, and young, White professionals are moving in, oblivious and insensitive to the destabilization they are a part of. Many of the professionals are merely "investing"—not occupying their fashionable reconstructed town houses until the neighborhood changes over from poor to middle- or upper-class hands.

The drug crisis exacerbates these conditions because it undermines the community unity necessary to challenge the incursion of drug markets and drug houses. Consequently, those who are suffering most will no doubt suffer more.

More Law, Less Order

Women are becoming addicts and going to jail for drug-related offenses at rates significantly higher than men. In addition to the impact on individual women, communities are becoming even more destabilized as women of color are incarcerated or destroyed by drugs. The disproportionate number of Black men in jail and in the military has often meant that women are forced to raise a family alone, and often in dire economic straits. Now that many more women are caught up in the destructive lifestyle of drug abuse, children are being raised by relatives—or simply abandoned.

The get-tough, mandatory-sentencing laws are forcing judges to send to prison first-time offenders who a short time ago would have gotten only probation or a fine. With the community pressure to arrest those involved in drugs, it is inevitable that women caught selling even the smallest amount of drugs will do time. As a result of the explosion in drug arrests, women's jails and prisons are overflowing. In 1984, women accounted for only 5.8 percent (1,996) of all federal prisoners. In 1989, that number had shot up to 6.8 percent (3,584).[2] That figure represented a 24.4 percent leap over the 1988 figure, while the male prison population grew just 12.5 percent. In 1987, the female prison population grew 54 percent in Washington, D.C., 40 percent in New York, and 35 percent in Virginia. From 1980 to 1989, female incarceration rates were higher than for men.[3] California women's prisons are having one of the nation's greatest overcrowding problems. In 1990, female prisons at Stockton and Frontera were operating at 170 percent and 250 percent capacities respectively.[4] The increase in women's incarceration rates is a direct result of drug-related offenses and crimes, such as prostitution, theft, and even armed robbery—historically a male crime. In Washington, D.C., more than 80 percent of the crimes committed by women in the late Eighties were drug-related. Similar trends are reported in other major cities.[5]

Women are also finding themselves going to jail for child neglect at a much higher rate than ever before. As many women addicts abandon and abuse their children, child neglect has become one of the most serious social problems in the nation. In San Francisco, for example, between 1986 and 1989, foster care cases concerning drug-addicted families rose 148 percent, involving more than 900 children. Crack was involved in 77 percent of those cases.[6]

Congressman Charles Rangel of New York, Chairperson of the House Select Committee on Narcotics Abuse and Control, estimates that there are about two million women who use cocaine regularly. According to Rangel, about 10 percent of all pregnant women tried cocaine at least once during their pregnancy.[7] The National Institute on Drug Abuse (NIDA) estimates that women make up about 3.8 million of the regular 10 million drug users.[8] The great majority of these women are of child-bearing age (fifteen to forty-four). This group is disproportionately of color, poor, and abused. The tragic consequences befalling the Black women in this group threaten not only their lives and their community, but the future of Black America itself.

With the rise of crack addiction, there has been a rise in "cocaine mothers," pregnant women who pass their addiction on to their unborn children. Despite the fact that White women test positive for drugs at the same rate as Black women, as one reporter noted, the term cocaine mother has virtually become synonymous with pregnant Black women.[9] Racism is the reason for this erroneous perception. A Florida study done by the National Association for Perinatal Addiction Research and Education (NAPARE) discovered that physicians turn in Black women who test positive for drugs at a rate almost ten times that of White women.[10] In the forty-seven cases identified by the ACLU involving prosecutions of women for abuse of their "unborn child" where the mother's race could be determined, 80 percent involved women of color.[11] The rate of drug use among pregnant White women in the NAPARE study was 15.4 percent compared to 14.1 percent for Black users. The rate varied considerably, however, for specific drugs. For cocaine, Black women's rate of use was 7.5 percent while for White women it was 1.8 percent. For marijuana that relationship was reversed. White women had a use rate of 14.4 percent compared to 6 percent for Black women.[12]

As the law enforcement thrust grows, women are catching the worst of it. Fetal endangerment cases, where drug-addicted pregnant women are accused of endangering the life of their unborn child, are more frequent. In state after state, including South Carolina, Colorado, Florida, California, Massachusetts, Ohio, Arizona, Washington, D.C., and Indiana, charges have been filed and women have gone to jail.[13] The criminalization of pregnant drug addicts has required fanciful interpretations of current legal statutes. Laws prohibiting child abuse, drug distribution to minors, involuntary manslaughter, and even contributing to the delinquency of a minor have all been exploited to prosecute women whose problems have clearly been more health-related than criminal.

In 1985, Pamela Rae Stewart became the first victim of these new legal maneuvers.[14] The San Diego County district attorney's office charged Stewart with failing to provide support and medical care for her unborn child. This charge of criminal neglect—a misdemeanor dating back to 1925 that is usually reserved for fathers who don't take care of their child support obligations—was brought against her after her son was born brain-damaged and died six weeks after birth.[15] In court, Stewart was accused of not following her doctor's advice of abstaining from using drugs and of having intercourse during her last months of pregnancy. The San Diego County Municipal Court ruled that the law Stewart was charged with was too broad to be constitutional as applied to fetuses. Judge E. MacAmos, Jr. ruled against the district attorney's office in a pretrial motion and the charges were dropped, but not before Stewart spent a week in jail.

Since that time an avalanche of similar cases has appeared, and, where convictions have been won, the sentences have been longer and have held up in court. Several lengthy probations and a number of jail terms have been handed down.

In 1988, in the District of Columbia, Brenda Vaughan was sentenced to an extraordinarily long 180 days in jail after pleading guilty to forging $700 in checks. At the time, Vaughan was pregnant and using cocaine. Attempting to throw her in jail long enough for her to have a "drug-free" child, Judge Peter H. Wolf rejected the prosecution recommendation that Vaughan be put on probation.[16] It is fairly well known that illegal drugs can be obtained in any jail or prison in the country.

Wolf defended the decision by saying, "Obviously you want to protect society from a dangerous armed robber who is going to rob again. Is not an unborn baby equally entitled to protection from a mother who cannot stay away from cocaine?"[17] He went on to state, "I concluded that we taxpayers are going to pay for that baby anyway if it is born addicted or neurologically damaged. So, yes, it is a valid consideration. I also recognized that the damage to that baby may already have been done. I may have locked her up...too late."[18] Wolf's stab at judicial wisdom failed, because Vaughan was able to meet early release provisions and had her child outside of jail. In many cases, the zeal to enforce the law has not only been legally questionable, but also humiliating. In 1989, in Kentucky, Connie Welch O'Neal was convicted on one count of second-degree criminal abuse of her infant son for using drugs during her pregnancy. The jury deliberated for only thirty-five minutes.[19] In the public hospital in Charleston, South Carolina, women were selectively tested for drugs. Women who tested positive were handcuffed, arrested, and taken to jail, in some instances, within minutes after delivery. One woman went to jail still bleeding from the delivery and was told to sit on a towel.[20]

District attorneys' offices all over the country are rushing to get laws on the books that criminalize the pregnant user. In Butte County, California, District Attorney Michael Ramsey proposed that county hospitals attempt to identify which newborns are drug-addicted and, if they test positive, report the mother to authorities to be charged with drug possession. Those convicted would be placed in a drug treatment program or face a mandatory ninety days in jail.[21] An important point, conveniently ignored by Wolf, Ramsey, and other hard-liners, is that giving birth in prison, an environment where stress is high, prenatal care and nutrition are virtually non-existent, and illegal drugs rampant, is a cruel punishment for mother and child alike. Sudden withdrawal, for example from heroin, could very likely cause fetal death.

Rep. Louise Bishop of the Pennsylvania House of Representatives asks, "Where do we draw the line?"[22] In highlighting the dangers of imprisoning pregnant users, particularly under the pretext of concern for the "unborn child," she further chides those who would prosecute these women by asking, "Should smoking, drinking alcohol, exposing oneself to contaminants in the work place, or staying on one's feet too long also be subject to criminal penalty?"[23] The American Civil Liberties Union points out that women who are diabetic, overweight, stricken with cancer or epilepsy all may use drugs that are potentially harmful to the fetus. With some sarcasm, it notes that U.S. women who fly to Europe (adverse affects of radiation from the sun and the stars that could lead to retardation) or empty their cat's litter box (exposure to toxoplasmosis that could cause sudden abortion) could also be charged with fetal endangerment.[24]

Cases like Stewart's, Vaughan's, and O'Neal's have raised the ire of the American Civil Liberties Union, women's organizations, medical groups, health care unions, and political rights activists. Judith Rosen of the ACLU provides sharp rebuttal to these draconian trends. She says, "The real issue is that women are not getting the treatment they need before the baby is born."[25] In Butte County, women addicted to heroin had to travel eighty-five miles to Sacramento to a private outpatient program that charged $200 a month, an obviously unaffordable fee for most addicts.[26]

Jurisdictions are aggressively seeking to prosecute addicts essentially for not getting treatment before they were pregnant, yet have failed to make treatment facilities geared to drug-abusing pregnant women available. Further, as the ACLU testified before the House Sub-committee on Health and the Environment of the Committee on Energy and Commerce, "The length of waiting lists for treatment centers frequently extends beyond the pregnant woman's due date, thus rendering the benefits of treatment meaningless to fetal health."[27]

The prejudice against pregnant users is so strong that even treatment programs that have space often refuse these women. Some programs feel that they don't have the additional resources needed to handle the extra complications that pregnant users and crack addiction bring. Others, which have traditionally dealt mainly with men, are still adjusting just to having to treat women for the first time. A study of 78 drug treatment centers in New York found that 67 percent of those centers denied treatment to pregnant addicts even though they were eligible for Medicaid, and the treatment would be paid for. For those addicted to crack, the refusal rate rose to 87 percent even while on Medicaid.[28]

In addition, the fear of arrest has made more women reluctant to seek delivery in hospitals. This fear is justified. Here again we witness selective discrimination, because public hospitals, which are used more by poor people and people of color, tend to test for drug use more, whereas private facilities tend to test less and certainly turn in clients at a much smaller rate. As a result of such legal threats, many women are deciding to have their babies at home, a choice which greatly increases the risk of harm or even death for the mother and the infant. As one study concluded, "...in the end, it is safer for the baby to be born to a drug-abusing, anemic, or diabetic mother who visits the doctor throughout her pregnancy than to be born to a normal woman who does not."[29]

One of the problems with most current treatment programs for cocaine and crack users is that they are often modelled after past programs that targeted heroin-addicted men (and did not work). No model program has been developed that specifically treats crack-addicted women. For example, pregnant users who have other children also avoid treatment programs because of the unavailability of either childcare facilities or a relative to care for their children. Ideally, programs would include prenatal care, classes in parenting, skills and educational development, childcare facilities, and job preparedness and placement.

A couple of programs have taken steps in the right direction. In Detroit, the Eleanore Hutzel Recovery Center focuses on adult women users and has recorded some successes. With a staff of about forty-five, including physicians, nurses, social workers, psychologists, and therapists, it's one of the few programs that does not turn away any pregnant addict, no matter her financial situation. The program is funded mainly by the state of Michigan.[30] Another program in Hawaii is named Pohai Pono, which means "Circle of Wellness." The program works with the mothers and addicted newborns in their development skills.[31]

Even women who have no trafficking or abuse record are being victimized by the drug war. In Los Angeles, an attempt was made to jail a woman whose seventeen-year-old son was in a gang that raped a twelve-year old girl. Gloria Williams was arrested and charged under the Street Terrorism Enforcement and Prevention Act.[32] The law, passed in 1988, stated that parents could be jailed and fined for failing "to exercise reasonable care, supervision, protection and control" over their children who were minors.[33] But the interpretation of what is "reasonable" is broad enough to include any offense the city wants to bring against a parent. When it was shown that she had attended parenting classes, and with pressure from local and national civil libertarians, women's groups, and others, the Los Angeles Sheriff's Department was eventually forced to drop the case.[34] The ACLU is fighting to have such laws declared unconstitutional and has filed lawsuits against the Los Angeles District Attorney's office.

Drug Abuse Grows

The growth in drug abuse among women, especially young women, has potentially genocidal impact on innumerable communities. For the first time, health officials see more women drug users than men. In New York, Washington, D.C., Kansas City, Portland, and other major cities, women outnumber men in drug abuse.[35] Females of all ages are being affected. Girls as young as twelve trade sex for crack as prostitutes in crack houses, and even all-girl crack gangs have been formed.[36] This development is especially dangerous, as many poor women addicts, who unlike most of their male counterparts don't have a steady legal or illegal income, are driven fairly quickly to trading sex for drugs. Even outside of prostitution, drugs are also used as a means of breaking down resistance to male sexual overtures, especially for young teenage girls.

One Justice Department study pinpointed the role of "crack" cocaine as a reason for the increase in female drug addiction. Another researcher, who has worked as a child/family counselor in Queens, New York, believes crack doesn't violate what she calls "feminine body taboos," whereas women are more hesitant about using needles than men. In addition, the writer argues that the millions of dollars spent by tobacco companies glamorizing smoking have broken down women's inhibitions about using crack.[37]

The Justice Department study showed, for example, that a higher percentage of women than men in the District of Columbia tested positive for cocaine use: 65 percent of women as opposed to 62 percent of men. In New York, the numbers were 73 percent for women and 67 percent for men.[38]

And it's not just cocaine use that has grown. Historically, studies have shown that more than 80 percent of heroin users have been men. In 1989, according to the same Justice Department study, female heroin users outnumbered male users in a number of major cities. In New York,

28 percent of the women in the study tested positive for heroin as compared to 25 percent of the men. In the District of Columbia, it was 20 percent of women and 11 percent of men.[39]

Endangered Species: Mothers and Children

Drug abuse growth among women has led directly to the rise in boarder babies, that is, infants born mostly of drug-addicted parents and abandoned in hospitals. According to NAPARE, about 375,000 babies a year are born exposed to drugs.[40] In one study of eight hospitals in Philadelphia, about 16 percent of all women who delivered babies were cocaine users; of this group, 87 percent were Black.[41]

Washington's D.C. General Hospital, New York's Harlem Hospital, and other hospitals nationally have opened prenatal clinics for women addicts. At some Washington, D.C., hospitals, as many as 40 percent of women having babies are drug addicts, resulting in the highest infant mortality rate in the nation—32.3 per 1,000 live births.[42] In central Harlem, 21 percent of all pregnant crack users receive no prenatal care.[43] Howard University Hospital had no boarder babies until May 1988; in 1989, the hospital had twenty-one in one week, five with AIDS.[44] At San Francisco General Hospital, 12 percent of the babies born were crack addicted. In 1988, the hospital took care of about 250 crack babies born there.[45]

These infants suffer horrifying repercussions as a result of their mother's addiction. Cocaine's low molecular weight and high solubility in fat allows it easily to cross the placenta to the fetus. This often results in a process known as *abruptio placentae,* in which the placenta hemorrhages and causes premature birth.[46] One study found that the rate of premature births for drug users was over 30 percent compared with a rate of about 3 percent for non-drug users. In some cases with drug users, premature birth can be as much as fourteen weeks ahead of schedule.[47] These babies are generally smaller and sometimes weigh as little as one and one-half pounds or less.[48]

Pregnant drug users also have a high incidence of stillbirths. Cocaine causes blood vessels to constrict. As the arteries and the veins narrow and, therefore, transport less oxygen, the unborn fetus can die of a heart attack or stroke.[49] Soon after birth, many babies die from Sudden Infant Death Syndrome (SIDS). For the babies of drug users, SIDS has an occurrence rate of 15 percent versus that of 1 percent for non-drug users.[50]

For those babies who survive the trauma of the womb, life is not much better. Many children suffer from severe respiratory problems, have a higher incidence of congenital malformation in the nervous, gastrointestinal, and genitourinary systems, and universally experience

Neonatal Abstinence Syndrome (NAS).[51] NAS causes these babies to develop abnormal sleep patterns, extreme irritability, poor feeding habits, and inadequate coordination. More than half of these babies develop small heads and small abdomens.

Drug-afflicted babies stay an average of forty-two days in the hospital before they are placed, while the stay for a normal infant is three days. The cost of maintaining one of these babies is estimated to average $100,000 each year per baby.[52] The love and care that these babies receive depends on the whim and ability of the hospital staff. These children, unnaturally separated from their mothers, will generally struggle with the psychological effects of abandonment, a poor attention span, and an inability to cope with intimacy.

A study released by the Department of Health and Human Services states that most crack babies do not fit the stereotype of an underweight, wrenching, constantly crying infant, and that the effects of their prenatal drug exposure could take up to two to three years to appear.[53] In addition to the physical and psychological damage that the drug will have caused, these children will almost all live in a socially and economically disadvantaged setting. These conditions will only compound the problems not just for the children, and the parents, but for the society that must find a way to integrate these children despite the challenge they may pose.

The study estimates that special intensive services needed to adequately prepare these children for school could cost as much as $167,000 per child.[54] Between 1990 and 1995, the cost of caring for the estimated 100,000 cocaine-exposed babies born in 1990 will amount to more than $16 billion. With the continued growth of drug-exposed infants, there could be well over four million such children in the United States by 1995.[55]

Emergency in the Emergency Rooms

City services are collapsing even as they try to meet the expanded needs of drug users. Public hospitals, particularly in the inner cities, are taking the brunt of the drug-driven emergencies. Emergency rooms increasingly look like scenes from the television series "M.A.S.H." as hospitals implement war-like practices of determining under extreme pressure who will live—and who will be left to die.

U.S. army doctors are being sent to inner-city emergency rooms, such as the Martin Luther King, Jr./Drew Medical Center in Los Angeles, to be trained in the application of combat medicine, an experience that can otherwise only be gathered in war-torn situations. One reason that army doctors went to train in Los Angeles was because, in

1989, Los Angeles had more automatic-weapons gunshot victims than Beirut.[56]

As health care costs have skyrocketed, fewer and fewer poor people are insured. Millions of Americans have inadequate or no health insurance and, as *Time* noted, the result is that "the emergency room has become the family doctor."[57]

Hospitals are being inundated with patients who have no medical coverage or means of paying large hospital costs. Cuts in Medicaid and Medicare have forced many poor patients, out of financial concerns, to delay going to the doctor until medical problems have become too serious to ignore. By the time they finally seek medical help, it is often much more costly and more long-term. In the Eighties, public hospitals found themselves forced to take on more and more patients who had virtually no medical coverage. Among these patients were also the numerous victims of the illegal drug trade.

Urban and rural hospitals are cutting staffs, eliminating critical medical functions, or closing down totally. In Spring 1990, several Washington, D.C., hospitals that service the city's poor people were forced to initiate mass firings. Complaining of diminishing resources due primarily to the overwhelming demands brought on by the city's drug crisis, Howard University Hospital, George Washington University Hospital, and the Washington Hospital Center released dozens of workers.

These firings occurred as the drug-driven violence and health-related problems continued unabated. The Washington Hospital Center, for example, reported that violent injuries (stabbings, shootings, beatings, etc.) rose 94 percent between 1987 and 1990. Gunshot wounds were up 150 percent, according to *Time*.[58]

Emergency care is disappearing as the high cost of maintenance becomes prohibitive for many hospitals or they shift their focus to more lucrative services such as drug and alcohol treatment or outpatient psychiatric care. The National Association for Hospital Development, *Time* reports, predicts that close to 900 of the 2,200 acute-care units (about 40 percent) will be closed or used for other purposes by the year 2000.[59]

A Search for Solutions

Law enforcement as a means of dealing with the growing number of women involved with illegal narcotics is retrogressive and doomed to failure. The most significant result has been an explosion in the population of women prisoners and an attack on women's rights. Congressperson Charles Rangel, Chairman of the House Select Committee on

Narcotics Abuse and Control, takes to task the drug warriors who blame addicted mothers for the problem. He states bluntly:

It would be easy to point a finger at the mothers of these children, but that will not solve our problem. These mothers are not responsible for the bumper crops of coca, opium, and marijuana in drug-producing countries. They are not to blame for the influx of drugs into this country, because our borders are, for all intents and purposes, a sieve. And, it is not their fault that we have not had, until recently, federal funds for drug education or prevention programs. It is not the mothers who have promoted slogans rather than policies as the primary weapon against drug abuse. Finally, it is not the mothers who determine the availability and accessibility of drug treatment and prenatal care.[60]

At the policy level, a number of steps have been taken to address the issue of addicted mothers-to-be. Going against the law-and-order approach of the Reagan administration, Congress in 1986 and 1988 passed legislation that provided more resources than ever before for helping drug-addicted, pregnant women. Although the Anti-Drug Abuse Acts of 1986 and 1988 made critical concessions to the law enforcement side and vastly underestimated funding needs, hundreds of millions of dollars were appropriated that specifically addressed this problem.

For 1989, $806 million was provided for the federal alcohol, drug abuse, and mental health block grant. The acts also required states to set aside at least 10 percent of that block grant funding specifically for programs and services for women, especially for pregnant women and their children. An additional $75 million was made available to reduce treatment programs' waiting lists. Also authorized under the two acts was funding for model drug- and alcohol-abuse prevention, education, and treatment projects for pregnant and post-partum women and their infants.[61]

As important as this funding was, the need remains great, and public policy must broaden its scope and commitment to this issue. Among the work that must be done, as Rangel has identified, is the establishment of critical prenatal drug- and alcohol-abuse prevention and education programs and services. Outreach to the target community must be extensive and well-planned. Prevention and education projects must be combined with general health care programs and access to social services, such as job training and public housing, if success is to have a long-term effect.

In a broader sense, an entire overhaul of the U.S. medical system should be on the agenda. While poor people have been reduced to interacting with the medical community only in times of emergencies, even those with medical insurance are finding the costs of health maintenance, let alone prevention, increasingly prohibitive. What's amazing is not that the health care system has collapsed, but that the collapse is so invisible to policy makers, journalists, and the established medical community. Given the depth of the health crisis, a national health care system that addresses the needs of poor people is urgently lacking.

It is critical that the women's movement play a more active role in the struggle against drug abuse and the violations of the drug war. Racism and class biases have historically isolated the mainstream women's movement from the needs and issues of poor women and women of color. The drug issue, with its uneven impact on women of color, can be the bridge that unites. Much more investigation needs to be done on why women are becoming more addicted to cocaine, crack and heroin in this period. The current and long-term consequences of this phenomena are frightening. The powerlessness of women of color is becoming even more acute as a result of the drug crisis.

As the drug war has escalated, its victims have extended beyond the Black community and women. Families and communities, already in crisis, are imploding with blinding fury. Nearly every sector of society is being drawn into this war. While drug use continues, fragile democratic rights are being revoked, and many innocent individuals have been taken prisoner.

Chapter 4

THE WAR ON DRUGS
AND OTHER LIVING THINGS

If you want to lose the war on drugs, leave it to law enforcement.

—U.S. Attorney General Richard Thornburgh[1]

Bush's Opening Move

On September 5, 1989, following months of speculation and anticipation, President Bush released the long-awaited $7.8 billion federal anti-drug plan, titled the National Drug Control Strategy. The plan, drafted principally by Drug Policy Director William Bennett, was almost universally condemned by drug experts and laypeople alike as inadequate, misfocused, and doomed to failure.

More than he realized, Bush's decision to dramatize his televised speech by holding up a bag of crack he claimed government agents were able to buy in Lafayette Park (located across from the White House) provided a glaring indication of the focus that his drug war would assume. His deceptive attempt to illustrate that the drug epidemic was so pervasive and monstrous that crack could be bought anywhere, even in front of the White House, backfired.

As reporters discovered in the days immediately following Bush's speech, there was much more to the story about that bag of crack. Bush did not mention that Keith Timothy Jackson, the eighteen-year-old Black high school senior who sold the three ounces of low-grade crack, had never heard of the park and had to be given written directions to get there. In fact, Jackson reportedly asked what the White House was and where it was located. When told that it was where the President resided, he apparently thought that Reagan still lived there. In the end, Jackson was driven to the park by a DEA informant. Even worse, Bush did not mention that neither crack, nor any other drugs, had ever been bought in the park until the U.S. government sent agents out to buy them.[2]

The staged event, which involved DEA agents and local police, was so poorly executed that they had to lure Jackson to the park twice because, on the first try, the government agent who was filming the transaction was attacked by a homeless person.[3] This comedy went even further. After buying the crack, the agents who were supposed to arrest Jackson lost him. Jackson was not arrested until September 26, twenty-one days following the speech.

The judge who presided over Jackson's trial was Stanley Sporkin, who had worked as general counsel for the CIA from 1981 to 1986. In at least once instance, Sporkin attempted to help a former CIA employee named A.J. Maillis, who had been arrested for selling cocaine to an undercover agent. The CIA provided Maillis with legal assistance, with the consent and guidance of the general counsel's office headed by Sporkin, and successfully lobbied to have his fifteen-year conviction reduced to three.[4]

In one final irony, Jackson was found not guilty on the Lafayette Park charge, due to entrapment by the government agents. After four days of jury deadlock, a mistrial was declared. Cherry Adams-Huff, foreperson of the jury, said that eleven of the twelve jurors felt that he should be acquitted. Jackson was convicted, however, on other drug charges and has gone to prison with no possibility of parole until 2001.[5]

Why go through so much trouble to put out so much disinformation? Why not use another icon of the drug problem such as a bag of laundered money or a jar of urine that had tested positive? In the aftermath of Bush's speech, Keith Jackson became an unambiguous rallying symbol. Just as the Bush team had used a Black rapist and murderer named Willie Horton to fan the flames of racism and law-and-order during his presidential campaign, Bush would play the race-baiting card again. Keith Jackson would become the Willie Horton of the drug war.

The Bush/Bennett War Proposal

When stripped of its hype, President Bush's war on drugs masks the continuation of Reaganism at home and abroad. During the 1988 presidential campaign, Bush issued a slew of promises concerning the drug problem. Most of these commitments were re-phrased Reaganisms. Among the actions he promised to take were to encourage public housing authorities to develop neighborhood watch programs, to make sure no one made bail or got probation without passing a drug test, to restore the death penalty, to double the federal prison budget, to expand prison treatment, to oppose drug legalization, and to establish "zero tolerance" as a "way of life."[6]

Bush made very little mention of expanding education, treatment, or prevention programs. He made even less mention of the poverty that is the root of drug trafficking and drug abuse in the inner cities and rural areas. He gave lip service to building urban enterprise zones and providing housing vouchers to poor families, but in effect Bush offered no new direction in eliminating America's extensive poverty.

Bush's anti-drug plan continued Reagan's strategy of law enforcement and attacks on civil liberties rather than prevention, education, and treatment. Like Reagan, Bush failed to adequately address the development needs of the international community, ignored the collaboration of U.S. intelligence agencies in drug trafficking, and evaded any responsibility for the economic and social policies of the Reagan era that provided the basis for the current crisis.

More than 70 percent of the funds allocated to Bush's original plan was aimed at halting drug supplies to the United States, with the remaining 30 percent targeted at reducing demand. Of the 70 percent focused on ending supply, about 40 percent was for increased law enforcement efforts, 22 percent for interdiction, 6 percent for international aid, and 2 percent for intelligence gathering. Of the 30 percent allocated for reducing demand, 14 percent went toward treatment, 12 percent to education, and 4 percent to research.[7]

Federal funding for treatment and prevention proposed for Fiscal Year 1991 amounts to less than one-half of one percent of the total economic costs of illegal drugs to United States. It's estimated that every dollar spent on treatment services saves $11.54 in social costs.[8] The majority of funding for treatment does not come from the federal government. While federal funds account for 23 percent of all treatment dollars, states pay 49 percent, local areas 9 percent, and the rest comes from other transfers.[9]

By manipulating the budget, Bush made it seem he was greatly increasing anti-drug funding, though in fact he would have brought funding only up to its previous levels. Rev. Jesse Jackson said in a television interview, "Bush's plan calls for less of the same," because it projects taking money from other important federal programs to run a drug plan that is already in place—and not working.

The plan called for war-like tactics and legislation. Drug czar Bennett made clear his emphasis when he stated that "a massive wave of arrests is a top priority for the war on drugs." This included building and maintaining military-style boot camps for nonviolent, first-time offenders; eviction of unprosecuted "dealers" in public housing; use of warrantless searches; and more aggressive actions against casual users. Users, Bennett suggested, should lose property, have their driver's licenses taken, have their names published in local newspapers, face stiff fines, and do weekend jail time.

Undaunted by the already overwhelming bureaucracy that coordinated the federal anti-drug programs, including thirty congressional committees and subcommittees and thirty-two federal agencies, the new plan added at least four new structures.[10] The new coordinating bodies were the Supply Reduction Working Group, the Demand Reduction Working Group, the Joint Intelligence Collection Center(s), and the Drug Control Research and Development Committee.

In May 1990, a new legislative package, the National Drug Control Strategy Implementation Act of 1990, was submitted to Congress by Bennett. This new package, which covered national and international policy, continued the law enforcement thrust of Bush's earlier plan. The plan recommended the death penalty for "major drug kingpins" and for those convicted of aggravated drug-related crimes such as murder. Other government agencies, such as the Immigration and Naturalization Service and the Coast Guard, were given expanded enforcement powers. For the first time, immigration agents could arrest aliens on non-immigration charges; and for drug-related convictions, the deportation process would be accelerated. The Coast Guard, under the proposed legislation, would have the authority to interdict planes. One provision would allow seizure of legally obtained properties as substitutes for properties suspected of being bought with drug money that could not be found.[11]

Bush's proposal is more a declaration of war on the Bill of Rights than on drugs. Efforts to limit peaceful assembly violates the First Amendment; unwarranted searches directly violate protections guaranteed under the Fourth Amendment; forced urine testing goes against the self-incrimination immunity of the Fifth Amendment; backlogged drug cases transgress the right to a speedy trial as stated by the Sixth Amendment; overcrowded and dangerous prisons desecrate the Eighth Amendment's protection against cruel and unusual punishment; and federal anti-drug statutes are believed by many lawyers to override the rights of states as outlined in the Ninth and Tenth Amendments.[12]

The Camps

The plan drew criticism in many other areas. It called for vigorous prosecution of casual users, although even the administration acknowledged that casual use was declining and had fallen 37 percent since 1985. Rather than address the overcrowded jail situation or the inequity of sentencing laws, the plan advocated "alternative" sentencing solutions such as boot camps and house arrests. In 1990, in at least eighteen states, nonviolent drug offenders were being "voluntarily" sent to the camps. While the camps are supposed to rehabilitate first-time offenders and steer them away from the hard-core drug dealers, they are actually little more than militarized prisons. Most of the camps housed youth offenders who were disproportionately Black and Latino. Known as

Special Alternative Incarceration, Disciplinary Rehabilitation, Challenge Incarceration, or Shock Incarceration, these programs inspire the best in submission training that the U.S. system of justice has to offer.[13]

The Michigan program is a typical example. Inmates sleep in military-like barracks, correction officers dress military-style, and military-oriented discipline and humiliation set the tone of the camp. Perhaps this is why a presidential commission was considering turning closed military bases into more of these boot camps.

The camps focus on creating discipline through harsh manual labor, marching, and drilling, although some programs offer classes in reading skills, vocational education, and job training. Many of the camps have instituted drug counseling programs.

In the Michigan example, inmates are called "maggots" and "quitters" and, if not properly servile, they are sent to regular prisons. Applying even more rigid standards than a normal penal institution, prisoners are only given about ten to thirty minutes of free time each day.[14]

The notion of setting up camps for drug offenders was suggested years ago. In the early Seventies, New York Governor Nelson Rockefeller had asked President Nixon to set up emergency camps to quarantine all of New York's addicts. Although Nixon was not personally opposed to the idea, he felt that the political costs, not to mention the ineffectiveness of the scheme, were too high, and the plan was abandoned.[15]

Stronger Law Enforcement

The law enforcement bent of the plan strengthens the mandatory-sentencing thrust of recent years. Mandatory sentencing began as a liberal reform movement that attempted to address the discriminatory and arbitrary nature of sentencing in U.S. courts. Many of its earlier proponents now admit that success has backfired.

The chief impact of mandatory sentencing has been to clog the courtrooms as more offenders opt to go to trial. Plea-bargaining is severely limited, and most offenders would rather take their chances with a jury. This often means that courts take ten to fifteen times longer to bring a case to completion. Under these guidelines, only truly big dealers have anything to trade.

The federal prison population is expected to double by 1995. Drug-related offenders are projected to grow from 47 percent in 1990 to about 70 percent in 1995.[16] Although emphasis on law enforcement has been demonstrated to show no appreciative effect on drug-related crime or use, the federal trend continues in that direction. In 1970, the federal government spent about 44 percent of its anti-drug monies on law enforcement. By 1987, that number had grown to 76 percent.[17] In 1988, more than 750,000 people were arrested on drug-related charges, mainly possession. Despite the focus on cocaine and crack, most arrests for possession involve marijuana.[18] In 1988, close to 400,000 were arrested on charges involving marijuana.[19] The draconian anti-drug "Rockefeller Laws" of the 1970s in New York had virtually no effect on heroin trafficking or use. Under those statutes, being caught with one pound of heroin or cocaine could get you life in prison. Being arrested with one ounce of marijuana meant fifteen years. Governor Nelson Rockefeller, whose great-grandfather ironically began the family fortune selling an opiate-based "cancer" medicine in the 1800s, tried but failed to halt the drug epidemic in his state.[20]

Appropriately, the Pentagon has not been left out of this war. The Air Force reportedly has assigned the over-the-horizon Backscatter radar, designed to detect nuclear cruise missiles launched from Soviet submarines in the Gulf of Mexico, to be part of the Pentagon's $627 million drug "detection and monitoring mission." NORAD has been brought on board to support drug interdiction and surveillance efforts as well as to detect a Soviet nuclear-missile attack. AWAC airplanes, the U.S. airborne radar war stations, now spend 40 percent of their time tracking drug dealers. One overzealous submarine captain at the National War College has suggested converting billion-dollar ballistic-missile submarines into "high-capacity-strike warfare platforms" for use against the "drug cartels."[21]

Congressperson Charles Rangel commented on these developments by saying, "Now that we hardly have any communists left, it doesn't surprise me that the Pentagon might be looking for drug traffickers too." Only a few years ago, when it appeared that the Soviet and Eastern European threat would keep the armed services in perpetual and exorbitant funding, army officials were saying that they believed that the drug war was an "unwinnable war."[22]

The international aspects of the bill also maintained the enforcement angle and an unbalanced focus on the Andean region of South America. While the amount of anti-drug aid to the drug-producing countries of Colombia, Peru, and Bolivia was to increase three-fold to about $300 million, very little funding was aimed at alternative crop development or debt relief. A number of provisions appeared to cross the line of respect for the sovereignty of nations and edged toward unhealthy intervention. For example, the bill suggested that the United States remove a prohibition on the provision of training and equipment to certain law enforcement agencies in those nations. In addition to strengthening the law enforcement apparatuses of these governments, the U.S. plan called for intervention into the judicial processes of these nations. The United States, for example, sought to have these countries rewrite their extradiction laws to make it easier for the U.S. government to extradiate accused drug traffickers from those nations to the United States.

Democratic Critique

The Democratic opposition in Congress responded immediately. Most Democrats criticized the Administration's focus on law enforcement and called for an increase of $2.2 billion over Bush's plan that would emphasize ending the demand for drugs. Senator Robert Byrd proposed devoting 53 percent toward law enforcement and interdiction and 47 percent toward education, prevention, and treatment.[23]

In recent years, the federal government has spent about $4 billion a year in the drug war, with about 75 percent of that being aimed at halting supply. While the funding request for Bennett's plan appeared to be a significant increase over the Reagan years, the $7.8 billion price tag for the plan is misleading. Actually, Bush proposed only $716 million in new funds to state and local governments because the rest of the funding that was requested was already contained in monies approved by Congress.[24]

Bush proposed to fund his program by taking money from state and federal programs rather than raise taxes or cut the military budget. An analysis by the Democratic Study Group detailed how the Bush plan gave with one hand—while taking with the other. The Bush plan, in effect, provided states and local governments with $499 million while taking away $604 million.[25] As a result of his administrative sleight-of-hand, forty-three states would have received *less* federal aid. Alabama, for example, would have obtained an estimated $7,300,911 from the plan, but would lose $6,594,500 as a result of cuts in the federal programs. Alabama would only receive $706,411 in new funds. Twenty-three states, including several with severe narcotics epidemics, would have a net loss after balancing the added drug program moneys and the cuts. This includes Texas (-$25,462,347), California (-$149,608,762), Florida (-$6,499,228), and Washington, D.C. (-$1,148,796).[26]

Bush proposed to shift funds from programs that were geared to help principally low-income families. Under the plan, cuts would occur in four areas: juvenile justice assistance programs, many of which run anti-drug projects; programs for newly legalized immigrants; Economic Development Administration grants; and subsidies for public housing.[27]

About $900 million for treatment was being requested; however, that funding would bring treatment costs only up to the level that existed before Reagan made cuts. Treatment programs for children under sixteen in the juvenile system and pregnant addicts would cost four times more than the amount proposed, which was roughly $3.9 billion.[28]

It is estimated that 6.5 million Americans need immediate treatment, yet facilities are available for only 250,000.[29]

William Bennett: Portrait of a Drug Czar

> "My question is to Mr. Bennett. Why build prisons? Get tough like Arabia. Behead the damned drug dealers. We're just too darned soft."
>
> So spoke a caller on a talkshow featuring William Bennett. Bennett responded: "It's actually—there's an interesting point. One of the things that I think is a problem is that we are not doing enough that is morally proportional to the nature of the offense. I mean, what the caller suggests is morally plausible. Legally, it's difficult. But say—"
>
> LARRY KING: "Behead?"
>
> BENNETT: "Yeah. Morally, I don't have any problem with that."
>
> —The Larry King Show, June 15, 1989[30]

William Bennett, dubbed "drug czar" by the mainstream media, was actually an ideal candidate to lead the conservative-oriented war on drugs. In temperament and style, Bennett embodied the politics of intolerance and anti-progress that characterized the Reagan Presidency. As Reagan's Secretary of Education, he had mercilessly cut programs that were widely viewed as instrumental in allowing working-class students and students of color to attend college.

Reportedly, Bennett had flirted with leftist politics in the Sixties. Political positions that gave conservatives of the time apoplexy were embraced warmly by Bennett. He had opposed U.S. involvement in the Vietnam War and had supported the Civil Rights movement. The Bennett of the Sixties played in a rock band called "Plato and the Guardians" and even considered joining the ultra-radical Students for a Democratic Society (SDS) while attending Williams College.[31]

In an almost unbelievable twist of fate, rockin' Bill had even gone on a date with rock goddess Janis Joplin, who later died of a drug overdose. Known for getting stinking drunk during her performances, Joplin came to symbolize for many conservatives the excesses (and the tragic consequences) of American youth's infatuation with drugs, sex, and radical politics. As for the date, Bennett drily states that they "just drank a couple of beers."[32]

Somewhere along the way, however, Bennett experienced a conservative conversion—although it appears that the seeds were there all along. As the proctor in a freshmen dorm at Harvard, Bennett prophetically acted out his drug czar-to-be future. He states proudly, "I was tough on drugs." He pressured the Harvard administration to permanently expel students who sold drugs.[33] In 1982, Bennett was appointed chairperson of the National Endowment for the Humanities. He was a full-fledged conservative by then and gleefully carried out a right-wing assault on numerous projects. He cut off and refused to fund projects that he deemed leftist. Following the Reaganist line on civil rights, he also refused to set numerical goals for the hiring of women and people of color.[34] Bennett, however, did not reach his full conservative stride until he became Secretary of Education in the mid-Eighties. Poor college students came under attack as Reagan and Bennett called for severe cuts in financial aid programs. They proposed a reduction in Pell Grants, the elimination of Supplemental Grants, a 28 percent decrease in work-study programs, and more difficult and punitive restrictions on loans.[35] He instituted the Loan Default Program that functioned as a financial-terrorist program that threatened students who did not pay back their loans with all sorts of punishments, including bad credit references. He pushed Reagan's position of providing vouchers and tuition tax credits to private schools. Contrary to state and federal law, he advocated "voluntary" prayer in public schools.[36]

During Bennett's tenure, education and those who most needed access to it suffered. According to a report examining the Reagan/Bush years issued by the Democratic National Committee, the number of poor students receiving federally supported basic-skills training fell from seven million in 1980-81 to 5.7 million in 1988-89. At the same time, those needing assistance grew to about 8.5 million.[37] In general, federal education funding fell from 2.3 percent of the federal budget to 1.7 percent in the period 1980-1989. The impact of these cuts increased the dropout rate to between 15 and 20 percent nationally, although in a number of major urban areas, the rate was as high as 65 percent. Nationally, 4.2 million children drop out of high school each year.[38] As head of the Education Department, Bennett managed a budget of $18 billion. Yet only a paltry $3 million was slated for drug- and alcohol-abuse programs.[39]

Bennett created a mild controversy concerning his own addiction to cigarettes. As a well-known chain smoker, when first announced as the new drug czar, Bennett was challenged by reporters on the obvious contradiction of attacking the addictive behavior of others without addressing his own. Bennett pledged to give up cigarettes for the duration of his term as drug czar. Some time later, when reporters noticed a constant "gum" chewing on the part of Bennett, they discovered Bennett was chewing nicotine gum, which contains more nicotine than an average cigarette. Meanwhile, the surgeon general had just issued a report stating that tobacco is as addictive, if not more so, than heroin and cocaine. This whole saga was played out in Garry Trudeau's *Doonesbury* cartoon strip.[40]

In November 1990, Bennett announced that he was quitting his post after only twenty months on the job. At the press conference announcing his resignation, the always combative Bennett called Congressperson Charles Rangel a "gasbag" and referred to the District of Columbia as a "basketcase."[41] Within days of Bennett's resignation, President Bush announced that he had nominated Bennett to become chairperson of the Republican Party. Desperate to replace the highly skilled and politically savvy Lee Atwater, who was incapacitated by inoperable brain cancer, Bennett seemed like a perfect choice. Bush was hoping to take advantage of Bennett's high profile and aggressive political style. However, after initially declaring that he would accept the position, Bennett backed out of the deal a week later to the shock and embarrassment of the Republican Party. Bennett had discovered that he would be unable to earn the level of income that he had planned to make from speaking engagements and other contracts. In his capacity as Republican Party chairperson, it would have been improper, though legal, for him to take money for speaking engagements from the same people who were trying to influence the Party.[42]

Bush then nominated former Florida Governor Bob Martinez to replace Bennett. Martinez was a hard-line conservative who stiffened drug penalties and nearly doubled the number of prison beds. As governor, he had signed more than 130 death warrants. He achieved national notoriety when he asked the state prosecutor to build up the obscenity case against the rap band 2 Live Crew. The response to his nomination was far from favorable. U.S. House of Representatives Government Operations Committee Chairperson John Conyers said, "What we don't need in the next drug czar is someone whose principal recommendations are to put people in jails or simply put them to death."[43]

The Drug Warriors

Without question, the longest war in U.S. history has been the war against drugs. For almost a century, not counting the alcohol prohibitionists, federal drug warriors have launched campaign after campaign and passed law after law in a fruitless effort to end America's illegal drug use.

Nearly every President since World War II has declared a "war on drugs." In 1961, President John F. Kennedy held a White House conference on drug abuse. Out of the conference came the President's Advisory Commission on Narcotics and Drug Abuse. The Commission issued a report in 1963 that called for an expansion of the federal role in providing treatment to drug addicts.[44] During the first year of Kennedy's administration, the United States (along with seventy-three other nations) signed the Single Convention on Narcotic Drugs. Like other international drug agreements, it called for more international cooperation to end drug trafficking and abuse.

Only two federal drug treatment facilities existed at the time. In 1929, Congress had passed an act establishing two narcotic rehabilitation facilities in Lexington, Kentucky, and Fort Worth, Texas, for addicts who had been convicted of drug offenses. The CIA, twenty-five years later, would use the Lexington facility for LSD experiments on unsuspecting recovering Black addicts. The Community Mental Health Centers Act of 1963 for the first time provided federal assistance to non-federal programs for treatment.[45]

Richard Nixon came to the White House in 1969 at the height of the heroin crisis. Congress, under pressure from local and state legislatures, attempted to attack the problem. In 1970, Congress passed the Controlled Substances Act and its companion piece, the Controlled Substances Import and Export Act, in an effort to consolidate the scattered pieces of drug legislation.

In January 1972, Nixon created the Office of Drug Abuse Law Enforcement (ODALE) and ordered a "concentrated assault on the street-level heroin pusher."[46] In September 1972, Nixon declared a total war against drugs. In a flurry of rhetorical statements, he said that people who deal drugs "are literally the slave traders of our time. They are trafficking in living death."[47] Six months later, in March 1973, Nixon created the Drug Enforcement Agency (DEA) in an attempt to control the federal inter-agency struggles over who was in charge.

The Carter era was marked by a more liberal approach to the drug issue. Drug abuse was down during Carter's administration and, therefore, was not made a priority. Although advocacy for the legalization of marijuana never emerged as a policy option under Carter, many of his top aids dealing with the drug issue had close ties to legalization proponents such as the National Organization for the Reform of Marijuana Laws (NORML).

Reagan had also declared an all-out war on the drug trade, and the White House Office of Drug Abuse Policy was created to oversee it. In 1987, Reagan created the National Drug Policy Board, headed by Attorney General Edwin Meese, to coordinate the government's anti-drug efforts.[48]

Despite all of his anti-drug discourses, Reagan's "just-say-no" drug activities primarily consisted of slashing programs that had been put in place under former administrations—and increasing the prison population. From Fiscal Year 1981 to Fiscal Year 1988, Congress was forced to restore money to anti-drug programs to which Reagan had made budget cuts. In total, Congress restored more than $5 billion above Reagan's budget requests. Anti-drug funding grew 39 percent during that period due to the restoration or increase in funding by Congress in eleven major anti-drug programs. Reagan requested cuts in programs operated by the Department of Education; Customs; the Coast Guard; the FBI; the Federal Bureau of Prisons; and the Alcohol, Drug Abuse and Mental Health Administration (ADAMHA).[49]

The result has been the same in each anti-drug campaign: a failure to halt either supply or demand. In fact, numerous critics have asserted that every effort to stop drug trafficking has led to increased supplies of illicit drugs. In the early Seventies, when Nixon applied pressure on Turkey and France to break the heroin traffic through their countries, he succeeded in spreading and enhancing opium growing and heroin manufacturing to a vast network of regions around the world. Since that time, the United States has watched helplessly as the flow of heroin into this country has see-sawed between Mexico, Afghanistan, Pakistan, and the countries of Southeast Asia.

Reagan's effort to stop the flow of marijuana from Mexico at the beginning of his term resulted in a tremendous leap in domestic production, estimated in 1991 to be about 25 percent, while there had been virtually no large-scale U.S. marijuana growth since the 1930s. When Reagan went after domestic production, he drove it inside where growers could more easily conceal their activities. This had the effect of sparking scientific breakthroughs in indoor cultivation that has made U.S.-produced marijuana more potent than it has ever been.[50]

George Bush was involved in the so-called war on drugs long before he became President. In 1982, Reagan created the South Florida Task Force, whose main mission was to halt drugs coming into the country via southern Florida, and put then-Vice President Bush in charge. Enforcement was emphasized and Navy destroyers and other military resources were brought to bear on the problem. Eight years later, the year Bush was elected President, south Florida still remained the number-one entry point for drugs. The task force Coast Guard Chief of Operations stated that the project was a failure and that "there was nobody in charge and not much was achieved."[51]

Bush also headed the National Narcotics Border Interdiction System created in 1983. Within a year of operation, DEA Administrator John Lawn was calling for its abolition. He was quoted as saying that the program "had made no material contribution" to dealing with the drug problem.[52]

Fighting the war against drugs has certainly been made more difficult by the fact that several of those leading the war have been involved in drug use. One of the most appalling examples is that of Henry G. Barr, a former top aide to Attorney General Richard Thornburgh. In August 1990, Barr was indicted on charges of repeated drug use and deliberate deception of federal authorities in order to receive a high-level security clearance. The indictment stated that Barr used cocaine as late as April 1989, while he was still on Thornburgh's staff as a Special Assistant. In that capacity, Barr attended meetings of Reagan's National Drug Policy Board and helped settle disputes between the FBI and the DEA.[53]

Scope of the Problem

Benjamin Disraeli once wrote that there are three kinds of lies: lies, damned lies, and statistics. Historically, one of the most deadly means of justifying and implementing oppression and prejudice has been through the use of well-crafted statistics. Social data, from Census surveys to estimates of literacy, contain a social bias rooted in the views, methods, and aims of those doing the collecting. Statistics have been used to justify every injustice known to the world. In the modern era, dissembling statisticians, assisted by computers and advanced mathematical theories, have created all types of fabrications to justify social inequality and the public policy to perpetuate it. Statistics having to do with race—the number of Blacks or Latinos in the United States, the number of households headed by single Black women, the crime rate committed by people of color—are notoriously discriminatory and erroneous.

Despite these cautions, we should shoot for accurate statistics. Most honest social researchers state their bias from the beginning. Even grossly inaccurate statistics are useful in that they expose the views and methodology of those who researched, compiled, and analyzed them.

Virtually all the statistics associated with illegal narcotics—number of users, amount of drugs available, costs of drugs, amount of money laundered, etc.—involve a great deal of guesswork. Doing research about drugs, like most underground enterprises, is a case of "those who know, don't say, and those who say, don't know."

Numbers are also distorted for political purposes. Politicians, who have a vested interest in exploiting the fear of drug use, often exaggerate use figures. Conversely, others who want to appear to have made some advances in dealing with the drug problem downplay the numbers. Peter Reuter, a researcher with the Rand Corporation who has authored numerous studies on illegal drugs, has been one of the most vocal critics of the figures used by government agencies and congressional committees concerning drug use. He believes that figures are grossly inflated to justify big anti-drug budgets. He calls the government numbers "mythical" and says that, "[t]here is a strong interest in keeping the number high and none in keeping it correct."[54]

Taking into account the validity of some of these criticisms, statistics are still very important to the debate over the drug crisis. They help to raise the level of argument from mere slogans and impressions to a more scientific sense of reality. Statistics are critical to determining what programs are funded and to what degree. Knowing the rationale and methodology of how government and other statistics are used is essential in shattering many of the myths about the use and trafficking of illegal drugs.

Whatever figures we choose, however, no one disputes the fact that the amount of illegal narcotics entering the United States is growing. The House Select Committee on Narcotics Abuse and Control (HSC), using figures from the National Institute on Drug Abuse (NIDA), estimates that in 1986, over twelve tons of heroin, 150 tons of cocaine, 200 tons of hashish, and between 30,000 and 60,000 tons of marijuana were imported to the United States.[55] Although the United States is only 6 percent of the world's population, this nation consumes 60 to 70 percent of the world's illegal narcotics.[56] The HSC estimates the value of these drugs at between $100 and $150 billion annually. This is about twice the U.S. market for oil and half the value of all U.S. currency in circulation. Illicit drug sales, including domestic and foreign production, are estimated to have increased by $10 billion annually since 1978.[57]

No numbers are debated as hotly as those that are used to determine the number of U.S. drug users and addicts. The principal government source for drug-related data is NIDA, which functions under the U.S. Department of Health and Human Services. NIDA monitors and collects drug-related data from more than two dozen metropolitan areas around the country. This data includes emergency room citations of drug-related incidents, drug-test results from jail and prison inmates, and information gathered from public and private treatment centers. NIDA conducts studies and obtains data from local and federal law enforcement agencies. Alcohol and tobacco statistics are also maintained by NIDA.

According to NIDA's 1990 National Household Survey, the United States has 500,000 active heroin addicts, about 1.6 million current cocaine users, and nearly 25 million regular marijuana users. The Survey states that there are about 662,000 hard-core cocaine users. The *Economist* reported that roughly 30 million Americans use an illegal drug regularly.[58]

In 1990, NIDA noted that casual use had declined—which the Bush administration heralded as a sign of success of its anti-drug program—but that the number of weekly users was up 33 percent and daily users up 19 percent. In other words, addiction is growing.[59]

The methodology used in the survey to arrive at figures for hard-core cocaine addiction was challenged by Senator Joseph Biden. He criticized NIDA for polling only households, and not including other areas where drug addiction is rampant, such as the homeless population, prisons, and drug treatment centers. Gathering data from these sources and using the skills of private and public researchers, Biden used their most conservative estimates and concluded that there are closer to 2.2 million hard-core cocaine addicts, nearly three times the government's official estimate.[60] According to Biden, there are 2.4 million weekly cocaine users, not 660,000 as NIDA reported, and about 940,000 weekly heroin users rather than the government estimate of 500,000. While NIDA claims that there are only about 115,000 teenage cocaine users, Biden cites data that shows that in three cities alone (New York, Chicago, and Los Angeles) more than 60,000 teens were arrested on cocaine charges. Washington, D.C., was number one in per capita cocaine addicts at 40.5 per 1,000 population. The next nearest state was Nevada at a distant 24.9 per 1,000. About 180,000 heroin addicts reside in New York, accounting for 20 percent of all heroin addicts in the United States. Other states with large numbers of heroin addicts are California with 150,000 and Illinois with 105,000.

Although the Household Survey has served as the government's official report on drug use in the United States, even William Bennett questioned its usefulness. He said on one occasion, "We have never used the Household Survey's cocaine addict estimate. It is inaccurate." Biden's staff were skeptical about how truthful respondents were to the Household Survey. One researcher said, "A lot of people just won't tell the nice man from the government that they smoked crack recently."

The implications of Biden's higher figures are tremendous. It means not only should treatment be greatly expanded, but that special treatment emphasis must be given to the homeless and those who are incarcerated. In addition, research into cocaine addiction and cures must be given a higher priority by policy makers than ever before. Biden recommended that cities hardest hit by the cocaine/crack epidemic be given more federal aid, new prisons be constructed (including the brutal "boot camps") with advanced treatment facilities, 400,000 new beds be added to treatment centers, state and local law enforcement grants be doubled, and drug treatment research be expanded.

The Struggle for Mo' Better News

The media's role in the drug war has been less than honorable. As Al Giordano wrote in the *Washington Journalism Review,* "Who Drafted the Press?" in the drug war.[61] In a rush for ratings and sales, the media has consistently bought the administration's view on the drug crisis and parroted White House press releases. Bennett's goal of reducing drug use by 5 percent annually, a reduction that will not offset the national trend, was never exposed as lame. Similarly, Bush's position that he did not know that Panamanian General Manuel Noreiga was involved in drugs when he was head of the CIA or later when he was Vice President never became a real issue during Bush's presidential campaign, nor during his launching of the drug war.

Numerous inaccuracies and errors have been broadcast and printed by media monopolies driven by sensationalism and profits. For example, the inaccurate claim that "a person would crave cocaine for as long as they lived" after trying it once, a gross fabrication, was broadcast by ABC's Peter Jennings.[62] Very few drug experts who differ with the administration or who advocate some form of legalization or decriminalization appear in the mass media. In another example, studies show marijuana is not the harmful killer of youth that groups like Partnership for a Drug Free America like to propagate. Furthermore, the Partnership was allowed to distribute media advertisements that stated that five million people received cocaine-related emergency medical care, when the actual number was only 62,141.[63]

Network television has been the most aggressive of all media in exploiting the drug war. Numerous television shows and specials sensationalize the drug crisis, from the "reality-oriented" mass vigilante programs such as "America's Most Wanted" and "Cops" to regular programs like Fox Channel's short-lived *DEA* and specials such as CBS's *One Nation, Under Siege* and ABC's *A Plague Upon the Land.* Between August 1 and September 13, 1989, the networks, the *Washington Post* and the *New York Times*—America's media cartels—produced 347 stories on the drug crisis.[64]

Many of those stories were racist. Rare was the interview with a young Black person who had avoided drugs and the drug culture. Night after night, images of young Black men lying dead or being arrested were splattered across the screens. This bombardment squeezed into the public mind the notion that young Black men are the heart and core of the drug problem in America. The media fed into the law enforcement bias, building profiles of drug dealers that overwhelmingly target young Blacks, especially young Black men. Rather than examine seriously the issues at the root of youth involvement with drugs, such as the relationship between unemployment and trafficking, the media sensationalized their plight.

One drug story that the media chose not to cover involved none other than Vice President J. Danforth Quayle. In November 1988, on the eve of the presidential election, a story emerged from El Reno, Texas, about a prisoner at the El Reno Correctional Institution who claimed that he had sold marijuana to Quayle in the early Seventies. Brett Kimberlin, who was doing time on marijuana smuggling and bombing charges, told the *El Reno Daily Tribune* that he had sold marijuana to Quayle on fifteen to twenty occasions between 1971 and 1973 while Quayle was in law school at Indiana University.[65]

Kimberlin's announcement, made only four days before the election, was followed by series of strange events. A press conference called by Kimberlin was quickly canceled by prison officials. Kimberlin was then put in isolation. None of the networks or corporate media would touch the story. Weeks later, the Washington-based *Legal Times* revealed that prison officials, government personnel, and the Bush/Quayle campaign management had all intervened to hush Kimberlin. When these details were uncovered, the networks and the corporate press still refused to see a story. Only the *New York Times* ran a story, but that one was filled with inaccuracies and misleading statements.[66]

Is a New Ice Age Coming?

> Don't try it once. It's too good. You'll never get it out of your mind.
>
> —Dr. Alex Stalcup, Director of Haight-Ashbury
> Free Clinic Detox Program, San Francisco[67]

Even as anti-drug resources and energies are being galvanized to attack the flow of cocaine into the United States, a new and more dangerous drug has emerged. Ice, the street name for smokable methamphetamine, has law enforcement and health officials alike scrambling for solutions to what may become the next drug emergency to hit the inner cities.

Although much is unknown about ice, it is considered more addictive than crack cocaine and produces a powerful high that can last for as long as fourteen to twenty-four hours. The most frightening aspect of ice is that it is easy and cheap to produce. Virtually anyone can set up an ice factory in their basement and purchase the chemical ingredients locally.

Methamphetamines were invented by the Japanese in 1893.[68] It wasn't until the 1930s that amphetamines were introduced into the United States, and methamphetamine quickly became the drug of choice for many, after marijuana and cocaine were outlawed. Both the Allies and the Axis forces gave the drug to tired munitions plant workers and weary soldiers to stimulate them. Hundreds of thousands of Japanese became addicted as a result. It was believed that both Hitler and Goebbels indulged regularly.[69] After a period of disuse, amphetamines, called "speed," became popular again in the 1960s and caused numerous overdoses. "Speed kills" campaigns forced amphetamines into disfavor by the end of the decade. In the 1980s, methamphetamines, known as crank, became popular among White bikers, White working-class and poor people, and rural Whites. Ice, sometimes called crystal meth, developed in Japan and South Korea and first surfaced in Hawaii around 1987. Called *shabu* by the Japanese, *hiroppon* by the Koreans, *batu* by the Filipinos, by 1989 ice had become Hawaii's number-one drug problem. Initially, most of the ice that arrived in Hawaii came from labs in South Korea, Taiwan, and the Philippines.[70]

In the Fall of 1989, ice sold on the streets of Hawaii came in a package called a paper, which is about the size of a penny, that sold for roughly $50 and contained about a tenth of a gram. The drug, which is odorless, has a crystal-like, icy appearance.[71]

According to Major Mike Carvalho, commander of the narcotics/vice division of the Honolulu Police Department, ice is affecting people of all ages. He said, "What we're finding is that ice is being used by everybody, even school kids."[72] In fact, Hawaii already has "ice babies," children born to ice-addicted mothers. Nurses and physicians who have worked with these babies believe that their problems are even greater than those of children born to mothers addicted to cocaine. The ice infants tend to have horrible tremors and often cry non-stop for twenty-four hours or more.[73]

Authorities and health workers outside of Hawaii are frightened that ice has crossed the ocean and increasingly is showing up on the streets and in the hospitals of a number of cities, including San Diego; Portland, Oregon; and New York.

Although ice has only shown up in a few areas, most notably the West Coast, methamphetamine trafficking and use exists in nearly every state. Ice has been found in Florida, Texas, and New York. One San Diego narcotics officer insists that ice has been in his area since the beginning of the Eighties. Further, as the AIDS danger grows due to the mixing of cocaine and heroin that has become common among crack users, many addicts, such as prostitutes, may switch to ice, which gives a powerful high for what is believed to be a lesser risk.

According to the Drug Enforcement Agency, methamphetamine is easy to manufacture and inexpensive. For only about $200 to $400, chemicals can be purchased that produce a pound of pure methamphetamine. Profits from just a pound can be as much as $90,000, says the DEA.[74] Ice can be made from mixing methamphetamine with ephedrine—an ingredient in many over-the-counter prescription drugs—and hot water. It is only a matter of time, according to officials, before methamphetamine producers here master the process of creating ice. For the most part, outlaw motorcycle groups and Asian gangs control the trafficking.

Every sign indicates that the spread of ice brings even greater health problems than crack. Methamphetamines and ice, in particular, can cause severe and sometimes irreversible psychiatric problems. Schizophrenia, paranoia, auditory hallucinations, toxic psychosis, and brain damage are common among long-time users. Many of these effects stay around for weeks, sometimes months after an individual has cleaned his or her body of the drug.[75] The physical side effects are equally deleterious. Even short-term users experience convulsions; vitamin and mineral deficiencies; rapid loss of weight; and heart, lung, liver, and kidney damage. Users can also risk the fluid-filled-lung syndrome called pulmonary edema and inflamed and shrunken pulmonary arteries known as vasculitis.[76]

Other than hearings held by Congressperson Charles Rangel, very little has been done to prevent and prepare for the devastation that will come from more widespread use of ice. Hawaiian Congressperson Patricia Saiki fought with William Bennett to declare Honolulu a high-intensity drug-trafficking area so that the city could qualify for additional federal drug monies. She warned that if ice was not stopped in Hawaii, that would quicken its migration to the United States.

At Rangel's hearings, a number of recommendations were put forth by witnesses from areas that are already experiencing the deadly effects of ice. In addition to more law enforcement efforts, it was suggested that more education and public awareness campaigns be started, that chemicals necessary to producing methamphetamines be removed from easy access, and that more intelligence sharing among law enforcement and health agencies be developed.[77]

Fear grows daily that methamphetamines and ice can cross the race and class barriers that have kept them out of the hands of inner-city

Blacks and Latinos. An administration drug war that focuses on "the drug of the week" approach will only see a parade of drug epidemics and will have little success in abating the havoc and harm caused by trafficking and abuse.

Conclusion

The drug war has served the administration well, allowing the government to tread on civil liberties long regarded as unnecessary by conservatives. It has also given new life to federal and local law enforcement agencies as substantial amounts of monies become available for drug-related law enforcement. In addition, the White House drug war has been a valuable propaganda vehicle for issues as far-ranging as the death penalty, abortion, gun control, and foreign aid.

This is not to say that the administration does not recognize a drug problem, only that it has defined the parameters of that problem in a different way from the way that working-class people, poor people, and people of color might. For the administration, corporate America and many conservatives, illegal drug trafficking and abuse affects productivity and creates unstable social conditions. The prospects of continuing property theft, loss of productivity, and a zonked-out working population does severe damage to the bottom line. These conditions are unacceptable in the long run and must be abated with deliberate speed. The simplest and least expensive approach is to jail all the traffickers that can be caught and neutralize the users through punitive measures and quick-fix, drug-induced solutions such as methadone.

While some conservatives who favor legalization see the drug problem in pragmatic terms, most see drug use as a burning moral issue. While alcohol and prescription-drug addiction generates no moral stigmatism, illegal drug use raises questions of character and human worth. Drug users are referred to in terms usually reserved for those who have committed crimes such as child pornography or incest.

For most people, however, the drug problem arises out of a crisis in economic development, political empowerment and democracy, and social equality. Aggression against people of color, poor people, and the Third World is at the core of the current drug war. Until the distinction between the interests of the administration and its allies and that of the majority is made clear, little progress will be made in ending the harm of drug trafficking, drug abuse, and the drug war itself. The following chapter details the many layers and dimensions of distinctions that exist between those who profit from the illegal drug industry and those who don't. Only by addressing the real underlying political and economic issues that the illegal drug crisis exposes can the drug problem actually be resolved.

Chapter 5

WHO BENEFITS
(AND WHO DOESN'T)

Things happen to people who let things happen to my dope.

—Words of a New York street dealer

With billions of drug dollars floating around, one obvious question is who gets the largest share of these illicit profits. Money is made at all levels of the drug trade, from producers to chemists to distributors to street sellers, but the amount varies depending on class, race, and nationality. Trying to sort out who gets what part of the drug profits requires an analysis of the political economy of the drug trade and its relationship to the legal drug market.

In third world countries, peasants who grow opium or coca leaves receive more than they would for other crops but still receive only a fraction of the profits eventually derived from their labor. In Bolivia, a "carga" of leaves (45 kilograms) sells for about U.S. $55 to $100. This comes to about U.S. $1.20 to $2.20 per kilogram.[1] It is estimated that the markup from coca leaves to the final product of cocaine can be as high as 700 percent. It's even higher for crack cocaine. For heroin, the markup is estimated to be 2,000 percent.[2]

As the coca leaves transform into coca paste then into coca base, which is then made into cocaine hydrochloride (cocaine powder), the profits to be made at each stage take huge leaps. This is the major reason why many peasants have expanded from growing coca leaves into producing coca paste, which sells for about U.S. $250 per kilogram. It takes about 100 to 200 kilograms of coca leaves to make one kilogram of paste.[3]

Although profits are raked off unevenly, the illegal drug industry is the most equal opportunity employer in the world. There is room for corporate-like structures with thousands of employees that deal with transactions involving millions of dollars daily, as well as mom-and-pop operations that are run out of the back seat of a car. Individual entrepreneurs, limited partnerships, and financial syndicates all function side-by-side.

Many others may be tied to drug trafficking but never come in contact with any narcotics except, possibly, for personal use. Accountants, bankers, lawyers, pilots, arms merchants, real estate agents, jewelers, chemists, and others function as fronts for drug traffickers.

Finally, there are also those who benefit by the commercial and cultural exploitation of the drug crisis. Numerous products are sold that would otherwise sit on shelves or not exist at all if not for the spending trends of drug dealers, users, or the architects of the war on drugs. Expensive sneakers, gold chains, particular automobiles, and other extravagant commodities that are favored by drug dealers or their imitators rake in millions. Drug paraphernalia such as rolling paper, pipes, and weapons have also made fortunes. As for the drug war industry, the manufacturers of medical drugs used in drug treatment, such as methadone, or those involved in drug testing have made untold millions over the years.

Third World Cartels: The First Tier of the Drug Economy

Similar to other multi-nation businesses, the organizational control and the division of profits is determined through the prisms of race, national origin, and class position. Rivalry within the industry, attacks from without, and ever-changing market conditions mean that a constant flow of new players and power plays make it difficult to determine exactly who gets what. Despite these factors, drug trafficking becomes better organized and more sophisticated daily.

For many regions and nations around the globe, drug production and trafficking is not just a major component, but the center of their economy. In Southeast Asia, for example, opium growing and trafficking were the major factors in the growth of the economy of that region. In the 1950s, after mainland China became communist, and Chinese criminal syndicates scattered throughout the region, every area from Hong Kong to Thailand to Burma became engrossed in the opium trade. Very little distinction could be made between the public and private sectors when it came to the drug industry, as many government officials facilitated or participated directly in trafficking.

Corruption of political institutions is the normal method of operation for the drug lords, to the degree that elected officials and drug kingpins function as one. In Colombia, Bolivia, and Peru, for example, ties to the drug cartels exist at the highest levels of government. In Colombia, several presidents and, it's currently estimated, at least one-third of its members of Congress have been bought and paid for by the cartels.

In Bolivia, the Hugo Banzer regime and other military governments that followed created what one journalist termed a "narco-nation." These regimes were based mainly on long-term, large-scale ties with drug capitalists.[4]

The government of former President Alan Garcia of Peru was one of Bush's strongest allies in the war on drugs. It was widely believed, however, that despite his rhetoric, Garcia was deeply tied to drug traffickers. While his administration focused most of its anti-drug attention on the renowned coca-leaf growing region of the Upper Huallaga Valley in northern Peru, where more than 50,000 hectares are planted with coca, the United Nations and others documented that Quilabamba-Cuzco in the south was producing 40,000 hectares of coca leaves, a rate of production that is more than four times the official government figures.[5]

In 1990, Garcia was replaced by Alberto Fujimori, a Peruvian of Japanese descent. While there has been no indication of any links to drug traffickers, Fujimori announced soon after his election that he does not want any "outside interference" in his country's effort to deal with the drug problem. In September 1990, he rejected $35 million in military aid from the United States that was to be the first installment of a $2.2 billion anti-drug package geared for Peru, Bolivia, and Colombia. As the largest producer of coca leaves in the world, Peru's participation in the U.S. anti-drug plan was critical.[6]

There are three general tiers within the structured illegal drug economy: the top level that includes the "CEOs" (Chief Executive Officers), who principally control production, manufacturing, and international export; the middle level of managers and administrators, who control national and regional distribution, marketing, high-level security, and money laundering; and the bottom rung, which includes the couriers, peasant farmers, street-level retailers, crack-house operators, and local enforcers. It's at the bottom level where entry into trafficking is most fluid and virtually open to anyone who can and wants to invest.

Trafficking in illegal drugs has been, to say the least, very profitable for the top echelon of the trade. They engage in a vortex of obsessive profit-making that seems boundless. According to *Forbes,* cocaine sales created at least three billionaires among Colombia's Medellin drug cartel leaders: the late Gonzalo "the Mexican" Rodriguez Gacha, who was killed in a shootout with Colombian police in December 1989; Jorge Luis Ochoa Vasquez; and Pablo Escobar Gaviria.[7] The Medellin and Cali cartels, along with the smaller Bogota and North Coast cartels, dominate the world's cocaine industry.

The Medellin cartel is run by the brothers Miguel and Gilberto Rodriguez Orejuela and their partner, José Santacruz Medellin. While the Medellin cartel once numbered an estimated 70,000 operatives and workers, it has lost a significant number of members as its leaders have been driven underground or jailed. As the Medellin cartel fell on hard times in the late 1980s, the fortunes of the Cali cartel rose accordingly. By mid-1990, the Cali cartel controlled about 50 percent of the cocaine export to the United States, up from about 25 percent only a few years earlier. The leaders of the smaller, more tightly-run Cali cartel, with an estimated 5,000 workers, are seen as respected community and business representatives whose association with the country's elite is not viewed as scandalous.[8]

Partnership with the cartels has been profitable for many. Honduran billionaire Juan Ramon Matta Ballesteros made his money, according to authorities, by setting himself up as an equal opportunity cocaine distributor for the Colombian cartels. He is credited with inventing the "Mexican trampoline" method of smuggling, whereby Colombian drugs are given to experienced Mexican smugglers who would bring them into the United States. After entering the country, the drugs are "bounced" back to Colombians in the United States tied to the cartel.[9]

Heroin traffickers have not missed the boom. Kuhn Sa, leader of the 15,000-member Shan United Army in Burma and reportedly the world's largest heroin dealer, has made countless millions over the last thirty years. He is believed to control about half of the opium that is grown and 70 percent of the heroin that comes out of the Golden Triangle.[10]

In Mexico, seven families have traditionally controlled the Mexican heroin market: the Herreras, the Maciaces, the Romeros, the Favelas, the Sicilia-Falcons, the Valenzuelas, and the Aviles-Quinteros. These families and other trafficking groups have controlled the law enforcement entities of the Mexican government for many years.[11]

Chinese gangs, some tied to Chinese secret societies known as Triads, control the estimated $200 billion-a-year heroin trade based in Hong Kong and Nationalist China. They have increasingly moved in on the heroin trade in New York.[12]

Traditional organized crime, in the form of the Mafia families known as La Cosa Nostra, plays a more muted role in drug trafficking these days. Most observers believe that the infighting, the blitz of investigations by federal authorities, and competition from the new Sicilian Mafia has decimated the once all-powerful families. The Sicilians, on the other hand, control heroin and cocaine distribution operations through what federal agents call the "Pizza Connection," where

Mafia-owned pizza shops are used for selling drugs. They also suffered large-scale busts in the late Eighties.

The individuals who rule these organizations occupy a tier of the drug industry that many aspire to, but few will ever achieve. They command immense political and economic power, own millions of acres of land, and have personal armies at their disposal. They provide employment for hundreds of thousands globally and function as powerful and untouchable capitalists in their native lands. And, when required, they murder to achieve their ends.

Gangs: The Second Tier of the Drug Economy

At the next level are the national and regional suppliers and distributors, along with their managers and administrators. In the United States, the Justice Department estimates that there are hundreds of drug-trafficking organizations. This includes inner-city street "gangs" such as those affiliated with Los Angeles' Crips and Bloods, Chicago's Vice Lords and El Rukns, and Miami's Untouchables. These groups control a significant proportion of the cocaine, crack, and PCP distributed around the country.

No unity exists among law enforcement agencies on a definition of a gang, though the broadest interpretation seems to be on the West Coast and the narrowest on the East Coast. These differences make it difficult to assess more precisely what the so-called youth gang problem actually looks like. What would be called a gang in some cities, such as Los Angeles or Chicago, is not seen as a gang in other cities, such as Washington, D.C., or New York. According to an article in *Social Service Review,* officials have sometimes changed their definition of what constitutes a gang, as they did in Chicago, in order to reduce gang violence and gang homicide figures.[13]

Youth gangs often function as surrogate families. Gang members identify with the gang more so than with their real family, which is often broken apart and/or dysfunctional. Although an overwhelmingly male activity, women's participation is not uncommon, especially in situations where a female relative had been involved with the gang. Gang identity, collective and individual, is often shaped by the amount of violence and victimization that is exhibited.

Los Angeles, a city famous for its "gang problem," has about 450 gangs with about 45,000 members. But to refer to Los Angeles' renowned Crips and Bloods as gangs is misleading because they are not really gangs—that is, no central controlling group called Crips or Bloods exists. Both the Crips and Bloods are names that the city's prolific array of Black gangs have identified with. Police officials speculate that there are close to 200 smaller gangs, known as "sets," that identify with the name Crips, and about sixty-five to seventy sets that identify with the Bloods.[14] A Crip set is as likely to fight another Crip set as it is to fight Bloods, and the same holds true for Bloods. There are other Black and Latino Los Angeles gangs that don't identify with either.

Media sensationalism has propagated the erroneous and racist notion that all of the city's Black gangs traffic in drugs. The truth is that not all of Los Angeles' street gangs deal drugs and not all drug dealers are in gangs. Actually, Blacks make up only 39 percent of the Los Angeles County Sheriff's department gang records. Latinos are 59 percent and Asians account for about 2 percent. Supposedly, only seventy-two White gang members are known.[15] Local critics point out the discriminatory geographic patterns of police sweeps in Los Angeles and surrounding areas that register more Black and Latino youth as gang members.

One Black youth gang in Detroit, Young Boys, Inc., grew from twenty-four members to 300 members, with estimated weekly sales of $7.5 million in heroin and cocaine. In 1982, they grossed close to $400 million. According to Michigan State University criminologist Carl Taylor, who has written an authoritative book on Detroit's youth gangs titled *Dangerous Society,* the gang began with an investment of $80,000 that came from an insurance claim by two of the original members. By all accounts the group was extremely organized, highly disciplined, and unabashedly brutal. It imposed a "no drug use" policy on its members, and the penalty for violation was death.

Young Boys, Inc., was able to exploit the financial crisis that Detroit's Black community found itself facing in the Seventies. The gang functioned as a bank for many Black Detroiters by giving loans at usury rates for house purchases and starting small businesses, since Detroit's financial institutions had been chastised by the banking industry for not making loans to Blacks in the city. Gang members themselves bought homes in the suburbs and houses and apartments in the city to process and sell drugs. Some members opened legitimate businesses such as video and record stores.[16]

Although some of the money derived from drug trafficking was reinvested into the community, the structural and entrenched economic crisis confronting Detroit's Black poor, particularly that of males, went unaddressed. The social and economic crisis of the community was exacerbated by Young Boys, Inc.'s, care and feeding of Detroit's estimated 50,000 heroin addicts. Their activities accelerated the city's social deterioration and wrought uncalculated suffering.[17]

The posses, who control much of the East Coast crack, cocaine, and marijuana trade, grew out of Jamaica's political turmoil in the 1970s and 1980s. Seasoned in the political gun battles of Kingston's streets waged between the backers of Michael Manley's People's National Party (PNP) and Edward Seaga's Jamaica Labor Party (JLP), the Shower Posse (linked to the PNP) and the Spangler Posse (linked to the JLP) grew large and deadly. Transplanted to the United States, along with many other posse groups named after various neighborhoods and regions in Jamaica, these gangs spread from coast to coast.[18]

The drug networks provide start-up capital, management, resources, security, and muscle for their operations and sales territories. They defend their markets with brazen violence, buying off judges, law enforcement officials, and prison guards without pause.

Third World Peasants, Immigrants, and African Americans: The Third Tier of the Drug Economy

On the bottom of the drug economy pyramid are the growers and retailers. Hundreds of thousands of peasants around the world make up the frontline of drug production. Subject to eradication attacks, struggles between different cartels, and a volatile market, peasants often risk all to produce and sell the only profitable crop they can.

In the United States, the front line is occupied by street sellers, lookouts, couriers, workers in heroin "shooting galleries," and crack-house operators. These workers, many of whom are inner-city Black and Latino youth, are the first arrested and the first killed. Although profits can sometimes be high (a low-level lookout can earn $75.00 an hour on a good day), the risks are deadly and unforgiving.

Neither peasants nor inner-city dealers have any financial security, health insurance, or legal options that their middle- and upper-class employers have. They are the first and hardest hit when the market declines and they lack the skills and resources to invest and create long-term legitimate sources of income. The cycle of poverty and disempowerment that was for many the catalyst for entering the drug trade often remains the only way of life, other than death or imprisonment.

Many experts feel that while it is easy to enter the drug trade as a drug seller, particularly selling crack, few become rich. The Joint Center for Political and Economic Studies sponsored a roundtable discussion titled *Crime, Drugs, and Urban Poverty*. During the discussion, Rutgers University sociologist Jeffrey Fagan said that, "Crack really is a deregulated market. It is totally open...people have access to raw materials...and to selling locations." This view was echoed by Steve Rickman, of the Washington, D.C., Office of Criminal Justice, who said, "anyone can set up shop" on the unprofitable street corners that are not already under control.[19]

The big profits made from street sales are restricted to a few. According to Bruce Johnson of the Narcotics and Drug Research, Inc., "less than 20 percent of the people engaged in drug dealing have a net-worth cash return of as much as $1,000." This view appears to be backed up by a Rockefeller Foundation-funded study that reported that street-level dealers in Washington, D.C., made between $740 to $1,000 a week. Crack-house workers, as opposed to owners, appear to make very little. In one East Harlem neighborhood, studied by San Francisco State University's Phillippe Bourgois, crack-house workers made $50 to $70 for an eight-hour shift. This worked out to only 50¢ per vial of crack.[20]

The most significant conclusion from these discussions is that it is highly likely that low-level employees in the illegal drug industry, who profit little and face the most danger, may be won over to the legal labor market. Contrary to popular belief, winning these workers over does not mean dangling a large salary in front of them. It does mean making available meaningful, nonviolent, productive, and career-oriented work.

Doing the Laundry: White Professionals in the Drug Trade

Probably the biggest problem facing drug dealers is what to do with the mountains of $5, $10, and $20 bills that they accumulate. In these drug-conscious (and federally-observant) days, it takes considerable and creative financial acumen to turn drug dollars into "honest" money. As a pamphlet titled *Money Laundering: A Banker's Guide to Avoiding Problems* notes: "For money laundering to be successful, there must be no 'paper trail.'" The pamphlet, put out by the Supervision Policy/Research Office of the Comptroller of the Currency, notes a number of laundering schemes that banks knowingly participated in, including opening fictitious accounts and hiding behind phony real estate loans.[21]

A whole new cottage industry now exists of professional money launderers, many of whom work on one-time-only contracts and often for rival drug dealers or gangs simultaneously. These individuals, for the most part, are respectable White professionals with no criminal record. They include people like former Rep. Robert Hanrahan (R-IL) and Richard Silberman, former fundraiser for Jerry Brown in California, both of whom were convicted of laundering drug money. They include a former attorney general for the state of Kansas;[22] a consortium of Pennsylvania airline pilots, called the Air America Organization, who smuggled drugs and money for the Colombian cartels;[23] and three former DEA agents indicted in November 1988 for laundering more than $600,000 in drug money, to name a few.

Launderers range from cash-and-carry types, who pack suitcases and bags with cash, to more elaborate operators with electronic money-wiring facilities, telex machines, and automatic bill-counting equipment.

The most frequent vehicles for the laundering of drug money are banks in the United States, the Caribbean, and Hong Kong. Colombian traffickers prefer to use banks in Aruba, the Cayman Islands, Panama, and Uruguay. Chinese heroin dealers prefer Hong Kong and Taiwan. And there are at least twenty-nine nations that have virtually no barriers to laundering money. This includes nations such as Austria, Bahrain, Barbados, Bermuda, Costa Rica, Grenada, Liberia, Liechtenstein, Monaco, Singapore, and Switzerland, as well as virtually unheard of islands such as Channel Islands, Caicos Islands, Isle of Man, Nauru, and Vanuatu.[24]

One indication of how profitable the illegal drug industry has been for certain areas of the United States is the growth in cash surplus at local banks. In the United States, a cash surplus results when all the banks in an area receive more money from a local Federal Reserve Board than they pay to it. In 1970, banks in Florida, a key drug entry point, had a currency surplus of $576 million. By 1976, this figure had grown to $1.5 billion. By 1982, the cash surplus in Jacksonville and Miami alone amounted to $5.2 billion. Similar trends exist in southern California, Texas, and New Orleans. Los Angeles had a surplus of $2.7 billion, while San Antonio's grew to $1.2 billion.[25]

Large-scale drug traffickers in these regions are being overwhelmed with drug dollars from buyers around the country. Traffickers, and the banks that they deposit in, are making overnight fortunes, and are able to make legal investments with this money in areas such as real estate and high finance that reap additional profits.

Although some government action has been taken against laundering, such as the Bank Secrecy Act of 1970, the Money Laundering Control Act of 1986, and the Anti-Drug Abuse Act of 1988, it's estimated that prosecutors catch only two percent of laundered money circulating in the United States. Actions against high ranking launderers has been limited, due to strong lobbying by banks to curtail government regulations and oversight. Many of these bankers have close financial and personal ties with Bush and Reagan administration officials. Consequently, prosecution of launderers has not been a high priority for either the Bush or Reagan administrations.

As a result, billions of drug-tainted dollars are pulsing through the nation's financial system, according to federal banking officials. In fact, there appears to be so much drug profit money flowing into the nation's banks that tests show virtually every bill in circulation to be covered with microscopic traces of cocaine.

A 1982 federal investigation entitled "Operation Greenback" discovered that a Capital Bank of Miami branch office had accepted $242 million in drug-tainted cash over a period of eighteen months. The investigation, however, was stymied by the Reagan administration's easing of banking regulations and resistance from the banking institutions. The investigation eventually phased out, and today the Capital Bank has expanded its operations with a brand new office two blocks from the White House.[26]

The S & L Connection

The 1990 Savings and Loan scandal illustrates the utility of banks for highly-motivated operators. The *Houston Post* conducted an eight-month investigation into the S&L disgrace and found links between twenty-two of the failed banks and the CIA, the Nicaragua contras, organized crime figures, and drug traffickers. According to the *Post,* former CIA contract agent Richard Brenneke stated that the CIA successfully plotted to "siphon funds from financial institutions" to fund the contras after Congress banned contra funding in 1984. Of the twenty-two banks that they investigated, all had made substantial loans to people tied to the CIA, organized crime, or both. In fact, eighteen of the twenty-two were owned or controlled by people tied to the CIA and/or organized crime.[27]

Neil Bush, President Bush's son, was on the board of directors of the failed Silverado Savings and Loan in Denver, Colorado. In the Summer of 1990, he was accused by the Office of Thrift Supervision (OTS) of not disclosing a conflict of interest while extending a $900,000 line of credit to Kenneth Good, his partner in JNB Exploration Company.[28] Neil Bush became an outside director of Silverado in 1985 and stayed until October 1988, one month after his father won the Republican nomination. Four of Silverado's biggest borrowers had ties to Robert Corson, who authorities called a "known money launderer" in Houston. In 1986, Corson, a developer, had purchased and then four months later caused the failure of Vision Bank Savings in Kingsville, Texas. The collapse occurred after the bank lent $20 million to a group of investors that included CIA operatives and organized crime figures, according to the Christic Institute. Helping to negotiate the loan was convicted money launderer Lawrence Freeman, who had "washed" money for the CIA and Florida organized crime kingpin Santo Trafficante, Jr.[29] According to the *Houston Post,* $7 million went to a company tied to drug traffickers and launderers in the Isle of Jersey located in the English Channel.

Another central figure in the S&L scandal is Mario Renda, who brokered billions of dollars in deposits into the nation's S&Ls. Renda, a Long Island money broker, is linked to the Gambino and Lucchesse organized crime families, which have both been involved in drug sales and drug money laundering. Renda is in federal prison for racketeering and bank fraud. In one failed Texas bank, Empire Savings and Loan, Renda alone accounted for more than half of the bank's money deposits, approximately $150 million.[30]

Perhaps the most notable involvement is Frank Castro, long linked to anti-Fidel Castro activities in Florida and throughout Latin America. According to research conducted by the Christic Institute, Frank Castro was part of a drug-smuggling group that bought Miami Sunshine State Bank. The bank failed, but not before it had laundered millions of dollars tied to the CIA, organized crime, and the contras. Castro was caught bringing 425,000 tons of marijuana into the United States, but the charges were dropped in June 1984, when he began training contras for the CIA in Naples, Florida.[31]

It's not just banks that are involved in money laundering. Similar to banks, businesses are required to file an IRS Form 8300 when they handle cash transactions over $10,000. National investigations have shown, however, that many businesses that handle large cash transactions, such as jewelers and automobile dealers, ignore the regulation shamelessly. One jeweler in Atlanta, attempting to sell two high-priced Rolex watches to undercover investigators posing as customers, was willing to evade the reporting requirement even as IRS agents were in the back of the store at that moment going over his books.[32] Many businesses have not only been willing to ask no questions, but a large number of them were willing to facilitate the violation. Well aware of the law, corrupt businesses get around the reporting rule by splitting a purchase into two or more transactions or using cashier's checks and money orders, which do not have to be reported. The situation in Washington, D.C., is indicative of how casually the reporting rule is snubbed. In 1988, only eleven forms were filed, and in 1989, only fifteen. As of September 1990, only four had been filed.[33]

Many other professionals have sullied their hands. High-powered lawyers are hired not only to defend traffickers and dealers against criminal charges, but also to lobby the U.S. Congress and other governments on behalf of the illegal narcotics industry. Michael Abbell, who once worked as director of the Justice Department's Office of International Affairs, is now the Washington representative for leaders of the Cali Cartel. He makes no apology for this transformation and states in a *Washington Post* interview, "My impression is you can work with these people."[34] Other attorneys also deny the obvious. Medellin Cartel lawyer Bill Moran states without blinking that "It's just hard if not impossible for me to believe that cartel boss Jorge Ochoa is involved in that kind of behavior." He speaks of Ochoa as a dear friend and goes on to say, "I've met his family and been in his house."[35]

Lawyers from Los Angeles, Washington, and especially Florida have sought the plentiful profits that come from defending high-level drug dealers. One of these lawyers, Joseph Vodnoy of Los Angeles, speaks for all of them when he says, "There's no question the U.S. crackdown is good for business."[36] According to *Newsweek,* Vodnoy used to go to Colombia two or three times a year to pass out his business cards.

Chemicals, Drug Production, and Environmental Destruction

Cocaine powder is impossible to make without certain chemicals. The general method is as follows: at the beginning of the process, after the leaves are harvested, they must be dried and treated with either lime, sodium carbonate, or potash. Next, the leaves are soaked in kerosene to extract the leaf's fourteen alkaloids, one of which is cocaine. Sulfuric acid is then mixed with the kerosene to form cocaine sulfate which takes the form of salt. When the kerosene is separated from this concoction, what is left is cocaine paste.

The cocaine paste must then be turned into cocaine base by adding potassium permanganate to eliminate all non-cocaine alkaloids and impurities. Next, ammonium hydroxide is added. After the resulting substance is filtered and dried, cocaine base remains.

The final stage is to transform cocaine base into cocaine hydrochloride, better known as cocaine powder, by adding either acetone or ether with hydrochloric acid. This mixture is converted to the white crystalline salt powder that dominated the U.S. drug crisis of the 1980s. Many of the same chemicals used to make cocaine, such as lime, ammonium chloride, acetic anhydride, acetone, hydrochloric acid, and ether, are also used in the process of transforming opium to morphine base and then heroin.

Manufacturers of chemicals needed for narcotics production have seen nothing but rising profits in the last decade. Ether and acetic anhydride, both of which have legal uses, are necessary to produce cocaine and heroin, respectively. According to the *Christian Science Monitor,* the United States makes 95 percent of these and other drug "precursor" chemicals. Between 1983 and 1986, U.S. exports of ether and acetic anhydride tripled. In 1988, an estimated 47 percent of the 10,000 tons of ether exported to Colombia, Ecuador, Peru, and Bolivia went to cocaine production.[37] Eastman Kodak, which produces about one billion pounds of acetic anhydride annually, admits not being able to account for the destination of at least one million pounds of their product. Other chemicals, such as acetone, the solvent toluene, and methly ethyl ketone (MEK) can be used as substitutes. Exports of these drugs to Latin America doubled during the early 1980s.[38]

The destructive use of these chemicals goes beyond just drug production. These chemicals have also had an extremely ruinous effect environmentally. Buenaventura Marcelo, a Peruvian engineer at the National Agrarian University, estimates that in 1986 alone 15 million gallons of kerosene, 8 million gallons of sulphuric acid, 1.6 million gallons of acetone, 1.6 million gallons of toluene, 16,000 tons of lime, and 3,200 tons of carbide were dumped into the Huallaga Valley waters in Peru.[39]

In the Amazon Basin region, the most dangerous impact of these chemicals has been the deoxygenation of the water sources; meaning waters that most aquatic life, such as fish and amphibians, cannot survive in. Many species of fish, aquatic reptiles, and crustaceans have already been rendered extinct. According to Marcelo, World Health Organization pollution standards have been greatly exceeded to the degree that many of these waters can no longer be put to normal use.[40]

As water and animal life is affected by these developments, so are the people who live in the region. Forced to drink from these contaminated waters due to a lack of potable and safe water supplies, the health of people in the region will deteriorate over time.

For third world peoples, many of whom live in rural areas and depend on the health of the environment for their livelihood and survival, drug production has a most detrimental long-term impact on their lives, communities, and environment.

More Drug War Profiteers: The Multinational Component

Just as war profiteers are enriched from the expenses incurred in fighting and maintaining a conventional war, so too are the current "drug war profiteers" that have sprouted and grown wealthy from the sale of legal drugs, from the never-ending federal drug wars, and from exploiting the drug culture.

Companies that produce medicines and operate programs that treat or test addicts have made millions over the past ten years. Multinational pharmaceutical corporations, such as Eli Lilly, Dupont, and others, have produced methadone and other addiction "cures," monopolizing the drug treatment market. George Bush is more intricately tied into the pharmaceutical cartels than any other President to date. The Bush family has had substantial stockholdings in a number of large pharmaceutical corporations, including Abbott, Bristol, and Pfizer. From 1977 to 1980, the period when Bush was head of the CIA, Bush was made a director on the board of Eli Lilly by James C. Quayle, the father of Vice President Dan Quayle. Eli Lilly is one of the largest producers of methadone in the world.[41]

Methadone was invented by Germans during World War II as a substitute for scarce morphine. It is a synthetic drug with similar analgesic properties as those of morphine, heroin, and meperidine. After World War II, Lilly chemist Dr. Ervin C. Kleider joined the State Department's Technical Industrial Intelligence Committee that was investigating Nazi drug companies. Kleider's team first brought methadone to the United States, marketed by the Lilly corporation as a cough medicine named Dolophine (the Nazi brand name for methadone in honor of Adolph Hitler). Eli Lilly became the first company to manufacture methadone, then used in government hospitals to detox heroin addicts. Following the war, methadone was used to treat middle-class heroin addicts in Europe and then in the United States.[42]

Col. Eli Lilly founded the company in 1876. Lilly produced heroin-based cough syrups as recently as the turn of the twentieth century. The company sold at least four kinds of heroin cough medicines up until 1919, five years after the passage of the Harrison Act.[43] Although best known for the inventions of Salk polio vaccine and insulin, through which it came to dominate more than 85 percent of the legal drug market, Lilly also produced the toxic, "non-narcotic" painkiller, Darvon, which was responsible for 11,000 deaths and 79,000 emergency room visits during its shelf life.[44]

When Bush joined the Lilly board, it was unsurprisingly all White and all male.[45] In 1980, Bush owned $180,000 in Lilly stock. Russell Mokhiber's book, *Corporate Crime and Violence,* raised suspicions that Vice President Bush had played a biased role in the Justice Department's case against the company regarding Darvon. The Justice Department had charged Lilly and Dr. W. Ian H. Shedden, Lilly's vice president in charge of its research labs, with withholding information to the Food and Drug Administration (FDA). Mokhiber speculates that Bush's tie to Lilly was the reason that the company and Shedden were charged only with misdemeanors and not felonies.[46]

Lilly's international policies also came under question. Despite worldwide sanctions against South Africa, Lilly maintained its South African operations and charged prices that were out of reach for most Blacks.[47] Lilly is also the maker of the herbicide tebuthiuron, sold under the brand name Spike, that was specifically developed to destroy woody plants like the coca leaf. In 1986, while Bush was Vice President,

Congress appropriated $1 million for research that led to the development of Spike in March 1988. After a trial run, however, environmentalists and the EPA raised enough questions about the product's safety that Lilly withdrew its bid to sell Spike to the U.S. government.[48]

Other companies that produce or are researching, through large government grants, legal narcotics to be used in treatment programs include Norwich Eaton, Merrell Dow, Searle, Dupont, Geigy, Marlon, and Sandoz. According to NIDA, these companies are involved in the development of drugs to be used in maintenance therapy. The treatment goal is essentially to switch addiction from one drug to another rather than ending the user's addiction.

Not coincidentally, all of these companies are already involved in the production of highly addictive legal prescription drugs. According to a report by the Washington Area Council on Alcoholism and Drug Abuse (WACADA), more people die from valium overdoses than from PCP. The report, using data from the Drug Abuse Warning Network (DAWN), also points out that the number of teenagers admitted to emergency rooms for overdoses on legal tranquilizers was eight times the number admitted for heroin abuse.[49] In 1987, in Washington, D.C., over 800 people were treated in emergency rooms for abuse of prescription drugs.[50]

The most dangerously addictive of these drugs are Benzedrine, Librium, Trilium, Dalmane, Novoflupan, Dilaudid, Demerol, Ativan, Darvon, and Xanax. Former Washington Mayor Marion Barry confessed upon his return from two drug treatment centers that one of the drugs he had been addicted to was Xanax. Ten times more powerful than valium, Xanax sells on the street for as much as $8.00 a pill.[51] Halcion is the most popular sleeping pill on the market. Yet from 1982 to 1990, the FDA received more than 2,000 complaints stating that the side effects of Halcion included retrograde amnesia, aggression, delirium, hallucinations, seizures, and suicidal urges.[52]

Most of these anti-stress drugs are in the benzodiazepine family. More than sixty million prescriptions are filled per year for these drugs, to the tune of $800 million. In 1986, anti-stress pills were involved in more than 500 fatal drug overdoses and accounted for 52 percent of all drug-related emergencies.[53] In 1987, according to *Business Week,* the top fifteen pharmaceutical companies made $43 billion in sales. Eli Lilly had sales of $3.6 billion while Smith Kline, the producers of the mind-numbing Thorazine, made $4.3 billion.[54]

Alcohol and Tobacco—No Need for Firearms

> Once upon a time, way back in 1934, the American Tobacco
> Company set out to sell Lucky Strikes to women, who had
> only recently started smoking in large numbers. Market
> research revealed that women disliked the brand because
> the package, which used to be green, clashed with their
> clothes! The solution? Popularize green as the fashion color
> of choice. First, the director of a major society ball was given
> $25,000 to turn it into a "Green Ball!" Then, a "Color Fashion
> Bureau" was set up to herald the new green season! Fashion
> editors and interior decorators were enlisted, and even the
> cooperation of the French couture houses was secured!
> Before long, green was the color of American fashion.
> Hordes of women started buying and smoking Lucky Strikes
> as an accessory. And they all died happily ever after!
> Thousands of 'em!
>
> —*Doonesbury,* September 9, 1990

The tobacco and alcohol industries, along with the pharmaceutical companies, spend billions per year on advertising—much of it aimed at people of color and White working-class communities. The tobacco industry alone spent $2.5 billion a year on advertising in 1988.[55]

A 1987 study in St. Louis found three times as many billboards in the Black community as in the White. In the Black community, 62 percent of those billboards advertised tobacco and alcohol as compared to only 36 percent for the White community.[56] A similar pattern was found in Detroit. Nearly 43 percent of the billboards in the city advertised alcohol and tobacco. Only 24.7 percent did so in the surrounding White areas.[57]

Marketing strategies aimed at the Black community reflect an adjustment to the national trend of decreasing consumption of tobacco, hard liquor, and cheap wine among Whites and the affluent. In 1965, 40 percent of the population smoked. By 1987, that number had dropped to 29 percent. In the Black community, however, use of these substances has risen and is a significant factor in the increasing health problems among Blacks. For example, the Black lung cancer rate has grown four times faster than the White rate, according to the American Lung Association.[58]

In 1990, RJ Reynolds announced plans for a new cigarette brand, Uptown, to be aimed at Blacks. The cigarette was to be field tested in Philadelphia, but Black community groups in the city vowed to block its promotion. RJ Reynolds bowed to the resistance and decided not to market the cigarette.[59]

Secretary of Health and Human Services Louis Sullivan, at one point, invited Black magazine owners and editors to meet and discuss tobacco ads in their publications. All refused to attend the meeting. Some Black newspaper representatives did attend, but no one stopped taking the advertisements.[60]

Some Black spokespeople have defended these advertisements. NAACP Executive Director Ben Hooks dismissed the argument that these advertisements influence Blacks. He stated: "Buried in this line of thinking…is the rationale that Blacks are not capable of making their own free choices and need some guardian angel to protect their best interests."[61] However, this simplistic viewpoint is immediately contradicted by the fact that tobacco companies do not spend billions yearly on advertising campaigns that do not show results.

The tobacco industry is the number-one lobby group in Washington, D.C. For individual companies and through the industry think tank called the Tobacco Institute, lobbying is intense and aggressive. And there is plenty of reason to lobby, as the deaths caused by tobacco use require the industry to recruit at least 1,000 new smokers every day to replace the 1,000 who die daily as a result of cigarette smoking.[62] Between 350,000 and 400,000 people die each year—accounting for approximately one out of every seven deaths in the United States.[63] Lung cancer has surpassed breast cancer as the leading cause of death among women.[64]

Alcohol abuse continues to be another major killer in the United States. As Mothers Against Drunk Driving (MADD), Students Against Drunk Driving (SADD), Alcoholics Anonymous (AA), and other anti-substance abuse groups can attest, alcoholism remains one of the most deadly diseases in America. It's estimated that alcohol abuse results in 100,000 to 125,000 deaths per year, not including traffic deaths and other accidents. More than 8,000 teenagers are killed and over 40,000 maimed each year from alcohol-related driving accidents.[65]

The Native American community, in particular, has seen the destructive consequences of alcoholism. Prior to instituting prevention and treatment programs, many Indian tribes suffered nearly complete alcoholism among their adults. As a result of these programs, the Alkali Lake and Shuswap Indians in British Colombia went from nearly 100 percent alcoholism to 98 percent sobriety in fifteen years. An Aleut village in Akhiok, Alaska, went from 90 percent alcoholism to 80 percent sobriety.

Alcoholism affects both men and women. In 1988, Indian women aged fifteen to twenty-four had a cirrhosis mortality rate three times that of Indian men and thirty-seven times that of White women of the same age. Fetal Alcohol Syndrome was as high as one in 100 in some Indian communities.

By creatively using a combination of Alcoholics Anonymous methods with traditional Native American healing rituals, such as the sweat lodge, great success was achieved. Native Americans saw a 55 percent decline in alcohol-related deaths.[66]

The pharmaceutical, tobacco, and alcohol companies attempt to deflect the criticism of the death they bring by effectively buying off their opposition. Donations are given to Black causes such as the United Negro College Fund and to Black groups such as the Congressional Black Caucus Foundation and the Urban League, and massive advertising is purchased in Black publications such as *Essence, Ebony,* and *Emerge.*

The beer company Coors, whose record on race, labor, gender, and international issues is one of the most reactionary of any major corporation, has been particularly deft in going after Black patronage. *New Horizons,* the quarterly publication of its National Program Office of the Community Relations Department, is saturated with pictures of Black celebrities at Coors-related events. Its twelve-page August/September 1989 issue alone includes Eddie Murphy, Sinbad, former Superbowl quarterback Doug Williams, basketball great Walt Frazier, Detroit Mayor Coleman Young, Whitney Houston, Glynn Turman, Marla Gibbs, Danny Glover, Muhammad Ali, and Spike Lee. A number of these individuals give a significant amount of their time and money to worthy causes and probably would have some reservations about having their efforts exploited by a company whose history is as sordid and tainted as Coors.

The death and destruction caused by the legal drugs of alcohol and tobacco merits little criticism from the administration and Congress. Large donations and effective lobbying by alcohol and tobacco companies silence, for the most part, any official denunciation of these merchants of death. Politicians are able to hide behind the proverbial fig leaf that says that since these products are legal, their consumption should be controlled by the invisible hand of the marketplace.

Less than 10,000 people die annually from consumption of illegal drugs. That figure pales considerably when we look at the estimated more than 400,000 Americans who die as a result of smoking and another 100,000 who die of alcohol-related illnesses every year (not to mention the thousands more who die from incidental smoke or from alcohol-related car accidents). In 1990, alcohol abuse cost the United States an estimated $136 billion in lost productivity and medical expenses. Even as Americans are smoking less, U.S. tobacco companies are rapidly expanding their export to markets in other lands. In 1989, U.S. cigarette exports totaled about 150 billion cigarettes, bringing in $5 billion in revenues.[67]

The harm caused by alcohol and tobacco addiction must be fought as vigorously and as seriously as that caused by illegal drugs. The legality of these products functions to mask their social destruction while allowing their promotion to a degree unseen with most other commodities. When alcohol is used in moderation and with appropriate health-oriented education, alcohol-related deaths and illnesses can be significantly reduced. Tobacco, on the other hand, is legal suicide. A health-conscious society must confront the real possibility of eventually banning all tobacco production and products. Until public and governmental commitment to ending the harm of legal drugs is as strong as the rhetoric and energy employed against illegal narcotics, substance abuse will remain a self-destructive and costly burden in U.S. society.

Drug Culture Profits: The Problems of Drug Testing

As the mania to identify drug users has escalated, so have the profits of the drug-testing industry. Virtually unheard of until the late 1980s, drug testing has boomed in recent times. Now, at the beginning of the Nineties, about one-third of all U.S. companies have some sort of drug testing program for employees, compared to only about 3 percent in 1984. Over half of the Fortune 500 corporations do some form of drug testing. Some experts estimated that the drug-testing industry is bringing in revenues of between $73 million and $115 million a year.[68]

The random and often mandatory nature of the tests has become a serious civil rights issue for workers. While unions have conceded that drug tests can play an important role in areas such as public transportation and security, their use across the board has been severely criticized.

In addition to the issue of privacy, there is mounting evidence that the tests are unreliable. Drug users have discovered creative and effective methods for passing urine tests, such as substituting apple cider for urine, while innocent non-users can test positive for drugs based on their eating poppy seeds or drinking herbal teas. Over-the-counter drugs, such as Ibuprofen, can also cause positive test results.[69]

When drugs or other substances such as food are taken—whether orally, smoked, or injected—they undergo chemical changes in the body so that all that is not absorbed or used can easily be excreted. This transformation or metabolism creates what are called metabolites. The logic behind urine testing is that drug metabolites are released from the body primarily through urination. Urine testing can involve either testing for simply the presence of a particular drug or for the actual amount of a particular drug. Some drugs, such as marijuana, take longer to metabolize—up to two weeks—and are easier to detect in urine. Others, such as cocaine, are metabolized quickly and so thoroughly that virtually none of the original substance remains.

Despite these problems, drug testing continues to expand, along with the profit margins of the companies that perform the tests. Many businesses use the cheaper and inaccurate Emit d.a.u. (drug abuse urine) test and do not confirm results with the more reliable and expensive Gas-Liquid Chromatography (GLC), Thin Layer Chromatography (TLC), or Radioimmunoassay (RIA) tests, as recommended by testing experts.

Several studies conducted by the Centers for Disease Control from 1972 to 1981 assessed the reliability of urine drug testing. The Centers concluded that while some testing methodologies were more proficient and accurate than others, none was 100 percent accurate. A 1985 study by the Centers found the error rates for cocaine testing ranged from zero percent to 100 percent. In the same study, tests for amphetamines ranged from 19 percent to nearly 100 percent.

Hair testing for drugs has proved to be even more error-prone than urine testing. The largest commercial hair testing company is Psychemedics. Dr. Werner Baumgartner, the company chairman, has promoted the company by making spectacular claims regarding the accuracy and efficiency of his company's hair testing. He boasted that Psychemedics could tell when, how much, and which illegal drug had been used from any hair sample. Baumgartner backed these assertions by claiming Psychemedics has done more than 17,000 tests and over 100,000 hair analyses.[70]

It is interesting to note, however, that Psychemedics' chief medical advisor, Dr. Robert Dupont, was the former head of NIDA and, before that, director of the Narcotics Treatment Agency in Washington, D.C., where he implemented the city's large-scale methadone maintenance program in the Sixties.

When Washington Mayor Marion Barry was arrested on charges of cocaine possession, samples of his hair were taken by the FBI and used later by the government as evidence of drug abuse prior to his arrest. However, after a special investigative report on Psychemedics was aired by WJLA, a Washington television station, during the early weeks of Barry's trial, the prosecution judiciously decided not to introduce drug-tested hair samples as evidence.

The reporters created a fictional company, appropriately called Bald Eagle Security, and sent six hair samples to Psychemedics for drug testing. Some of the samples had been pre-treated with particular drugs or came from admitted drug users. The inaccurate results, dramatically broadcasted over a three-day period, not only demonstrated the unreliability of the tests, but also the possibility of racial bias.

Only two out of the six samples were correctly diagnosed by Psychemedics: the hair sample treated only with PCP and the sample treated only with marijuana. Psychemedics' identification of the other four were completely false. One sample that contained cocaine, PCP and opiates was identified by Psychemedics as only containing marijuana. Another sample that was treated with a substance similar to cocaine was identified as not only containing cocaine, but marijuana and PCP as well. The two largest errors occurred on the sample of a frequent marijuana user and on a sample that had been exposed only to crack-cocaine smoke. No drugs were detected on the hair from the marijuana user, while the smoke exposed hair was incorrectly identified as belonging to a heavy cocaine user.

According to the report aired by WJLA, a group of scientists who met in Washington in May 1990 to review the data available on hair testing reached this consensus: "The use of hair analysis for employee and pre-employment drug testing is premature." Dr. Naresh Jah of the University of Southern California School of Medicine, an acknowledged expert on hair testing, says that hair testing results are not worth the paper they are written on. Other critics have charged that there are too many variations of hair and too many variables, such as dye or bleach, that impact on testing for it to be seriously considered reliable.

Dr. David Kidwell of the U.S. Naval Research Laboratory, who has conducted experiments on different types of hair, believes that thick hair and dark hair seem more likely to test positive than thin hair or light hair, even when exposed to the same substances. Hair from people of color overwhelmingly falls into the first category, making the already flawed process even more discriminatory.

Psychemedics' methods are harmful and insidious precisely because they promote a false notion of accuracy, implying that companies don't need a second (usually more expensive) confirmation test. One Psychemedics employee estimated that perhaps only 20 percent of their customers request confirmation tests. After being told by Psychemedics that a prospective employee has tested positive for drugs, many companies simply write off the individual and hire someone else, especially since current law does not require potential employers to give test results to those tested.

A number of researchers and scientists have drawn a link between illegal drugs and melanin, pigment which is more prevalent in the skin of people of color, particularly people of African descent. Scientists in Atlanta discovered that melanin was chemically similar to tetrahydro-cannabinol (THC), the active ingredient in marijuana. James Woodford, a forensic chemist and researcher, believes that this similarity is a contributing factor in why many Blacks test positive for drugs.[71]

The drug testing market has also led to entrepreneurial efforts on the part of private individuals. One enterprising Texan, who adopted the name Jeff Nightbyrd, opened up a factory to produce powdered urine. The company's witty and politically succinct slogan was, "Pee for Plea-sure, Not for Employment."[72] For $19.95, customers who worried about passing a urine-based drug test would receive two vials of powder and an instruction book. Ironically enough, Nightbyrd initially procured his urine from church seniors, but was forced to seek other sources when he discovered that high levels of prescription drug use would make the urine test positive.

Corporate manufacturers also take advantage of the drug crisis to create and market their cultural commodities. Carl Taylor points out that U.S. urban centers have been a gold mine for certain businesses. Gucci, for example, makes expensive gym shoes sold only in three U.S. cities: Las Vegas, Atlantic City, and Detroit.[73] Similarly, large companies have set up businesses that sell beepers, cellular phones, and auto customization services geared to the lifestyle and business needs of individuals employed by the drug trade. Paradoxically, these companies exist only in the wealthiest and poorest neighborhoods. And it goes without saying that the multinational companies producing these goods are headed by White corporate elites—completing the circle of exploi-tation whereby drug money originates in the ruling class and eventually returns to the ruling class via the consumer market economy.

Conclusion

Sorting out the division of drug profits is a complex, fluid, and speculative science. It is clear, however, that the most substantial profits go to a third world and White ruling class and that those funds are routinely channeled toward legal, financial, and business enterprises. The federal government, on the other hand, continues to deprive, penalize, and prosecute those occupying the lower strata of the illegal drug trade while providing economic incentives to the venture capital-ists who join this super-profitable industry. For people of color and poor people, nothing changes economically; the "drug industry" constructs itself much like any other corporate "industry." African Americans and Latinos earn less, go to jail quicker, and suffer the institutionalized racism and classism of federal policies that perpetuate inequity even in illegal endeavors.

Chapter 6

THE INTERNATIONALIZATION
OF THE
ILLEGAL DRUG TRADE

In the years to come, the rhetoric of Dope War will replace the rhetoric of Cold War as the justification for foreign military intervention. Instead of sending in the Marines, Washington will send in the narcs.

—"Dope Dictators: The Vietnamization of Mexico, Jamaica, Colombia and the Third World," *High Times,* March 1977

According to *Fortune,* worldwide trade in illegal narcotics is a $500 billion a year industry.[1] By many accounts during the 1980s, trafficking in illegal drugs became the number-one growth industry in the Third World. And as with other multinational businesses, the organizational control and the division of profits is largely determined by the intersection of class, race, and nationalism.

More than 100 countries are directly involved in drug trafficking as producers, processors, distributors, or money launderers. Many smaller nations have become involved in other aspects of the drug trade. Nations such as Haiti and Ecuador serve as transshipment points, while others such as the Cayman Islands and the Bahamas are major laundering sites.

In the 1980s, this menagerie of nations was united by the two themes that characterized the Reagan/Bush international agenda: economic assault on developing nations and support for anti-communist allies in the name of national security at any cost.

With the Cold War receding and changes in Eastern Europe and elsewhere consolidating, the clarion call to fight communism has a hollow sound. Instead of a re-examination of the priorities and dictates of the intelligence agencies in light of these changes, there is every indication that the agencies will justify their existence by creating a new international danger: the narco-terrorists. Ivan the communist has been replaced by José the drug dealer. In the words of right-wing, techno-novelist Tom Clancy, the drug traffickers of today are for the cold warriors still in power "a clear and present danger."

Debt Crisis in the Third World

The aim of U.S. foreign aid, despite predictable protests to the contrary, has never been to eliminate poverty or to expand democracy. The dismal record in these two areas is glaring. U.S. foreign aid—whether economic, developmental, or military—has always served the dual purposes of politically rewarding our perceived friends and forcing U.S. capital into foreign markets.

In the ground-breaking book, *Betraying the National Interest,* authors Frances Moore Lappe, Rachel Schurman, and Kevin Danaher detail how U.S. foreign policy has undermined the economic and political stability of the Third World. According to the authors:

> Our government's view of the world as a battleground between "them" and "us" not only contributes to a military-dominated foreign policy, but powerfully shapes the content of the strictly economic portion of United States foreign aid. Washington believes that any economic system not like ours, must be like theirs.[2]

In particular, the "them" versus "us" mentality that guided U.S. foreign policy and shaped America's aid disbursement in the Eighties established the conditions that would force innumerable national economies into the illegal drug industry.

During the Reagan era, nation after nation was forced to adjust to a new period of debt capitalism and its consequent legacy of increased poverty and unemployment. Third world debt grew from $500 billion in 1980 to over $800 billion by 1985.[3] Latin America and Asia, key sources for illegal drug production, accounted for $368 billion and $304 billion of this debt, respectively.[4] By 1990, third world debt had grown to a colossal $1.2 trillion.[5] In Latin America, the foreign debt has ballooned to about $420 billion. Interest payments on this debt are estimated to be about $25 billion annually.[6]

Third world debt is escalating in an upward spiral that appears to have no limit. In complete antithesis to the fundamental law of capitalism, as explained by Karl Marx in *Capital,* third world nations find themselves in the position of being forced to "sell cheap and buy dear."

Dragged into debt by risky loans in the 1970s, third world nations began to take out new loans just to pay the interest on the old loans. Almost 80 percent of new loans fell into this category.[7] Jamaica, for example, had a foreign debt of $3.5 billion in 1988, according to the

Economist, and about 45 percent of Jamaica's export earnings went toward debt service.[8]

In Reagan's first term, export earnings from non-oil-producing third world countries fell from $104 billion to $87 billion. At the same time, capital flight from those countries exceeded $200 billion. Latin America alone lost $105 billion between 1983 and 1985.[9]

Through its self-serving economic policies, the United States has consistently undercut any chance developing countries have had to move from producing illegal drug commodities to legal ones. In 1965, only 27 percent of commodity imports to the United States had nontariff barriers. By 1986, that number had grown to more than half.[10] As one economist pointed out, third world nations are on a permanent cycle of "being forced to market fatter and fatter volumes of commodities at lower and lower prices in return for higher-priced imports."[11]

A farm bill passed by Congress in the mid-1980s, which reduced sugar imports to the United States, is estimated to have left 100,000 Caribbean workers unemployed.[12] This hit nations such as Jamaica and Belize especially hard and resulted in those two countries becoming two of the largest exporters of illegal drugs to the United States. Since then, Belize has become one of the biggest exporters of marijuana to the United States.[13] In response to the somewhat successful marijuana eradication campaigns that drove production down from 645 metric tons in 1985 to seventy-three metric tons in 1989, cocaine has become more available.[14]

The London-based International Coffee Organization, a seventy-four-nation organization, composed of twenty-four coffee-consuming and fifty coffee-producing member countries, has determined global coffee prices and import-export quotas since its establishment in 1962. In September 1989, during a meeting of the ICO, the United States let an international coffee agreement collapse, causing a 50 percent fall in coffee prices internationally, according to the *Washington Post.*[15] The fall of the agreement, experts estimated, will cost Colombia $600 million a year.[16] Providing 80 percent of the cocaine available in the United States, Colombia's cocaine revenues are estimated to be between $2.5 billion to $3 billion annually.[17] Coffee is Colombia's largest legal export and employs over 500,000 growers. In 1988, coffee exports—mainly to the United States—were $1.6 billion and accounted for one-third of its legal exports and 30 percent of its export earnings. Mexico, another principal supplier of illegal drugs to the United States, was projected to lose $195 million as a result of the agreement debacle.[18] These U.S. economic and political policies were enough to push thousands of peasants to the brink of survival and opened the door for enterprising big-time drug dealers to move in. Under Reagan, military aid was three times that of food aid.[19] Unemployment grew, and peasants and workers found it nearly impossible to survive under these new conditions. Soon, the opium fields of Pakistan and Mexico; the coca-leaf fields of Peru, Colombia, and Bolivia; and the marijuana fields of Jamaica and Belize became their main source of employment, income, and relative economic stability. Latin America experts estimate that there are about 1.5 million coca farmers in the Andean nations of Peru, Bolivia, and Colombia.[20] According to the *Christian Science Monitor,* more than 500,000 people are involved in the illegal narcotics trade in Bolivia alone.

In Myanmar (formerly Burma), the per capita income in 1989 was $180. About 1.4 million people in the country are dependent upon opium production and trafficking.[21] Myanmar is the largest producer of opium in the world, growing nearly five times as much as its nearest competitor, Afghanistan.

These countries are locked in an economic dependency on the "underground" drug trade. Billions of dollars enter the region through illegal narcotics channels and are integrated into sagging economies. In Colombia, drug dollars are about 10 percent of the export earnings. In Peru and Bolivia, the numbers are 25 percent and 50 percent respectively.[22] It's estimated that in 1988, third world nations produced at least 2,433 metric tons of opium, 173,745 tons of coca leaves, 15,042 tons of marijuana, and 1,185 tons of hashish.[23]

Bolivia, which is the second-poorest nation in the hemisphere after Haiti, saw cotton prices fall sharply in the mid-1970s, and many farmers found growing coca leaves their only alternative. Tin prices dropped a decade later, and Bolivia laid off over 20,000 tin workers. Prices fell so fast that, in 1985, tin lost half its value in the span of one month. Unemployment doubled, income dropped by 30 percent, and inflation rose to a stunning 24,000 percent. As a consequence, these same tin workers had no recourse but to find their way to the coca fields in Chapare Valley, where they comprise up to 20 percent of the coca farmers of that region.[24]

In Bolivia, 4 percent of all landowners control or own 68 percent of all arable land. Within this percentage, the drug lords are estimated to own between 400,000 and one million hectares.[25]

In none of the drug-producing nations do legal crops compare with the profits to be made from growing opium poppies, coca leaves, or marijuana plants. With the sharp decrease in traditional commodity exports during the 1980s, not only are these drug crops more profitable, but they are generally easier to grow and harvest. Cash crops such as rubber or coffee often require two or three years to mature before they can be harvested. Coca leaves can grow in poor soil, mature rapidly, and can be harvested, in some cases, six times in one year.

In Peru, coca leaves earn 2.4 times as much as cocoa, the country's second most profitable cash crop, and 39.9 times as much as corn maize. In 1989, a farmer could bring in an average $4,500 a year per hectare from coca leaves, compared to the meager $600 a year for cocoa.[26]

An important point in the debate against eradication of these plants is the cultural and historic significance they have for the people who grow them. In their non-toxic form, coca plants are safe in moderation and have played an important role in the lives of the farmers and the communities which cultivate the plants.

From Turkey to Pakistan to Laos to Burma, the opium plant has been the staple of local communities for centuries. Every part of the plant is put to use by farmers and villagers. Oil from the plant is used in cooking, its leaves go into a traditional salad, its seeds flavor homemade bread, and its pods are fed to farm animals. Even the stalks are utilized when woven into cottage ceilings.

The clay-like gum that is scraped from the opium, obtained by making an incision in the pod and allowing the liquid that oozes out to harden on the pod overnight, is its most prized possession. For many generations, the gum was used as a natural medicine that could either be eaten or applied to the skin. Families used the gum to cure illnesses such as colds, upset stomachs, fevers, and pain.

Coca leaves in the Andean region of South America have had similar importance. For centuries, people in the region have chewed on the leaves for cultural, social, and political reasons. To fight off the cold of the high altitude and the backbreaking long hours of farming, farmers chewed the leaves for energy. Hard-working miners have chewed leaves for the same reason and in the past received some of their pay in coca leaves. Medicinally, the leaves are also used to combat altitude sickness, labor pains, headaches, and other ailments. They are also widely used in commercial products such as soft drinks and teas. It should be noted that even Pope John Paul II felt it safe to consume quite a bit of coca tea during his visit to Bolivia in 1988.[27]

The transition from growing opium, coca leaves, and marijuana for local use to growing them as commodities which are integrated into a worldwide economic system is directly and fundamentally tied to the penetration of Western capital into the Third World. Once these traditional herbs were subject to control by the ironclad laws of capitalism, their historic purpose became greatly obscured. Invoking more than just the politics of supply and demand, the economic driving force behind the new role that these products play is the relationship between local labor, on the one side, and national and international capital on the other. The result has been the unprecedented impoverishment of the Third World.

Unholy Alliances in Drug Trafficking

> I want to emphasize in the strongest possible terms that the CIA neither engages in nor condones drug trafficking.
>
> —CIA Spokesman Mark Mansfield[28]

While the economic crisis in the Third World worsened, the CIA and other U.S. government agencies were forming alliances with right-wing drug pushers such as the Mujahedeen in Afghanistan, General Manuel Noriega in Panama, and the contras in Nicaragua.

The international and national drug crisis cannot be understood without understanding fully the significance of past and present relationships between Western intelligence agencies, organized crime, and anti-communist organizations. Historically, the driving force behind the production, distribution, and sale of illegal narcotics has been the collaboration and alliance of these forces. The drug crisis of the 1990s is rooted in increased unity among these groups under the Reagan/Bush administrations. In exchange for assisting in Reagan's anti-communist assaults, *carte blanche* has been given to known narcotics traffickers.

In his classic work, *The Politics of Heroin in Southeast Asia,* Alfred McCoy states: "American diplomats and secret agents have been involved in the narcotics trade at three levels: coincidental complicity by allying with groups actively engaged in drug trafficking; abetting the traffic by covering up for known traffickers and condoning their involvement; and active engagement in the transport of opium and heroin. It is ironic, to say the least, that America's heroin plague is of its own making."[29] Although McCoy was specifically addressing the heroin epidemic of the Vietnam War era, his words ring true of nearly the entire period of 1945 to the present.

The war against drugs has always been secondary to the war against communism. Indeed, in many instances, U.S. international drug policies have facilitated the efforts to contain the "communist menace" and essentially allowed anti-drug policies to become an extension of U.S. foreign policy.

The involvement of U.S. intelligence agencies in drug trafficking dates back at least to World War II. In that period, the Office of Strategic Services (OSS), the immediate predecessor to the CIA, formed an alliance with the heroin-dealing Corsican underworld to defuse the influence of French Communist Party-dominated trade unions in post-war France. Other Western intelligence agencies are also involved with U.S. intelligience services and organized crime networks. Britain's MI5, France's SDECE, West Germany's Gehlen Organization, and Italy's SIFFAR have all made agreements with organized crime as well as right-wing organizations in an effort to stop the advance of the communist parties, which, like their counterparts in Eastern Europe, had played a critical role in the defeat of Hitler.[30]

A similar relationship was established with the Sicilian Mafia whereby organized crime figures in the United States attempted to halt the growth of the Italian Communist Party.[31] One such figure, Charles "Lucky" Luciano, had dealt heroin since 1915 and was in control of the mob's drug distribution networks in the United States.[32] Although other Mafia dons saw drug dealing as taboo, Luciano and his Florida lieutenant, Santo Trafficante, Sr., uninhibitedly became the major importers of heroin to the United States. When Trafficante died in 1954, his son, Santo, Jr., became Luciano's right hand. In 1936, Luciano, one of the biggest Mafia kingpins ever produced in the United States, was sentenced to prison for White slavery, a victory which then New York District Attorney Thomas Dewey used to propel himself into the governor's mansion.[33]

It soon became clear, however, that Luciano's value to Dewey and the OSS would supersede his prison obligations. Operation Underworld, one of the OSS's first major operations, was the first and perhaps the most decisive step in forging a unity between the U.S. government and the drug dons of organized crime.[34]

In 1942, Dewey, through his partner, Mafia boss Meyer Lansky, and the OSS negotiated the use of Luciano's "thugs" to rid New York City docks of Nazi agents and union organizers in exchange for a pardon and an early release date. At the same time, the OSS asked Luciano to use his contacts in Italy and throughout Europe to help prepare for the Allied invasion of Italy. Following World War II, in coalition with the CIA and Italy's right wing, Luciano would also use his mob in Sicily and other cities to stop the growing influence of the Italian Communist Party. Former CIA operative Miles Copeland stated it clearly when he said, "...had it not been for the Mafia, the communists would now be in control of Italy."[35]

Once released from prison in 1946, Luciano established more firmly his worldwide apparatus for heroin trafficking, extending from Sicily to Mexico to the streets of Harlem. He set up headquarters in Havana and later moved to the Bahamas after Fidel Castro overthrew Fulgencio Batista in 1959.[36]

Along with anti-communist campaigns in Europe, the CIA also began backing anti-communist drug dealers in Southeast Asia. During the 1950s and 1960s, the routes used by drug traffickers to smuggle opium were the same routes used to smuggle agents into southern China during the United States' covert war against China in 1949. The CIA also made sure to build strong ties with the Thai National Police Department, which was the largest opium provider in the world, and CIA operatives were stationed in Long Tieng in northern Laos, the central site for heroin production for the entire Golden Triangle.[37]

The CIA set up a number of fronts, such as Sea Supply, Inc., Continental Air Service (CAS), and Civil Air Transport (CAT), which later became Air America, to facilitate their missions in the region. CAS and CAT, 60 percent of which was owned by Taiwanese crime figures and 40 percent of which was owned by the CIA, flew weapons and supplies behind enemy lines in Laos and Cambodia in exchange for opium.[38] Paul Withers, a Green Beret who was sent on secret missions into enemy territory during the war, reveals how the operation worked:

> The mission in Laos was to make friends with the Meo people and organize and train them to fight the Pathet Lao. One of the main tasks was to buy the entire local crop of opium. About twice a week an Air American plane would arrive with supplies and kilo bags of opium which were loaded on the plane. Each bag was marked with the symbol of the tribe.[39]

This period coincided with the heroin epidemic sweeping U.S. inner cities during the Vietnam War, an epidemic that did not subside until the end of the war. As the United States pulled out from 1971 to 1974, traffickers began to ship large quantities of heroin to U.S. cities. For example, in 1970 only 8 percent of Seattle's heroin was from Southeast Asia. By 1974 that amount had risen to 45 percent. Overall, Southeast Asian heroin smuggled into the United States doubled from its 1970 amount to about 22.3 percent in early 1975.[40]

Following the end of the Vietnam War, heroin trafficking and production slowed in every country in the region except Thailand, which served as a transshipment point. Up until 1969, only Marseilles produced ample quantities of the extremely pure China White heroin, otherwise known as Number Four. In addition, from 1976 to 1980, the number of heroin addicts in the United States dropped from an estimated 500,000 to 380,000. During Reagan's presidency, the number escalated once again to over 500,000.[41]

During the Vietnam War, the CIA and the U.S. Army supported Vang Pao in Laos. Vang Pao was one of the largest opium dealers in Southeast Asia and a key financier of the 30,000 Hmong tribesmen who were used by the CIA for political and military operations.[42] In 1968, Vang Pao met with U.S. organized crime figure Santo Trafficante, Jr., who was to become the largest importer and distributor of China White heroin in the United States. At the advent of this meeting, Trafficante was preparing to shift his Mafia operations to Southeast Asia, because it was becoming increasingly clear that the trafficking of opium from Turkey through France—the infamous "French Connection"—was crumbling.[43]

Two years later, Number Four was showing up in Saigon, and addiction rates for U.S. soldiers rose dramatically. According to a report issued in 1971 by Congresspeople Morgan Murphy and Robert Steele titled *The World Heroin Problem,* about 15 percent of the GIs stationed in Vietnam were heroin addicts.[44]

This entire program was coordinated by the Special Operation Group commanded by General John Singlaub of Iran-Contra scandal fame and president of the World Anti-Communist League. Serving under Singlaub was then-Second Lt. Oliver North and then-Deputy Commander Lt. Col. Richard Secord.[45]

In Southwest Asia, around the region known as the Golden Crescent (where Pakistan, Afghanistan, and Iran meet), the United States became involved with the Mujahedeen in their war against the Afghanistan government and their drug-dealing supporters in Pakistan. Long before the Mujahedeen launched their "civil war," they had been involved in opium smuggling and heroin manufacturing to Iran and Egypt.[46]

Between 1980 and 1990, the United States gave over $2 billion to the Mujahedeen, despite it being fairly well-known that they were involved in illegal narcotics. Their largest base is in Peshawar, Pakistan, which is a major center for opium production.[47] The region is responsible for 75 percent of the heroin that reaches Europe and for more than 50 percent of the heroin that reaches the United States. In 1983, for example, 4.5 tons of heroin were shipped to the United States.[48] It is estimated that between 700 to 800 metric tons of opium were produced in 1988 in Mujahedeen-controlled territories, making them second in world opium production to Myanmar (formerly known as Burma).[49]

The Iranian government had banished the Jamiati-Islamic (Islamic Society), a key grouping in the Mujahedeen, because of its ties to the CIA and heroin smuggling. *The Herald,* a Pakistan-based English-language newspaper, has regularly published articles emphasizing that the main conduit bringing supplies and weapons to the rebels in the North is also one of the principal routes for moving heroin back to Karachi.

As the CIA moved in, the DEA was forced to suspend investigations along the border of Afghanistan and Pakistan, where the most abundant amounts of opium are grown. It is generally acknowledged that U.S. drug enforcement in the region has been subordinated to support for the Muhajadeen under all circumstances. A DEA official admitted that "The DEA has been ordered to roll back its men from Afghanistan and Pakistan."[50] The impact has been felt even in Pakistan. In the 1970s, Pakistan had only a few hundred addicts; today, it has nearly 400,000 and, according to European police, it's the source of 70 percent of the world's refined, high-grade heroin.[51]

Divisions within the Mujahedeen have unclothed their drug dealing practices, despite the extensive efforts on the part of the United States to keep them covert. Although there had been numerous reports given to U.S. officials, including some from dissenting Mujahedeen rebels, no serious investigations were ever conducted. One key guerilla commander supported by the United States, Gulbuddin Hekmatyar, is known as perhaps the biggest heroin smuggler in the region. He has received tens of millions of dollars in weapons and supplies from the United States, and at one point he was the foreign minister of the U.S.-backed Afghan Interim Government (AIG) that was set up as a counter-government to the Kabul regime. The AIG is linked to the principal supporters of the guerrillas in the region, the Inter-Services Intelligence (ISI). The ISI, which is the military intelligence arm of the Pakistan government, has supported Hekmatyar and his Islamic Party over other guerilla commanders.[52]

Reportedly, Hekmatyar has opium brought from Afghanistan, where he has strong ties, to his laboratories in southwestern Pakistan. The opium is refined into heroin and then sent to Europe and the United States via Karachi, Iran, and Turkey. These operations are done with the full cooperation of the ISI. The AIG and the ISI control nearly all roads that lead from Afghanistan into the region, particularly those leading to Rabat. This small town, at the crossroads of all three countries (Iran, Pakistan, and Afghanistan), has long been the center of drug trade in the Golden Crescent.[53]

In the Fall of 1989, U.S. Embassy officials attempted to curtail the rebels' trade in opium. They met with Nassim Akhundzada, a rebel commander in conflict with Hekmatyar, and apparently persuaded him to halt opium production in his region. Akhundzada, known locally as "The King of Heroin," cultivated more than 250 tons of opium in 1989 in

Helmand province alone. Without admitting to the agreement, the United States confessed that development aid was being considered for that area. The United States did, however, suffer a setback in April 1990 when Akhundzada was assassinated in Pakistan.[54]

Middle East Muddle

Bush's decision to wage war against Iraq was another setback in efforts to combat the problem of drugs. It is believed that, in the past, the United States has been a silent spectator with regard to Syria's role in drug trafficking, due to the key role Syria has played in hostage release negotiations. Bush's Persian Gulf war further compromised U.S. willingness to criticize Syria's drug trafficking, since it was functioning as an ally against Iraq.[55] One could also surmise that Syria maintains the position of middle man for the United States precisely because the U.S. government will turn a "blind eye" on its drug trafficking industry. Drug production in the Middle East, particularly in Lebanon, soared during the 1980s.

Over the last decade, drug production in Lebanon has soared. The drugs are grown principally in the Bekaa Valley region in eastern Lebanon, which has been controlled by Syria since 1976. By 1990, Lebanon had an annual production of about four million pounds of hashish and over 20,000 pounds of heroin. This amounted to more than $4 billion in profits in 1990 alone. Drugs have become Lebanon's single largest export commodity. A small portion is used internally, but the bulk, 75 percent, goes to Egypt, Israel, Europe, and North America. About 20 percent of all heroin in the United States, roughly 2,500 pounds, comes from Lebanon. More than half of Europe's heroin is from the region.

Drug trafficking is controlled by the Syrians and can be traced to an inner circle in the Syrian government. In 1989, this circumstance led to Syria being denied U.S. certification verifying that it was addressing the drug problem. The potential impact of this refusal could have cost Syria half the amount of money it normally received in foreign and military aid. This fact stands in opposition to U.S. policy in the 1970s, when Lebanese Christians controlled the drug trade and the U.S. government remained a silent ally.[56] This situation also led Reagan's national security advisor, Robert McFarlane, to convince Saudi Arabian officials in March of 1984 to supply the contras with $1 million a month.[57]

"Contra" dictions

In Central America, a similar relationship developed between the CIA and the contras, a covert military unit created and sponsored by the

Reagan administration to overthrow the revolutionary Sandinista government in Nicaragua. Many of the contra leaders had been involved in the corrupt Anastasio Somoza regime overthrown by the Sandinistas. Somoza had been a business partner with two of Nicaragua's major drug traffickers, and nearly one ton of cocaine was smuggled into the United States by the contras per week, according to estimates made by the Christic Institute.[58] Overwhelming evidence exists to prove that, in exchange for flying weapons and supplies to the contras during the period of the congressional ban on such activities, the United States allowed drug dealers freely to fly narcotics into the United States. According to General Paul F. Gorman, former head of the U.S. Southern Command: "The fact is, if you want to go into the subversion business, collect intelligence, and move arms, you deal with the drug movers."[59]

The Reagan administration used every arm of government possible to facilitate these narco-contra activities. One congressional report states that "the State Department selected four companies owned and operated by traffickers in order to supply humanitarian assistance to the contras."[60]

In his Iran-contra diaries, Lt. Col. Oliver North himself made numerous references to his own drug smuggling and money laundering adventures. A July 12, 1985, entry, for example, reads: "$14 million to finance [arms] came from drugs."[61]

Oliver North's activities led to his being banned from Costa Rica. A Costa Rican congressional investigation determined that "certain American authorities had permitted the shipment of cocaine to the United States through Costa Rica, with the objective of channeling illegal funds to the Nicaraguan counter-revolution." President Oscar Arias signed the order banning from Costa Rica North, Secord, former National Security Council Advisor Admiral John Poindexter, former U.S. Ambassador to Costa Rica Lewis Tambs, and CIA Station Chief Joseph Fernandez. Although this action was unprecedented and reflected extreme anger on the part of Costa Rican officials, it received very little coverage by U.S. media.[62]

After being found guilty at his Iran-contra trial, North was fined $150,000 and assigned 1,200 hours of community service at a youth facility in Washington, D.C., a sentence which clearly demonstrates the racism and nationalism which informs drug-related prosecutions in North America. North had the temerity and gall to respond in a right-wing magazine: "For most of my adult life I have been involved in one way or another with young people. First as a Marine, and today as a person helping to solve the problems drugs have created in our nation's capital."[63] North neglected to add that those problems were made a great deal worse by his illegal and hypocritical operations.

It was reported in *The Nation* that the DEA attempted to persuade Medellin Cartel leader Jorge Luis Ochoa to falsely implicate the Sandinista government in Latin American drug trafficking. Ochoa, who was under arrest in Spain at the time, was told that the DEA would arrange his release if he cooperated. He refused, stating explicitly that the Sandinistas were not involved in the drug trade, and was eventually sent back to Colombia by Spanish authorities.[64]

Just Say Noriega

If one were to read only the Bush administration's press statements, the fall of Gen. Manuel Noriega, following the United States' December 1989 invasion and overthrow of his government, meant the virtual end of illegal drug dealing in Panama. By implication and inference, President Bush and Drug Czar William Bennett asserted that with Noriega's fall an irreparable blow had been dealt to the flow of drugs reaching U.S. streets.

Whatever may result from Noriega's overthrow, it is highly unlikely that drug smuggling and money laundering through Panama will wane, for two very important reasons: first, because of the society-wide pervasiveness and institutionalization of Noriega's operations, and the heretofore willingness on the part of the United States to turn a blind eye to his drug dealing, anti-communist allies; and, second, because most of the new U.S.-installed leaders of Panama have substantial connections to individuals and groups in the illegal drug industry.

Noriega's known activities concerning illegal drugs date back as early as 1972.[65] As an army intelligence officer under then-President Omar Torrijos, he served as Torrijos's link to the DEA, the CIA, and other U.S. agencies. Torrijos developed Panama into an international banking center and tax haven. U.S. dollars became the official currency, and bank clients soon discovered that they did not have to worry about taxes or embarrassing disclosures due to strict bank security laws.

Between 1976 and 1979, according to Senate testimony, Noriega provided money laundering and security services for Colombia's ruthless Medellin Cartel through their Miami-based accountant Ramon Milan Rodriguez.[66] Eventually, billions of drug dollars would go through Banco Nacional de Panama—the country's bank—and most of the other banks in Panama.

It is believed that the few narco-traffickers turned in by Noriega at the time were rivals of the Medellin Cartel, and their incarceration conveniently and deceptively eliminated competition. To say that

Noriega got more than he gave from the DEA and other U.S. agencies is a gross understatement.

After Torrijos died in a mysterious plane crash in 1981, Noriega took control of the country. One of his first acts was to consolidate the National Guard, Air Force, Navy, Police, and Customs into one service—the Panamanian Defense Force (PDF)—under his rule. In a very short time, drug trafficking and related activities had become institutionalized in Panama. The PDF provided security and escort services as planeloads of cash arrived by the hour. More important, under Noriega the PDF was responsible for drug enforcement.

By the mid-1980s, Noriega's drug operations were in full swing. Cocaine processing plants were set up, billions in dirty dollars were being laundered, critical precursor chemicals, essential to producing cocaine, were being shipped, and drug fugitives were hiding out in Panama City. Reportedly, Noriega was getting $100,000 or more for every planeload of cocaine that passed through Panama.[67]

With all this activity, the unanswered question is: When did the United States become aware of Noriega's drug dealings and what did it do about them? Gen. Paul Gorman, former Commander-in-Chief of the U.S. Southern Command, claims that the United States heard nothing, except rumors, until 1986.[68]

During the 1988 presidential campaign, Bush stated that he did not know that Noriega was involved in drug trafficking until February 4, 1988, the day Noriega was indicted. He claimed that he had had no knowledge of Noriega's drug involvement while he headed the CIA from 1976 to 1977 or as Vice President from 1980 to 1988.[69]

Bush's claimed denial of knowledge concerning Noriega's trafficking is contradicted by none other than Oliver North. In March 1985, North wrote in his notebooks that the "VP [was] distressed about the drug business."[70]

When government spokespeople weren't claiming ignorance, they were praising Noriega. Imagine the smirks that abounded when Jack Lawn, DEA administrator, went as far as to herald Noriega and his DEA liaison Luis Quiel for their efforts in combatting drug trafficking.[71] In fact, Quiel was Noriega's point man in eliminating small Panamanian dealers who threatened Noriega's monopoly and his connection to the cartels.[72]

Many former U.S. officials, all in positions to know, tell a very different story. Dr. Norman Bailey, former senior staff member of the National Security Council (1981-83), told a Senate committee that there was not just "a smoking gun, but a 21-cannon barrage of evidence" linking Noriega to illegal drug trafficking.[73] William Von Raab, former commissioner for the Customs Service, said that "they, Customs, had evidence against Noriega as early as 1983."[74] According to the DEA's own records, between 1970 and 1987 Noriega's name appeared in more than eighty different DEA files.[75] Thomas Gepeda, former DEA agent, testified that as far back as 1978, the DEA had been informed that Noriega and Torrijos were meeting with Medellin leaders in Colombia.[76]

In spite of these well-known facts, Noriega was seen as a "friend" of the United States and had been on the CIA payroll since 1967.[77] Panama, under Noriega, was key in the U.S. monitoring of left-wing activities in Central America. The CIA also wanted to exploit Noriega's ties to Fidel Castro and to the intelligence communities of other radical nations and groups.

Noriega became especially useful during the Reagan era, when his anti-Sandinista assistance took greater precedence in his relations with the United States. According to testimony revealed during the Iran-contra trial of Lt. Col. Oliver North in July 1984, Noriega provided the contras on the southern front with $100,000.[78] He had also helped the contras detonate an arsenal inside Nicaragua and had offered to facilitate the assassination of Sandinista leaders.[79]

Noriega met directly with many individuals on Reagan's "secret team" that coordinated White House contra activities. He met with North in June 1985 and September 1986, with late CIA Director William Casey in November 1985, and with Adm. John Poindexter in December 1985. Yet Noriega's illegal narcotics maneuverings never received more than a slap on the wrist during these meetings.[80]

Francis J. McNeil, U.S. Ambassador to Costa Rica (1980-83), stated that in regards to Noriega, the United States took a "see no evil" approach. He went on to say that "a decision was made to put Noriega on the shelf until Nicaragua was settled."[81]

Despite the lack of will and effort on the part of the United States, Noriega's drug domain began to collapse under its own weight. His rift with the cartels over money in 1984 and his increasingly erratic behavior made Noriega-controlled Panama an unstable transshipment point. U.S. conservatives, still upset over the prospects of turning the Panama Canal over to the Panamanians in 1999, seized the opportunity to stifle Noriega's increasing nationalism through drug trafficking charges. In turn, Noriega's public rantings against the Reagan and Bush administrations also meant that he had outlived his usefulness to U.S. intelligence agencies.

In February 1988, Noriega was indicted by federal grand juries in Miami and Tampa on charges of drug trafficking, money laundering, and racketeering. The United States, first under Reagan and then under

Bush, spent the next two years in a verbal war with Noriega. While publicly threatening the unrepentant general, secret negotiations that would have given Noriega immunity from U.S. prosecution in exchange for his resignation were taking place behind the scenes.[82] When the talks finally fell through in late 1989, Bush sent the troops in with barely the pretext of a reason. Noriega was placed under arrest, a puppet government was installed, and U.S. troops, more than a year after the invasion, still occupy the country.

Yet Panama remains a key laundering center that for many traffickers is a more critical function than the use of Panama as a transshipment point. Also, many of the legal precursor chemicals used in producing cocaine, such as ether and acetic anhydride, continue to arrive in Panama and are then diverted to the cartels.

Until these areas are seriously targeted, the post-Noriega era will remain virtually unchanged from the recent past in terms of Panama's drug trade. More important, unless the United States redirects its foreign policy objectives and thinking toward Panama, it will continue to create (and support) more Noriega-style dictatorships.

Indeed, many of the new Panamanian leaders have links to the drug cartels. The current, U.S.-installed president, Guillermo Endara, has several ties to known drug dealers. As a corporate lawyer, he has long represented Panamanian business magnate Carlos Eleta, who was arrested in Georgia in April 1989 for conspiring to import more than half a ton of cocaine monthly into the United States. In addition to having represented Eleta for more than twenty-five years, Endara is a stockholder in one of Eleta's companies. Former Panamanian President Arnulfo Arias, who accumulated his wealth through drug smuggling, was Endara's political mentor.[83]

Panama's Vice President Guillermo "Billy" Ford, and Ambassador to the United States Carlos Rodriguez, also installed after the U.S. invasion, were co-founders of the infamous Dadeland Bank in Miami. Dadeland is well-known as a repository for the Medellin Cartel.[84]

Panamanian Attorney General Rogelio Cruz, Chief Justice of the Supreme Court Carlos Lucas Lopez, and Treasury Minister Mario Galindo all were board members of the First InterAmericas Bank. In 1985, the bank was shut down because of drug-related "irregular operations." Reportedly, First InterAmericas was owned by a Cali Cartel leader who also graciously laundered money for Medellin Cartel leader Jorge Ochoa.[85]

Even some of the United States' staunchest allies operate at cross-purposes when it comes to fighting drug trafficking. U.S. government officials have been noticeably quiet in regards to the revelations that Israeli nationals with direct ties to the Israel government have been involved with military training and covert arms shipments to the cocaine barons of Colombia.

It was disclosed in the Summer of 1989 that Mike Harari, Yari Klein, and Lt. Col. Amatzia Shu'ali—all leading operatives in Israel's security apparatus—and unnamed South Africans were training the paramilitary forces of the Medellin Cartel.[86] Israel's rapid and shallow denials of any involvement in the activities were unconvincing for a number of reasons. Harari, who was officially stationed in Panama at the time as a direct liaison and consultant to Gen. Noriega, is a long-time officer of Israel's intelligence service, Mossad. Klein and Shu'ali are both tied to Spearhead, an Israeli arms company that is suspected of being either a government front or completely under the control of the Israeli government.[87]

Israel has also been implicated in the sale of weapons to the cartels. In January and February 1990, weapons discovered on the raided ranches of Medellin Cartel leader Jose Gonzalo Rodriguez Gacha were found to have been manufactured by the government-owned Israeli Military Industries. This particular set of weapons, according to their consignment identification, were supposed to be sold to the Caribbean island of Antigua and Barbuda. Colombian officials confronted Israel on the issue, thereby setting off a war of denials between the governments of Israel and Antigua and Barbuda.[88]

One of the rifles used in the August 1989 assassination of Colombian presidential candidate Luis Carlos Galan, a Galil 7.62mm, was traced by the U.S. Bureau of Alcohol, Tobacco, and Firearms to this shipment.[89] The assassination, carried out by one of the elite paramilitary units belonging to the Medellin Cartel, forced the Colombian government to launch one of its strongest counterattacks ever against the drug lords.

In Central America, Honduras—the strongest ally of the United States in that region—is up to its nose in cocaine trafficking. Numerous DEA, media, and congressional reports state that Honduran military officers are deeply involved in the shipment of cocaine through Honduras to the United States. One report estimates that as much as three tons a month is coming to the United States.[90]

Although the traffickers are known both to the United States and to the Honduran government, little has been done to eliminate the traffickers or to stop shipments at the border. According to Frank McNeil, former U.S. ambassador to Costa Rica, the CIA and other U.S. agencies knew which military officers and political officials were corrupt and yet did nothing to bring them to justice.[91]

Over a fifteen-month period, ending in mid-1988, an estimated fifty tons of cocaine went through Honduras, of which about nine tons were seized. Fifty tons equal about half of the current U.S. consumption.[92]

General José Bueso Rosa was caught smuggling $20 million worth of cocaine into Florida in 1984. Bueso, who served as the liaison between the United States, the Honduran military, and the contras, claimed that he was planning to use the cocaine profits to finance the assassination of Honduran President Robert Suazo Cordoba. The Pentagon tried to get the case dropped while National Security Advisor John Poindexter, Lt. Col. Oliver North, and CIA Operations Chief for Latin America Duane "Dewey" Clarridge lobbied to free him.[94]

A number of U.S. officials do acknowledge what was going on. Elliott Abrams, Assistant Secretary of State for Latin American Affairs, told one reporter when asked about Honduran military drug trafficking that "without a doubt" some Honduran officers were involved.[94] One CIA spokesperson stated candidly, "We use smugglers, but we are careful what they do at our behest."[95]

In February 1988, *The New York Times* noted the participation of another high-ranking officer in the Honduran drug trafficking network. Col. Leonides Torres Arias, head of Honduran intelligence, was heavily involved in the operations and a close friend of Panama's General Noriega.[96]

Other military officials also have been implicated in the drug dealing. Medellin Cartel leader Jorge Ochoa was stopped in Colombia driving a Porsche Turbo convertible valued at $260,000. Upon investigation, the car was found to belong to the Honduran military attaché to Bogota.[97]

A key route of the drug traffickers is through Mexico, where links between drug dealers, Mexican officials, and U.S. intelligence have been exposed. Columbian cocaine first goes to Honduras on ships along the western Miskito Coast. From there it travels to Puerto Cortes, protected by the Honduran navy, and is then flown to a base within the United States or shipped via the Gulf of Mexico.[98]

Efforts to catch traffickers in Mexico have been hampered by conflicting interests between the CIA and the DEA. DEA sources have felt that traffickers' collusion with Mexican law enforcement officials— the now disbanded Federal Security Directorate (DFS) in particular— has been hidden by the CIA, at best, or facilitated, at worst. According to the DEA, the DFS worked in partnership with most, if not all, of Mexico's largest traffickers. One DEA agent felt that the DFS was so involved that he called the DFS badge a "license to traffic."[99]

The discord reached a breaking point when the Guadalajara Cartel drug organization, which was directly linked with the DFS, kidnapped and murdered DEA agent Enrique Camarena in February 1985. DEA agents were bitter and angry that the CIA, which had infiltrated the cartel and knew it was monitoring the DEA and Camarena, failed to warn them about the plan.[100]

The DEA's outrage grew even greater as it came to believe that the CIA was participating in the DFS's effort to cover up and block the investigation into Camerena's murder. Unfortunately for the DEA, the CIA did have a long history of collaboration with the DFS.[101]

From 1946, when it was founded, through 1985, the DFS was the principal security agency in Mexico. Similar to the CIA and FBI, it was responsible for both internal and foreign security operations. For decades, the DFS worked with the CIA to spy on Soviet and Cuban nationals in Mexico City. Intelligence was also shared on other Central American leftists who travelled through or lived in Mexico.

The CIA and FBI stations inside the U.S. embassy in Mexico attempted to protect corrupt DFS officials on a number of occasions. When DFS chief Miguel Nazar Haro was indicted in San Diego in 1981 on charges of being involved in a car-theft ring, both the CIA and the FBI aided his defense. The FBI office in Mexico sent a telegram that stated that Haro was "an essential, repeat essential, contact for CIA station Mexico City." William Kennedy, the U.S. Attorney in San Diego who was prosecuting the case, tried to resist the pressure. Kennedy was eventually fired by President Reagan.[102]

The CIA's reluctance to upset the DFS was understandable. The CIA had built an arms transport network to the Nicaraguan contras in Mexico that involved the DFS and drug traffickers.[103] The Camerena scandal led to the disbanding of the DFS, lingering hostilities between the DEA and the CIA, and a straining of ties between the two nations.

The DEA issued a report in September 1990 stating that the CIA trained Guatemalan anti-communist guerrillas in the early Eighties at a ranch near Veracruz, Mexico, owned by drug kingpin Rafael Caro Quintero, a central figure in the murder of Camarena. The CIA, according to the DEA, used the DFS "as a cover in the event any questions were raised as to who was running the training operation." CIA operations personnel stayed at the home of drug lord Ernesto Fonseca Carrillo.[104]

Drugs and Socialism

In the movie, *Red Heat,* Arnold Schwarzenegger's Soviet detective character goes to great lengths in order to hide the fact that there is a drug problem in the USSR. He fails.

As the Soviet Union, in the era of peristroika and glasnost, removes the masks that have hidden many of the uglier social problems that affect Soviet life, the depth of the illegal drug problem in the country is being admitted to and addressed at the highest levels of government. In the past, the Soviet Union has either denied that a drug problem existed, or when confronted with unassailable evidence, relegated trafficking and abuse to a few isolated and individual incidents.

In 1990, the Ministry of the Interior admitted that drug abuse and trafficking exists in every region of the country. Drug problems are most common in the regions of Central Asia, Kazakhstan, North Caucusus, Transcaucasus, the Ukraine, the Far East, and Moscow.[105]

As elsewhere, there are few hard statistics on drug use in the USSR. In 1989, the Interior Ministry had about 130,000 people registered as non-medical drug users. About 60,000 were considered addicts, while another 70,000 were seen as non-addicted "consumers." There were more than 5,400 rehabilitation clinics throughout the country with about 125,000 to 130,000 hospital beds.[106]

In terms of trafficking, about 25,000 to 30,000 drug-related cases are tried a year. Drugs seized in raids number as high as thirty tons annually.[107]

Drug-producing plants, such as marijuana, coca leaves, and opium, grow abundantly in the areas that comprise the Soviet Union, particularly in Central Asia. As in other nations where these plants are indigenous, they were used for many purposes, including narcotic joy.

Russian hemp, from which marijuana came, was used as food, for medical purposes, and as a relaxant. Russia's hemp production in the 1700s and early 1800s (80 percent of the Western world's cannabis hemp) was so large that it was the country's number-one trading product.[108] In fact, it was Russian hemp that led to the eventual entry of the United States in the war with Great Britain in 1812, when the United States formed an alliance with Napoleon, who invaded Russia to cut off its supply of hemp to France's enemy, Great Britain.[109]

Drug use grew in Russia and was fairly pervasive by the turn of the century. In Turkestan, for example, the rate of marijuana smoking was as high as eighty kilograms per thousand people in 1907.[110]

Following the October 1917 revolution, the Soviets made an effort to stem both production and use of drugs. The first laws passed to stop cocaine production occurred in July 1918, thus marking the beginning of communist anti-drug efforts.[111] For the most part, these efforts were successful for the next fifty years or so.

Then, drug abuse took a big leap forward in the early Eighties. This was partially due to the Soviet invasion of Afghanistan, a major producer of opium and hashish.

Major steps have been taken to deal with the growing problem. Special committees affiliated with local Soviets of People's Deputies coordinate the anti-drug work of the government. These committees involve law enforcement agencies, customs, labor unions, mass media, and other institutions and ministries of Soviet society.

Other activities to end drug use and abuse have focused on teenage use and include tobacco and alcohol prevention measures. Harsh penalties are given for drug trafficking. Being convicted for the sale of drugs usually means fifteen years in prison on the first offense. Growing almost any amount of opium or marijuana garners ten years. Under Soviet law, however, any individual who turns in drugs to authorities or volunteers for treatment is exempt from criminal prosecution.

Cuba, one of the last defenders of revolutionary Marxist-Leninism in power, also found itself facing a drug problem. Perhaps no other incident since the revolution has shaken Cuba so much as the arrest, conviction, imprisonment, and execution, in the Spring and early Summer of 1989, of fourteen high-ranking Cuban officials for drug trafficking. What stunned Cuba and its supporters most was that those involved were heros of the revolution and some of the most admired citizens in Cuban society.[112]

General Arnaldo Ochoa Sanchez, Cuba's third-ranking military leader, Antonio "Tony" de la Guardia Font, and his twin brother Patricio had fought with Fidel Castro and Che Guevara in the famed Sierra Madre mountains. Tony de la Guardia rose up to become a colonel in the Ministry of the Interior (MININT) that controls all of the island's police and national security forces. Ochoa and Antonio de la Guardia were both executed, and Patricio received thirty years in prison.

Ochoa and the others were accused of allowing Colombian cartel traffickers to use Cuba as a transshipment point in moving drugs from Colombia to other points of destination, including the United States. For about three years, by virtue of their positions and official sanction to coordinate Cuba's forced smuggling of vital materials due to the U.S. embargo, nineteen drug smuggling acts were committed. According to trial transcripts, the drugs were mainly flown in or dropped into the waters at Varadero, Cuba, which is east of Havana. From there, the drugs were loaded on boats that went directly to Florida. The drugs involved were cocaine and marijuana.[113]

In addition to the drug charges, Ochoa and others were also accused of black marketeering and planning to launder money for the cartels. The accused were never charged with actually dealing or using drugs or letting drugs into Cuba.

Anti-Castro conservatives have alleged that Fidel Castro and his brother Raul have long been involved personally in drug trafficking. These charges have generally been dismissed by U.S. drug officials as unsubstantiated.

Drug Use in Africa

While media attention on the international aspects of the drug problem has focused on other regions of the world, drug trafficking and abuse in Africa, on the western coast in particular, has flourished. Although the production of drugs such as marijuana, opium, and cocaine is negligible at this point, there is a very real potential for increased narcotics production. The economic crisis facing the rest of the Third World is having an equally hard impact on Africa.

In Africa, international market conditions on the one hand and local corruption on the other has created an economically desperate situation for poor people that many are attempting to alleviate by drug trafficking. In addition, tourism has exacerbated the problem. Tourists not only traffic in drugs, but also introduce into the local populations alien addictive narcotics that quickly have become abused.

All types of addictive drugs, legal and illegal, are being used and abused, including amphetamines and tranquilizers, as well as cocaine, heroin, and hashish. Nigeria, Niger, Senegal, and the Ivory Coast, in particular, are experiencing serious cocaine and heroin abuse problems. Reportedly, in 1990 these drugs could be purchased in Lagos for as little as five naira, roughly 80¢ in U.S. currency.[114]

The biggest problem facing these West Coast nations is that opiate-based drugs, such as heroin, coming from Pakistan and India travel through Nigeria on their way to Europe and the United States. Cocaine from South America headed to Europe also goes through Africa's West Coast nations.

In Nigeria, at least seven major trafficking organizations have been identified. These groups have been tied to heroin-trafficking groups in Washington, D.C., and New York.[115] Human couriers have often used the technique of swallowing plastic bags or condoms filled with heroin, which are later recovered through forced bowel movements once the couriers are safely through customs. In a number of cases, a bag has torn and the courier has overdosed and died.

Nigeria has found itself being forced to implement stringent measures in order to deal with the problem. Currently, life imprisonment is a common sentence, and drug dealers have been publicly executed in the past. Despite these efforts, prospects for stemming the drug tide do not look promising.

In 1990, a joint agreement was signed between the United States and Nigeria. The United States has agreed to provide appropriate technical and managerial training for Nigerian drug enforcement officials, and possibly also law enforcement equipment. However, the economic situation in the country continues to worsen, and, as of mid-1990, Nigeria had no sophisticated drug detection equipment. In 1989, Nigeria established the National Drug Law Enforcement Agency. It is also a signer of the 1961 Single Convention on Narcotic Drugs, the 1971 Convention on Psychotropic Substances, and the 1988 Vienna Convention Against Illicit Traffic in Narcotic Drugs and Psychotropic Substances.[116]

Women from West Africa, who have been recruited or forced to be couriers for the drug traffickers, are starting to fill the jails of Europe and the United States. In 1990 in Britain, Black women were a quarter of the country's 1,700 female prison population. Many of those women, mainly from Nigeria and Ghana, were sentenced as drug couriers. The shortest sentence for drug smuggling in England is a mandatory three years, although most of these women have received sentences of at least six years. Despite the efforts of social workers to explain the mitigating circumstances of these women, the British courts have shown little sensitivity or remorse. Many of these women are naive and from the countryside.[117] Out of economic desperation or coercion, they agree to carry heroin or cocaine, although often they have little idea what they are smuggling. Complaining of diminishing resources due to falling prices on world commodities, little has been done by Nigeria or Ghana to institute programs that address this specific issue.

Multinational Fightback

The international effort to eliminate drug trafficking has been hampered by a number of political issues. The issue of sovereignty has been paramount for many nations who feel that aid of any kind, except economic, constitutes interference in the internal affairs of that nation. Latin America, in particular, which has seen dozens of invasions by the United States in this century alone, views overtures by the United States with great suspicion.

From Panama to Mexico to Colombia, political leaders have spoken out against U.S. intervention. Too often in the past, the U.S. Congress and State Department have accused other nations of doing too little to address the issue of illegal drug trafficking. The standard and sometimes antagonistic reply has been that the United States has done little to address the issue of illegal drug demand within its own borders.

In a number of cases, corrupt leaders have used national sovereignty as a means of rallying support for their continued abuse of power. Noriega in Panama, Jean Claude "Baby Doc" Duvalier in Haiti, and other drug-involved dictators have all known that they could find public support by calling for nationalist unity, although there is little sincerity in their rhetoric.

Despite these problems, a number of efforts by multinational cooperations have been tried with some degree of success. The United Nations, a logical place to begin any effort at global cooperation, has had a number of programs in place to address the issues of drug trafficking and drug abuse.

On February 19, 1990, the General Assembly met in special session to address the illegal narcotics issue. Delegates declared the 1990s the United Nations Decade Against Drug Abuse.[118] A number of proposals were called for by delegates, and a global program of action was adopted, including reducing demand in consumer nations, economic compensation to drug-producing countries who curb illegal production, greater legal cooperation between nations, stronger anti-money-laundering initiatives, and the establishment of a new United Nations facility that would serve as a clearing-house and advisory center for the dissemination of information about the drug issue. There was also discussion of creating a multilateral anti-drug strike force similar to the United Nations peace-keeping force.

These new anti-drug programs, and those already in place, are vastly underfunded. Only $74 million was available annually as of mid-1990. This paltry amount must finance the operations of the United Nation's three drug-control bodies: the UN Commission on Narcotic Drugs and its secretariat, the UN Division of Narcotic Drugs (DND); the International Narcotics Control Board (INCB); and the UN Fund for Drug Abuse Control (UNFDAC).[119]

The Commission was established in 1946 and serves as the main drug policy-making body for the United Nations. It is composed of forty members, who are elected by the UN's Economic and Social Council. Through its secretariat, the Commission assists member nations in implementing drug control treaties and mandates from the General Assembly related to drug trafficking and abuse.

The INCB is principally focused on the law enforcement side of the drug issue and attempts to reduce supply. It works with countries to prevent the cultivation, production, refinement, manufacturing, and trafficking of illegal drugs. It also works with INTERPOL and conducts seminars and training programs in different regions.

The UNFDAC, created in 1971, is mandated to provide technical assistance to nations in fighting trafficking and abuse. Its activities include crop substitution, rural development, drug treatment programs, early prevention work, public education campaigns, and advocacy for legislative and institutional reform. "Masterplans" are developed for countries and regions that present a comprehensive analysis of the problem and its solutions. In 1989, through its 114 drug control projects, UNFDAC provided help to forty-nine nations in the Middle East, Africa, Latin America, and the Caribbean. It has invested $57 million in Bolivia and $25 million in Peru, started a $15 million rural development program in Mexico, and a $12 million demand reduction program in Brazil.

On February 15, 1990, at a drug summit gathering, a broad accord was signed between the United States and the Andean nations to further cooperation among the parties to address the drug crisis. Meeting in Cartagena, Colombia, President Bush, Bolivian President Jaime Paz Zamora, then-Colombian President Virgilio Barco, and then-Peruvian President Alan Garcia forced the United States to concede that extensive economic and social development was needed if there was any hope of putting a dent in drug trafficking. Among the points agreed on were: alternative development and crop substitution, mitigation of the social and economic impact of the fight against illicit drug trafficking, trade initiatives, and incentives to exports and private foreign investment[120]

A significant emphasis was given to the law enforcement aspect. Among the ominous actions decided upon were continued interdiction, sharing intelligence information, increased involvement of the armed forces of the respective nations, and eradication of drug crops.[121]

During the summit, the United States signed three bilateral agreements with Peru and three with Bolivia. The United States pledged to develop stronger controls on chemicals shipped from the United States and used in illegal drug manufacturing, to help create education and prevention campaigns, and to limit the flow of light arms to drug traffickers in the region.

Sending aid to fight drugs through a multinational body would perhaps avoid some of the problems that have so far accompanied U.S. efforts. Much of the aid sent to developing nations by the United States to fight the drug traffickers has been either stolen outright by corrupt civilian and military officials or diverted to waging war against the perceived enemies of the state, who are invariably leftists or progressives.

Efforts at eradication have failed. In an interview, one leader of a Peruvian peasant trade union said: "[T]he lack of any viable alternative to growing coca leaves and marijuana and opium means that the number of peasants who join the illegal drug industry will only increase."[122]

A House of Representatives Government Operations Committee study concluded that the DEA should "redirect" its efforts from raids in Peru and Bolivia. Drug corruption is endemic in both militaries, and, as a result, coca cultivation and trafficking continues to grow. In Peru's Upper Huallaga Valley, cocaine processing plants and small airstrips are located near Peruvian military facilities because they are protected. In Bolivia, the DEA has been fired upon by the Bolivian navy and receives practically no cooperation at all from the army and air force services.

Encouraged by the United States, it has become common for leaders in countries with active anti-government popular movements to label the activists in those movements as "narco-guerrillas." Many of these leaders, themselves involved in the illegal narcotics trade, use anti-drug aid from the United States to fight wars against their internal enemies.

Michael Skol, of the State Department's Bureau of Inter-American Affairs, made the administration's position quite clear on this point. Testifying on anti-drug aid to South America at a hearing before the House Select Committee on Narcotics Abuse and Control on June 7, 1989, he said: "These funds will allow the Colombians to continue their aggressive pursuit of the traffickers and guerrillas. The Administration's fiscal year '90 requests for security assistance for Peru and Bolivia also are consistent with this approach."[123] In country after country, this line of reasoning has either explicitly or tacitly been operative.

Mexico, which is the overall largest supplier of illegal drugs to the United States, has long combined its anti-drug work with attacks on rebellious Indian peasant activists. In 1978, 7,000 soldiers launched an assault against the Indian-controlled, marijuana-growing areas of Durango, Sinaloa, and Chihuahua in northern Mexico. Accompanied by DEA agents, peasants were tortured, detained illegally, and intimidated into making false confessions regarding their political activity, according to reports from the U.S. Catholic Conference.[124]

Argentine officials, themselves involved in drug trafficking, have been more explicit in using the drug war cover to go after leftists. In 1974 at a press conference attended by the U.S. ambassador to Argentina, Minister of Social Welfare José Lopez Rega said: "We have caught guerrillas after attacks who were high on drugs. Guerrillas are the main users of drugs in Argentina. Therefore the anti-drug campaign will automatically be an anti-guerrilla campaign as well."[125]

In Guatemala, similar "anti-drug" campaigns have been inaugurated. Although no coca leaves grow there, and marijuana and opium plant production is sparse to the point of being negligible, the DEA and the State Department have spent at least $400,000 in efforts at drug crop eradication. Most of the areas that have been sprayed with the deadly and dangerous herbicide Round Up are located near where Guatemalan army troops have fought with Indian guerrillas. At the same time, rich and powerful landowners rent out private landing strips, to be used as transshipment points, to Colombian cocaine traffickers. These influential non-Indian individuals remain untouched.[126]

The Dutch Gambit

Finally, it should be mentioned that some nations have instituted innovative programs to deal with their drug trafficking and abuse problems. One example that has often been severely maligned by Western media is the Netherlands.

In 1976, the Dutch instituted a set of initiatives that radically changed the modern notion of how to address the problems of drug abuse and trafficking. Marijuana and hashish, considered "soft drugs," were legalized, and hard drugs such as cocaine, amphetamines, and heroin, were in essence decriminalized. In Amsterdam, the capital city, more than 300 cafes and coffee houses sell a variety of types of marijuana, including renowned brands from Lebanon, Turkey, and Iran. Small packets, weighing from 1.5 to 5 grams, can be purchased for about $13 to $20. It's a felony to possess more than 30 grams. On any given day, however, one is more likely to find Germans and Americans as customers than Dutch citizens. These cafes are a particularly favorite hangout for U.S. soldiers. Hard drug use, while still illegal, is restricted to certain public areas where the police "look the other way." Health professionals rather than law enforcement authorities are mobilized to work with the addicts. More than 70 percent of Amsterdam's addicts are registered with the municipal health department, which allows them to receive methadone treatment and clean-needle exchanges. There is even an addicts' union know as the Medical-Social Union for Hard-Drug Users.[127]

A large-scale, nationwide education program has been very successful. The program, unlike most in the United States, targets young schoolchildren. Instead of giving them slogans and encouraging them to turn in their friends, the program arranges visits to jails where addicts can talk to the children directly, and equal emphasis is given to other addictions such as alcohol and gambling.[128]

The results of this approach have caused U.S. officials to take notice. In 1981, Amsterdam had about 12,000 heroin addicts. By 1990, the number had dropped to about 6,500. During that time, the average

age of addicts rose from twenty-six to thirty-one, indicating that fewer young people were becoming users.[129]

Although important advances have been made on the user end of the drug problem, trafficking is still a large hurdle to overcome. The Netherlands, as many experts assert, is the number-one distribution point to Europe for Asian heroin and Latin American cocaine through Amsterdam's Schipol International Airport and Rotterdam's busy harbors.

Dutch judges have shown themselves to be tough on traffickers despite the lax law enforcement approach of the government. More than half of those occupying Dutch prisons are there on drug-trafficking charges.

Conclusion

This assessment only touches on a far deeper crisis in the international arena encompassing not only economic and political issues, but social and cultural ones as well. The elimination of the multinational illegal narcotics industry will require a total transformation in U.S. foreign policy objectives and operations. Indeed, a precondition to successfully addressing the drug crisis is ultimately the establishment of a new global economic order and the building of democratic political structures in virtually all of the drug-producing and trafficking nations.

As long as the developing world is dependent on a commodities market system over which they exercise no control, the flow of drugs will not cease. Illegal narcotics remain second only to oil as the most consistently stable commodity exported from the developing world. For peasants struggling to survive, these economic realities are devastating.

It will take considerable struggle to institute a progressive foreign policy program. But this remains the only avenue for ending the economic, political, and social havoc that has been wrought by the international policies of the United States over the last forty-five years.

Part II

Drug War on the Potomac

Introduction to Part II

To understand how the drug crisis gets expressed in peoples' everyday lives, it is useful to examine a particular locale for concrete illustrations. Such an examination helps us to understand the true scope of the phenomenon. Many cities in the United States have a significant drug problem, as do many rural areas. Miami, New York, and Los Angeles are major points of entry for drugs into this country and have severe drug problems. The District of Columbia is also important because it offers a unique mix of international, national, and local issues that provide a wide range of information on the national drug epidemic. The District of Columbia was chosen by the federal government as the test case for its "war on drugs" policies. How these policies fared in the test city is a lesson for the rest of the nation.

Through the prism of the federal drug war in the District of Columbia the issues of poverty, racism, restrictions on democracy, attacks on civil liberties, the one-sided federal emphasis on law enforcement, and the criminalization of Black youth can all be examined. In addition, the need for a strategy which promotes empowerment and development for the Black community as an anchor for a larger progressive coalition in the United States can also be looked at.

William Bennett selected the District of Columbia in early 1989 as the test case for strong law enforcement tactics. Those policies have been an abject failure. But that Bennett could so freely choose the city without even the cooperation of the local political establishment was a stark reminder of a political phenomenon not well known by the American public: citizens of Washington, D.C. lack the fundamental power to determine their own destiny. The problem of empowerment facing many communities around the United States exists for the whole city of Washington. This city, where every day the White House and Congress issue calls for international democracy, is the only capital district in the world to deny its citizens the right to national voting representation. This denial, and other restrictions placed by Congress on the ability of the District to marshall its own resources, fetters any attempt to undertake an all-sided effort to conquer the city's drug problems.

The District of Columbia has been a majority Black city since the mid-1960s and has historically been an important center of African-

141

American life in the United States. Its national and international fame lies in its role as the center of the capitalist world, as a tourist paradise of beautiful parks and spacious monuments, and as home to middle-class White and Black neighborhoods. However, the vast number of poor and working-class Blacks who live in the rest of the city, who constitute the bulk of the population, make up the "secret city." These are the people who are arrested, incarcerated, and murdered, not isolated from the brutal side of the drug crisis as are the drug traffickers and abusers in the exclusive sections of Capitol Hill, Georgetown, or downtown on K Street. The devastation caused by drugs to the Black majority in the District takes the form of a health crisis illustrated by a growing number of AIDS cases; abandoned, drug-addicted babies; non-stop homicides; and an incarceration rate that is the highest in the world. To understand the life conditions of this sector of Washington is to gain a good deal of insight into the drug epidemic.

The stunning video arrest, farcical trial, and unsettling conviction of former Mayor Marion Barry on crack cocaine charges was the event that most dramatically propelled Washington's drug story from serious local news to a drama of international proportions. Barry's saga, followed with riveted interest by people around the world, highlighted the wide range of political and leadership questions confronting the Black community, not only in Washington, but across the nation.

Thus, the lessons of the District of Columbia are lessons for the nation. Washington, D.C., in all of its complexity and comedy, its accomplishments and its failures, is a mirror of our times and our conditions.

Chapter 7

THE DISTRICT OF COLUMBIA
A Tale of Many Cities

Washington, D.C., is a city in which the American dream and the American nightmare pass each other on the street and do not speak.

—Author Sam Smith

When most Americans think of Washington, D.C., they think of federal landmarks—the President and the White House, Congress and the Capitol, the Lincoln, Jefferson, and Washington memorials. Washington, D.C., is a world of glittering monuments and parks, well-kept gardens, and some of the most extensive and informative museums in the world. Washington is the center of a vast administrative, political, military, and intelligence-gathering system, perhaps the most influential center in the world.

But behind these images lies what historian Constance Green called the "Secret City"[1]—a place that few of the ten million tourists who visit the National Air and Space Museum go out of their way to see. About 67 percent of the city's population is Black. In the District, for every five Black workers, one earns more than $42,000 a year, another one lives in dire poverty. Washington boasts some of the nation's most elegant neighborhoods, including prosperous Black middle-class ones, while in other neighborhoods, people live in dilapidated housing projects located far northeast or east of the river, or even ten blocks from the Capitol where many of the open-air drug markets have flourished.[2] This secret city has existed from the founding of the nation's capital in 1800 and is a central theme to the city's character—a living symbol of the lack of political democracy not only in Washington but throughout the nation.

Metropolitan Washington, D.C., contains the wealthiest counties in the nation, including Montgomery County in Maryland and Fairfax County in northern Virginia. Outside of the District of Columbia, nearly full employment reigns, and employers who seek to hire skilled workers often overlook Black people in Washington and will sometimes recruit in places hours away in Pennsylvania or West Virginia. Beginning in 1979, the service industry surpassed the government as the region's largest employer.

Although government and the service industry dominate the regional economy, many private-sector firms established a foothold in the city around the end of World War II. Communications giants, like MCI and COMSAT, research and information companies, and other multinational corporations have set up offices in the District, often as secondary headquarters in addition to larger offices in New York City. The District has surpassed New York City as the largest venue of trade associations. The local business elite is centered in the real estate, banking, and retail industries. The District of Columbia has some of the most valuable real estate in the world. Among the wealthiest Washingtonians, real estate moguls predominate.

The District is also a multinational city. Today an estimated 80,000 Latinos live in Washington, mostly refugees from the war-torn countries of Central America, including many "illegal immigrants." About 70 percent of the region's population are foreign-born immigrants. According to the superintendent of public schools, students speak some 111 foreign languages. Clashes between Blacks and immigrants in the District, such as Korean shop owners, have received some media attention, but have not reached the level of ethnic or racial conflict experienced in other urban centers such as New York City.[3]

The District is fragmented in cultural, political, economic, and moral terms. Rock Creek Park, which runs through the northern corner of the city, separates most Washington Whites from Washington Blacks. Outside the federal government, few workplaces are integrated by race. Most law firms, lobbying offices, trade associations, and congressional offices are staffed by Whites, many of whom live in suburban Maryland or northern Virginia. Taken alone, the median income of Whites in the District would make it the wealthiest state in the nation. Most of the 120,000 White Washingtonians are fairly insulated from concerns of joblessness, drug dealing, poor education, and prison. Many absent themselves from local affairs altogether.[4] Most of the service personnel—the cab drivers, clerical workers, or restaurant personnel—are Black or other people of color. Other than the local professional football team, the Washington Redskins, most of the city's social and cultural events tend to be segregated as well.

Not all Black people in the region are poor. The District has the highest per capita income compared to any state in the nation and the highest number of Blacks who earn over $35,000 a year. The District government awards more contracts to minority businesses (38 percent in 1985) than any other American city.[5] Many Black doctors, lawyers, and other professionals live in neighborhoods once inhabited exclusively by Whites, having entered the middle class through positions in government.

According to all the various social indicators, poverty is concentrated in the District of Columbia. There, the Black community is fighting for its life. Poverty afflicts one in five residents. While Black unemployment in the District is lower than in some other American cities, such as Detroit, joblessness still stands at Depression-level conditions—about 25 percent for Blacks under twenty-five years of age.[6]

The District has the highest incarceration rate in the world, with the exception of South Africa (more than 1,500 people per 100,000 residents), and an infant mortality rate which is higher than any state (20.8 per 1,000 live births). The teenage birth rate is about one-third higher than the national rate, and the public schools have a dropout rate of about 45 percent. The city's poor must wait on an average of ten years to receive public housing, in spite of the fact that about 18 percent of the city's 12,000 public housing units are uninhabitable due to disrepair.[7]

This is the Washington riddled by drugs and violence. Considering the District's race and class divisions, it is easy to see how the "Secret City" became the locale for the drug trade, how it has become convulsed by battles over a lucrative crack trade. The high median income of the region, combined with the despair and lack of opportunity of the inner city, created a community ripe for drug traffic.

Federal Guinea Pig

As the crack epidemic mounted in the late 1980s, area business leaders worried about the regional economy. William Sinclair, president of the local business organization, the Board of Trade, told the *Wall Street Journal*, "Whenever anyone describes Washington as the 'murder capital,' I wonder whether we will become Detroit. That's the last thing we want. This is the capital of the country."[8]

When national drug czar William Bennett announced in April 1989 a $70 million plan to build new prisons, increase law enforcement in the region, bring in military intelligence analysts, and evict public housing tenants suspected of drug dealing, he was doing more than establishing the District as a "test case" in the war against drugs. He was also asserting that the District had acquired an embarrassing international reputation and that, to clean it up, the federal government was prepared to dispense with the formality of local self-rule.

The District of Columbia has always been a target for federal experimentation—but not necessarily for the sake of its inhabitants. The District was the first southern area to eliminate slavery, following a long and protracted battle by abolitionists determined to make an example of the nation's capital in the 1850s. In the Reconstruction period following the Civil War, the city, under pressure from the Republican administration, outlawed discrimination in public accommodations, restaurants, and utilities. When the still all-White electorate in the District voted after the Civil War not to allow Black suffrage, the abolitionist Congress abolished the city council and appointed a new one, which included Frederick Douglass.[9]

In the words of Julius Hobson, Jr. (the son of Julius Hobson, the civil rights activist in the 1950s and 1960s): "We live in a goldfish bowl, surrounded by members of Congress, none our full-fledged representatives. Any District issue is easy game for any member who wants to tee off on something, or…who just doesen't like Washington or its people."[10] In recent times, this interference has taken different forms, from the serious to the ridiculous. President Bush vetoed the appropriations budget of the District of Columbia in 1988 and again in 1989 because the budget contained funds to be used for abortions for poor women. These were local monies voted for by locally elected officials. In contrast, one congressperson from New Jersey, Dean A. Gallo (R-NJ), made an amendment to the District's Fiscal Year 1991 appropriation to strike down the city's residency requirement for city attorneys. His reason? His daughter, a lawyer, desired a job with the city, but didn't want to relocate into the District.

The ease with which the federal government intervenes in the District's local affairs is built into its political and economic structure. The District was chosen as the test case for federal anti-drug policies, against the wishes of local officials, because real power ultimately rests in the hands of politicians who are not elected by the citizens of the District. The federal presence is a fetter on the ability of the city to end the city's drug crisis. Full local control over these resources, accomplished by achieving statehood for the District of Columbia, is a prerequisite for the region's recovery.

The Politics of Limited Democracy

The District of Columbia, created as the nation's capital in 1800, is legally neither city nor state. Created and ultimately ruled by the federal government, the District's citizens even today have no voting representation in Congress. Between 1800, the year of its founding, and 1874, the District operated under a variety of limited-rule schemes imposed by Congress. These included elected and appointed mayors and city councils, and a territorial legislature and governor. From 1874 to 1963, residents were unable to vote for any national or local office, and the city was ruled by racist southern congressmen through congressional committees and by commissioners, appointed by the President, who frequently lived outside of the capital.

Under pressure from civil rights activists, residents won the right to vote for President in 1963, for school board in 1968, for a non-voting delegate to Congress in 1971, and for mayor and city council in 1974. The Home Rule Charter of 1974 allowed District citizens to vote for a mayor and a city council with powers to pass laws and resolutions. Some federal agencies were transferred to local control.

But all laws were made subject to veto by Congress, and Congress retained control of the District's budget. Congress can also initiate local legislation. Congressional committees maintain their oversight over the District. Judges are appointed by the President, and federal attorneys prosecute most of the District's cases. Congress also subjected the District of Columbia to other restrictions. The city council cannot, for example, pass a tax on commuter income. In the words of author Sam Smith: "It was a government with the power to tax but not spend; a government expected to lower crime but with no control over the courts; a government that could initiate but could not guarantee what it had initiated; a government expected to act but lacking the freedom to do so..."[11]

A number of the leading veterans and activists of the Civil Rights movement migrated to the District during the movement's waning days in the late 1960s. This migration was prompted by a number of factors. The District, as the nation's capital, was an an important place to do public advocacy work. The civil rights and anti-war movements also familiarized a lot of activists with the nation's capital. The Poor Peoples' March of 1968, conceptualized by Dr. Martin Luther King and others to move the agenda of the civil rights movement toward economic justice, ended up in the District of Columbia. As a predominantly Black city, the District offered activists an unusual opportunity for political representation, created by the movement. Importantly, Dr. King had advocated statehood for the District.

When these individuals arrived, they found a majority Black city completely lacking in voting rights, and ruled through congressional oversight committees by racist congresspeople, such as John McMillan from South Carolina, and by city commissioners who were at times incompetent and seemed to have little invested in the city. Even the conservative *Washington Times* opined of those days that "before Home Rule, a president of the United States could have installed the Marx Brothers as commissioners, and every now and then it seemed that one had."[12] Blacks were still excluded from positions of influence in the District in the local government and in business.

In 1975, newly elected District officials found the federal government had left the District of Columbia in a shambles. The District of Columbia today is still paying off the deficit accumulated in the pre-Home Rule years. Moreover, the District lost much of its tax base when hundreds of thousands of middle-class Whites, lured by speculative real estate developers, fled to the suburbs to avoid integration.

One of the dominant figures of this period was former Mayor Marion S. Barry. The son of Mississippi sharecroppers, Barry was a founder and first national chairman of the militant Student Nonviolent Coordinating Committee (SNCC). Barry became active in the Free D.C. Movement, led boycotts of city buses over fare increases and disrupted the city over a range of issues, from racism to the lack of voter representation. As brash and radical newcomers to the District, Barry and his fellow activists perturbed the local civil rights establishment as well as the elites of the city. Their efforts to organize the city's poor and their willingness to confront White power went a long way toward advancing the issue of self-determination.[13] In addition to Marion Barry, other civil rights activists were able to use the limited offices provided by Home Rule to gain positions of power in the city. Walter E. Fauntroy was elected in 1971 to the seat of non-voting congressional delegate, and activists John Wilson, Frank Smith, Dave Clarke, and Statehood Party leader Hilda Mason also eventually joined the city council. Barry was elected to the board of education, then to the city council, and later to the position of mayor, a post he held from 1978 to 1990.

The statehood movement began in earnest in 1969. At that time, the newly organized Statehood Committee declared that "statehood for the District of Columbia is a natural right which can no longer be denied and must be achieved by whatever means necessary by the people"[14] In the 1970s, a "Statehood Party" formed around Julius Hobson and other activists. In 1974, this party chose Julius Hobson as one the members of the city council. The Statehood Party, the "little party with the big voice," functioning to the left of the liberal D.C. Democratic Party, became one of the most vibrant third parties on the local level in the history of U.S. politics.

Conservative Onslaught on the District

Politics in the District of Columbia underwent a significant change in the late 1980s with the arrival of the crack epidemic, the soaring murder rate, the constant scandals involving former Mayor Barry, and his eventual arrest, trial, and conviction. These events emboldened conservatives to go on the offensive and to limit empowerment in the District, and made even Democratic members of the House less willing to support statehood.

Throughout the 1980s, skirmishes between conservatives on Capitol Hill and the District government intensified. Sen. Jesse Helms (R-NC) referred to the District as "the abortion capitol of the world." But Congress rarely used its veto power over District laws in those years. In 1979, it vetoed a law that would restrict the location of chancelleries and, in 1981, it vetoed a law that decriminalized sodomy. Today, however, in the words of *Regardies* magazine: "District bashing isn't just for the lunatic fringe. The ideological conservatives...have been attracting new converts."[15]

In 1986, the Washington, D.C., city council passed legislation prohibiting insurance companies from requiring AIDS tests as a condition for buying health and life insurance policies. In 1988, Sen. Helms managed to include in the District's appropriations bill an amendment that would have frozen all District spending on AIDS if the council did not withdraw its own proposal within three months. Congress accepted the Helms amendment, and the council was forced to back down. Congress tried a similar tactic to block a District law concerning human rights, which protected funding support for gay students' groups at Georgetown University. Congress threatened to freeze all city spending if the law was not repealed, but a federal district court ruled the Congress acted inappropriately.

To protect jobs for its residents, the District has over the years imposed various kinds of residency requirements for city workers. In 1988, supported by the city's police and firefighters' unions (many of whose members did not live in the city), Congress also prohibited the District from using any of its funds to enforce the city's residency requirement. In November 1989, delivering on a pledge to anti-abortion forces, President Bush vetoed the District's 1990 appropriations bill because it restored the city's authority to spend local tax dollars on abortions for the poor. District home-rule supporters were unable to muster the votes for a congressional veto override, and the District was forced to cede its authority. Sen. Gordon J. Humphrey (R-NH) dismissed complaints that the action violated the District's powers of self-governance by stating: "We are in effect the legislature for the District of Columbia."[16]

Future Outlook

Much of the current Black leadership and other progressives in the city face an internal crisis of strategy. The District today is largely administered by Black officials, many of them veterans of the civil rights movement. When these individuals assumed power, some sectors of the Black community prospered, predominantly at the professional and managerial level. Black capitalists and the Black middle classes gained jobs, income, business opportunities, and access to City Hall. The opening up of these professional opportunities was a positive development that allowed individuals like Reed Tuckson, the former commissioner of public health, to contribute their talents to the District.

However, the leadership of these officials has not tangibly improved the lot of most Blacks. Ordinary Black people have not reaped the benefits of municipal government. This discrepancy is rooted in a class- and race-based economy, fueled by governmental and business policies that have led to the virtual abandonment of other U.S. urban centers. A shrinking tax base, decreasing federal expenditures, and the flight of more affluent residents to the suburbs have left the leadership of the city without a base from which to meet the needs of its people.

But the city's leadership also faces its own crisis. During former Mayor Barry's second term in office in the mid-1980s, the instances of corruption started to mount. Barry's close associates as well as his ex-wife were found to have stolen public funds or abused their office for personal gain. Barry also became increasingly associated with the Washington establishment and, as he gained power over the years, he lost interest in the community that had brought him to power. In the early years of the Barry administration, for example, there was much talk about developing the depressed neighborhoods east of the river, but as time went by little was done in that regard and even the talk seemed to diminish.

To fund the prosperity that exists for some people in the District, Barry fostered a positive environment for the local real estate industry, a powerful group in a city with no traditional base as an industry. To enrich the tax base, Barry cut the red tape facing the city's White real estate developers, enabling them to build more new office buildings downtown and shopping centers on the outskirts of the District. But such activity meant little to the mass of untrained and undereducated people of the District. Barry should have, for example, linked the granting of all building licenses to a demand that low-income housing or a daycare center be constructed in return for the permit to build.

Such vacillation in defense of the 'least of these' was not confined to Barry. In 1985 about half of the city council joined with the real estate industry and Barry—by then ex-mayor—in trying to destroy the city's rent control laws. The city council also substituted a watered-down version of the progressive Statehood Constitution, already approved by the voters in 1982, hoping to win Congress's favor. In 1990, the council was prepared to delay indefinitely the election of statehood lobbyists until Jesse Jackson, among others, generated public pressure.

The public perception of the District's limited form of government varies widely. Conservatives in Congress, the media, and the public see a majority Black urban center, led by Black officials, which is incompetent at best and corrupt at worst. The scandals of former Mayor Barry and the epidemic of drugs and violence have become the handles for conservative criticism of the District. Barry's trial on crack cocaine charges in the Summer of 1990 became a referendum on the District's right to self-government, and more particularly on Black political power. The District is, in the view of these conservatives, a failed experiment, another example of failed liberal policies. They argue that the District's already limited home-rule powers should either be restricted further, or done away with completely, with the federal government once again assuming direct rule of the city. In the words of ultra-conservative Congressperson Robert Dornan (R-CA): "Congress has to move in and take control."[17]

The more fundamental antagonism in the city is between a majority Black city led largely by former civil rights activists and sometimes left-leaning ones, surrounded by White conservatives for whom the District is the shining example of what is wrong with America. The leadership of the city is under siege. The new city leaders who took office at the beginning of the 1990s—Mayor Sharon Pratt Dixon, Congressperson Eleanor Holmes Norton, and others—helped to ease some of the surface antagonism but left the underlying dynamic intact. The fundamental issue underscoring this crisis is: Who will control the city—the current Black leadership and its heirs, or a Congress bent on destroying home rule and any drive toward increased empowerment, in particular, statehood?

The strategy of the former civil rights movement activists who are now in public office—that of gaining empowerment for Black people through leveraging concessions out of the local elites—could be seen in the decade of the 1980s to have benefited mainly the middle classes. In the words of political scientist Acie Byrd: "Too much emphasis has been put on placating the system, resulting in the loss of accountability to the mass of people."[18] Activist Josephine Butler adds that "[j]ust distributing city contracts is not enough by way of leadership. What's got to ride in front is a vision...and a strategy to generate new wealth."[19]

The difficult social and economic problems in the District, as well as in other urban centers, will not be overcome by any single strategy. But surely they will not be reduced without new and massive government intervention in education, job training and creation, drug treatment, housing, and social welfare. That intervention, in the face of a shrinking economy and demands to "make the workers pay," will be mobilized only when the mass of people are mobilized to win new public policies, to protect and expand the fledgling democracy in the District. That mobilization can only happen through a militant defense of the most impoverished sectors of the city. Deteriorating life conditions demand that such an approach be taken.

Economic development of the Black community must be promoted. Relative to other ethnic groups in our society, Black dollars are invested outside of the community in higher proportions. But economic development cannot be divorced from the acquisition of political power. Nor can economic development be looked at exclusively in terms of ownership. As Acie Byrd notes, "most Black, and White people as well, do not own businesses but work for other people. We need to be about the business of providing decent and secure jobs for workers as well as promoting ownership opportunities."[20]

Chapter 8

THE DRUG CRISIS IN WASHINGTON, D.C. PART I

...I remember in a meeting with the President he said, "All right, Bud, I'd like you to stop crime in the District of Columbia," and I said, "Yes," I would do that. So I called the mayor, Walter Washington, and asked him to stop crime, and he paused for a moment and said, "Okay," and that was about it.
—Egil Krogh, Jr., Deputy Counsel to President Nixon[1]

Like most major cities in the United States, the District of Columbia has a long history of illegal drug trafficking and drug abuse. Unlike other jurisdictions, however, time and time again Washington has been the guinea pig for the numerous federal "wars" against drugs. From Theodore Roosevelt at the turn of the century to Richard Nixon in the 1970s to Ronald Reagan in the 1980s and George Bush in the 1990s, the District of Columbia has been a testing ground for programs and policies that the federal government has had little chance of implementing elsewhere. The District has been central to every stage of drug policy legislation that has developed in the United States. The District has thus witnessed a history of tension and struggle between the different administrations, local officials, and activists in the varying political structures that have governed the city in this century.

An understanding of this history is critical to sorting out the current animosity between the Bush administration and the local political forces. A central theme is the racial dynamic of White political power clashing with Black political and community interests. The image of dangerous Black drug dealers and crazed Black users is part of a scare tactic used to win national support for programs of law and order and the suppression of Black rights.

The demographic and political changes in the District of Columbia have shaped the debate between the federal government and the Black community. Prior to the Fifties, when the city was a majority White and had no political voice locally or on Capitol Hill, drug policies were met with only a token challenge, if any at all. As the District became a majority Black, grassroots and official opposition to the federal programs became more vocal and more organized, leading eventually to the election of a congressional delegate in 1971 and the advent of home rule in 1974.

Pre-War Trafficking and Substance Abuse

The battles over anti-drug legislation in the early part of the century took place on the District's turf. Bills to enact labeling on medicines and other products were beaten back again and again.[2] Pharmaceutical companies and opium importers lobbied fiercely to no avail as the 1906 Pure Food and Drug Act set the stage for a plethora of drug laws. The laws did not outlaw possession or use of opiates. Groups affiliated with the drug trade established the National Drug Trade Conference in Washington in January 1913. That conference became a powerful influence in shaping the most decisive federal anti-narcotics act in the first half of the century, the Harrison Act of 1914.[3] Whites overwhelmingly controlled the illegal drug trade in Washington up until the 1950s. Some Blacks functioned as runners and as small-time traffickers, but Whites tied to organized crime in New York, Miami, and other areas ruled the roost.

Prior to the 1940s, substance abuse among Blacks in the District of Columbia principally took the form of alcohol abuse. During this period, Blacks were concentrated in the southwest, Georgetown, and downtown sectors of the city. Most socializing among Blacks took place in these areas and involved very little interaction with Whites. As Marcellus Boston, a senior counselor at the Washington Area Council on Alcoholism and Drug Abuse, recalls, liquor stores were pervasive throughout the Black community. However, he says, alcoholics were viewed in a negative light. During that period, many people were arrested and locked up for public drunkenness.[4] Treatment for alcoholism was rarely considered an option. Beyond the liquor stores, alcohol was easily accessible at rent parties or at the hundreds of after-hours places that existed in the Black community all over the city. People were also skilled at producing their own home-made moonshine, known as "white lightning."

Illegal drug use was much more circumscribed. For the most part, heroin and cocaine were too expensive to be used casually by the majority of Black folks. For those who traveled the club circuit, these drugs were available in the back rooms, and dealers could always be found in club establishments. Up until the mid-Forties, according to

Boston, young people did not use and generally could not even purchase marijuana. While a very few young people sold marijuana, most that engaged in ongoing criminal activities were involved in the popular illegal numbers betting racket.

Odessa's Odyssey

The most colorful and unforgettable individual of this period was Odessa Marie Madre, dubbed the "Queen" of Washington's underworld. One friend called her the "Al Capone of Washington."[5] For fifty years, beginning in the early Thirties, Madre ran whore houses, numbers, gambling establishments, after-hours liquor places—known as "jill" joints—and provided drugs to friends and acquaintances.[6] Madre, an imposing, dark-skinned woman who weighed about 260 pounds, would make spectacular entrances dressed from head-to-toe in furs and diamonds followed by a bevy of beautiful women and handsome men, all for sale.[7] She owned and ran Club Madre, located in the heart of the city's Black cultural center. The club featured such stars as Billie Holiday; Duke Ellington; Nat King Cole; Count Basie; the great Black comedian, Moms Mabley, who became a good friend of Madre's; and many other Black celebrities of the period.

One reason that Madre was able to operate for so long was because she paid off and controlled a vast network of police authorities. At the infamous Kefauver Hearings on Organized Crime in 1952, testimony was given that she paid Police Superintendent James Barrett $2,000 a month in "ice"—her term for payoff money. In fact, the hearings revealed that Madre practically "ran the whole damn police department" through her contacts and influence.[8]

Madre's ties with key police officials, including Police Superintendent Pat O'Shea and Captain John Murphy, represented more than just business. Although she grew up in the fashionable Black neighborhood of LeDroit Park near Howard University, she spent most of her time on the streets of the Irish community of Washington, called Cowtown, with many of the children who would later join the police force. She and other Black youth had formed alliances with the Irish children, including O'Shea, Murphy, and others, in turf fights against the Italian and German kids.[9]

Her ability to survive during her youth was conditioned by the segregation that existed in the District during that time. The Black community was restricted to a few choice neighborhoods where they could gather and socialize. In the mid- to late-1950s, as the walls of segregation came down within the nation's capital, many middle-class Blacks began to frequent downtown establishments, and Madre saw her monopoly straining. However, Madre retained her popularity because she was generous to the community. She made loans or donations to those in need and bought clothes for children whose parents could not afford them. She would also act as a mediator in disputes between Black and White gangsters locally and nationally.[10] After a series of arrests and incarcerations for drug possession and number running in the Sixties and Seventies, Madre spent most of the Eighties living a quiet life. She died in February 1990, practically penniless. It took several days before someone claimed her body and, in the end, a local funeral parlor donated their services and a casket.[11]

Napoleon "Nap" Turner remembers the Thirties well. Turner, a spry and energetic man, has led a varied and multi-vocational life. He has been an accomplished jazz musician, playwright, writer, radio host, and, in his words, "an addict-criminal." Turner performed at Club Madre during its heyday and knew the legendary Madre.[12] Turner says that two types of addicts existed during that time. Addict-criminals, like himself, committed crimes solely in order to feed their drug habits. They shop-lifted, burglarized and, generally, did only petty property crimes. For the most part, they did not sell drugs in any large quantities and many resented being called "pushers." Criminal-addicts, on the other hand, were hard-core criminals who had become addicted to drugs. They committed serious felonies and some did become full-time dealers.

Turner also recalls the pervasive police corruption that exploited and perpetuated crime in the Black community. When dope houses were negligent or late in their payoffs, the police would go to the shooting galleries (houses where addicts shot up), take the dealer's dope, and give it to the junkies. Before the 1950s, the police would often arrest drunks, but other addicts were seldom bothered. The drug community, for the most part, blended into the community as a whole and was neither violent nor a significant threat to the youth.

One of the most significant developments of this period was the founding in 1949 of the Washington Area Council on Alcoholism and Drug Abuse (WACADA), known then as the Washington Area Council on Alcoholism, by a group of volunteers seeking a better understanding of the causes of and effective solutions to alcoholism. As illegal narcotics use became a large problem in the early Sixties, WACADA applied its methods and tactics to the drug issue. Currently headed by Joe Wright, WACADA has been in the forefront of region-wide substance abuse work, including training substance abuse counselors and running a drug hotline.[13]

The Great White Dope Comes to Washington

Rumor had it that Franklin D. Roosevelt had made a deal with the Mafia that they would never openly operate in the nation's capital.[14] The District's increased drug addiction rate among Blacks, however, made

Washington a critical market for illegal drugs. According to one local anti-drug activist who had been involved in the drug scene at the time, a large number of Blacks in the District first became exposed and addicted to Asian-based heroin during the Korean War. In the early 1950s, a Mafia-run heroin ring at its peak was bringing in a kilo a week into the city, an extraordinary amount of heroin at that time.[15]

Most of that heroin came from New York. Other cities, such as Detroit, Philadelphia, Chicago, and Baltimore, supported Washington drug trafficking, but New York was the central source. According to congressional reports and anti-drug activists of the time, the Mafia still remained outside of the District—though highly active in Maryland and northern Virginia—and was satisfied with using couriers, middlemen, and imported enforcers as a way of asserting authority over Washington's drug market.

The big traffickers in the 1940s, 1950s, and 1960s were always colorful, often dramatic, sometimes community-conscious, and businesslike in their work; this three-decade span included infamous dealers such as Polly Brown, Schoolboy, Catfish Turner, Blue Miller, the Thacker brothers, Willie Earl, Stampede, Rudy Lawson, Reginald "Ping Pong" Smith, Issac Tindle, Bubba George, Russell Sykes, and Dumptruck Smith. They controlled almost all of the heroin market, in some cases, for more than a dozen years.

Many of these dealers were seen as survivors or even shrewd businesspeople rather than as hoodlums or outcasts. More benevolent and community-based than the dealers of today, many of these dealers helped to pay rent or send a neighborhood youth to college. Very little violence was associated with the drug scene; in fact, drug abuse was seen as being no more harmful than excessive drinking, often with tragic results.

As the District of Columbia became a majority Black in the Fifties, the city enjoyed the full-scale social life of other Black cities at the time. The city remained highly segregated, however, and Blacks found severe discrimination in housing and employment, and circumscribed access to certain social and public functions and opportunities. Similar to New York's Harlem, Detroit's Black Bottom, and Chicago's South Side, the District created strips that contained the cultural and social life of Black workers and the Black middle class.

In the District, the 14th Street Corridor in the northwest section of town became the hub of the Black community's social and cultural scene. Most of the popular Black clubs, including Off Beat, Old Rose, Howard Theater, and Crystal Caverns, were located there. The well-known eatery, Ben's Chili Bowl, was where Bill Cosby and other Black youth and students hung out. The area's focal point was the intersection of 14th and U Streets, then a sprawling panorama of small shops, night clubs, apartment buildings and single-family attached homes. The area went as far north as Chapin Street, as far east as Georgia Avenue, as far west as 18th Street, and as far south as P Street.

The 14th Street Corridor was also the center of drug trafficking in the District's Black community. There were very few places in the southeast or northeast sections of the city to buy drugs. Certainly, if someone were looking for quality drugs, they went to the 14th Street Corridor. Drugs were also prevalent in the area bounded by P Street on the south, Massachusetts Avenue on the north, 13th Street on the west, and North Capitol Street on the east. This area was known as "The Glut." According to an *Evening Star* editorial by then-City Council Vice Chairman Sterling Tucker, open air drug markets operated on 14th Street NW, U Street NW, 9th and O Streets NW, 7th and T Streets NW, far Northeast, Anacostia, Cleveland Park, and even in parts of Georgetown. He estimated the heroin trade to be about $500,000 a day in the District.[16]

Overwhelmingly, however, most of the trafficking took place in the 14th Street area. At times, hundreds of users would fill the streets in a carnival-like atmosphere, waiting for the "candy man" to arrive. Weekends were especially busy, as occasional use "chippers" joined the regular users and addicts.

The District had a reputation for high-quality heroin. The purity percentage (the amount of pure heroin) was generally higher than heroin obtained elsewhere, even in New York. In the Sixties, the purity often would reach as high as 9 percent and never fell below 4 percent. Users in most other cities would consider 3 percent a very good buy, though most likely they would settle for the usual 1-2 percent range.[17]

Washington's common two-week pay cycle also affected the heroin market. Generally, the best dope was available close to payday around the 1st and 15th of the month. The Metropolitan Police Department often made its biggest bust of dealers from New York on Wednesdays and Thursdays, when the dealers arrived to prepare for the weekend sales boom. Drug sales also boomed on "Mother's Day," the day that welfare checks arrived in the ghetto, and absentee fathers and boyfriends made their appearance, often to take or cajole money from welfare mothers. Toward the end of the month, dealers of high-quality smack would leave, and the "garbage men" would take over. The garbage men dealt low-quality heroin (less than 2 percent purity) and usually found customers only among the hard-core addicts.

Heroin arriving in the District from New York was brought in either by couriers or by the dealers themselves. Once the heroin was in

Washington, it would be "stamped on" or "cut"—that is, diluted to cut its purity with lactose, baking soda, or some other suitable ingredient. The cut heroin would then be packaged and sold to street or dope-house pushers who would cut it again before putting it into capsules to be sold to users. The purchase and distribution of large amounts of heroin (more than a kilo) would go through Mafia-controlled sources. There were many small dealers who would go to New York and purchase two to three ounces from street dealers there. An ounce sold for about $1,000 and "caps" for about $1 to $2.[18]

Reportedly, only two Blacks had direct ties with New York's Mafia families that controlled drug trafficking on the East Coast. One of those was Rayful Edmond, Sr., whose name-bearing son in the late 1980s would become one of Washington's most notorious and flamboyant cocaine dealers and drug kingpins ever.[19]

Trafficking and abuse rose dramatically in the mid-Sixties. In 1958, the Department of Corrections sentenced only about fifty known heroin addicts to jail. By 1966, this number had risen to about 150 annually. In 1969, only three years later, the average had risen to 1,400![20]

Before 1966, heroin addicts had never constituted more than 3 percent of the District's jail population. By February 1969, the number had grown to 15 percent. By August of that year, the number had increased to 45 percent. The District of Columbia had about 10,000 to 15,000 heroin addicts. According to one study, 19 percent of all young men between twenty and twenty-four were addicts.[21]

Heroin use grew also in the areas adjacent to the District. In wealthy Montgomery County, northwest of the city, there were twenty-eight heroin arrests in 1969. That number was equaled in the first three months of 1970. In Prince Georges County, to the city's east, there were sixty-eight arrests in 1969, but sixty-one in the first six months of 1970.[22]

A pivotal ruling in 1966 was spearheaded by the Washington Area Council on Alcoholism and the National Capital Area Civil Liberties Union. On March 31, 1966, in the case of DeWitt Easter v. District of Columbia, the U.S. Court of Appeals for the District of Columbia Circuit unanimously ruled that "[c]hronic alcoholism is a defense to the charge of public intoxication, and, therefore, is not a crime." The ruling essentially underscored a 1947 Act of Congress that advocated a non-criminal approach to the problem of alcoholism and called for more treatment facilities for the problem.[23]

In 1968, the District of Columbia had only one treatment program. The Drug Addiction, Treatment and Rehabilitation Center (DATRC) was an outpatient abstinence program sponsored by the Office of Economic Opportunity and operated by the Department of Public Health.

Following an August 1969 study by the District's Department of Corrections that showed that heroin addiction was growing in the city, a new treatment program was established. The Narcotics Addiction Rehabilitation Center (NARC) used methadone treatment for heroin addicts in District jails.[24]

On February 18, 1970, the Narcotics Treatment Administration (NTA) opened in the District, headed by Dr. Robert Dupont. The NTA became the coordination center for all of the District's treatment facilities. Its three-year goal was to provide treatment service for all of Washington's estimated 10,000 to 15,000 addicts. The NTA's major components were:[25] extensive use of methadone treatment; use of ex-addicts as counselors; use of outpatient services; promotion of employment training for recovering addicts; cooperation with other city and private service and treatment providers; participant recruitment through self-referral and referral through the criminal justice system; and development of a computerized evaluation system of all of the city's treatment programs. Drs. Vincent Dole and Marie Nyswander, founders of the methadone maintenance treatment in 1964 and operators of one of the nation's first methadone programs at the Rockefeller University in New York, called NTA's approach the most dynamic in the country.[26]

Following the establishment of the NTA, a number of community-based methadone programs emerged. Among the most noted and the most controversial of all was the Blackman's Development Center, founded by the enigmatic and charismatic Col. Jeru-Ahmed Hassan. Hassan, a former hustler and street-wise activist, was a fiery nationalist who channeled his Black Power energies into the development of Blackman's Development Center, which operated in three locations. His main center was located in the 1300 block of T Street NW in the heart of the city's drug trafficking area; up to 600 addicts a day were treated there. The second center was at 1407 H Street NE, and the third was set up at 6406 Georgia Avenue NW. Hassan dispensed methadone to thousands of addicts, set up political education classes, dressed his "army" of volunteers in military garb, and sent shivers down the spine of the Metropolitan Police Department.[27]

Although the Blackman's Development Center was never accused of any criminal activities, Hassan and his followers became targets of police surveillance and infiltration. Federal and local law enforcement authorities felt threatened by many community-based groups at the time, especially if they espoused nationalist and revolutionary rhetoric. The spread of Hassan's Centers to other cities increased police authorities' paranoia that he was part of a growing subversive political campaign.

Hassan also became the target of drug dealers, according to the *Washington Star*. He stated on numerous occasions that he knew the identities of the key traffickers in the District. He said that there "were at least 11 Black dealers who operate large wholesale operations and above them about 30 to 40 White mafia operatives who bring drugs from New York."[28]

The Rise of Rap, Inc.

The NTA's use of methadone for treating heroin addiction did not go unchallenged. Rap, Inc., founded by the determined and sophisticated Ron Clark, was established in 1970 as an alternative to NTA.[29]

Clark, an adamant advocate for the rights of addicts, waged his own personal victory over heroin addiction in the 1950s. Clark had worked also at non-medical treatment centers such as California's well-known Synanon clinic and New York's Phoenix House. Determined to set up a free, community-based, non-methadone treatment center, Clark worked with two local priests to secure initial funds and space from St. Margaret's Church. They were told, however, that they only had ninety days to get at least fifteen people in the program or they would have to leave. Fortunately for the people of the District, Clark was able to meet this goal. Rap, Inc., along with the therapeutically-based Second Genesis treatment center, became one of the first non-methadone treatment operations in the city. It became clear from day one that Rap, Inc., was going to make its mark on Washington.

Clark and others around him viewed the battle against drugs as a continuation of the struggle against racism. He believed that low self-esteem by Blacks, in which racism played a direct and central role, led to drug addiction and other negative behavior patterns. Treatment programs that ignored racism (or worse, perpetuated it) could never be fully successful. For its first few years, Rap, Inc., did not accept any local or federal funding. Committed to maintaining its independence from government agencies, Rap, Inc., raised funds from the community through fundraisers and donations. It also worked with community and political groups to share food and clothing with the city's poor people. One of the political groups that Rap, Inc., worked with during the early years was the local Black Panther chapter. Panther leader Malik Edwards was extremely instrumental in helping Rap involve itself in the community. (Edwards, like Clark, remains very involved in the political life of Washington.)

Rap, Inc., initiated an aggressive attack on methadone maintenance as a treatment approach. Clark and others worked with a doctor from the National Institute of Health who had begun research on the negative effects of methadone. Rap, Inc., began to produce and distribute pamphlets about the dangers of methadone and the political menace of Nixon's so-called war on drugs. The pamphlets bore provocative titles like "Imperialism and Drugs" and "Nixon and Methadone." At least one ex-addict and activist, who supported methadone treatment, felt that the work done by Rap, Inc., did not contain enough legitimate research to substantiate its claims about the harm of methadone. For the most part, however, Rap, Inc., found a receptive ear to its arguments.

Rap, Inc., also challenged the D.C. Board of Trade and the private, mainly White, Federal City Council. The BOT and the FCC, both of which had significant influence over what happened in the city, had become concerned about increased property crime, particularly shoplifting, as a result of drug use. Methadone was a cheap, but effective, way of neutralizing addicts' need to constantly steal in order to satisfy a habit that had to be fed several times daily. As Clark pointed out, neither of these groups was really concerned for the general health and well-being of addicts, who were overwhelmingly Black.

In 1973, Dupont offered Rap, Inc., $100,000 with the provision that it do urine testing, according to Clark. The offer was flatly refused. Clark says that Rap, Inc.'s, good relations with its patients, known internally as "family," was based on trust and honesty. This trust, in part, accounts for the fact that in over twenty years, Rap has never had any serious incidents of violence, which are common in other treatment centers.

Rap, Inc.'s, success eventually caught the attention of the District's city council, newly established in 1974. Two council members, the street-smart and rambunctious Doug Moore (who is Black) and Polly Shackleton, a liberal White who represented the upper-class residents of Ward 3, paid a visit to Rap, Inc. They liked what they saw and, despite some opposition from then-Mayor Walter Washington, pushed through some city funds for the program.

Rap's work extended beyond the city's limits. Clark gave a well-received presentation to the founding convention of the National Black Political Assembly in 1972 in Gary, Indiana. He also travelled to the People's Republic of China, where he visited many cities, held talks with Chinese officials, and adopted for Rap the slogan used by Mao Tse Tung on the long march during the Chinese revolution: "Dare to Struggle—Dare to Win."

During the period of Rap's rise, estimates of the social costs of heroin abuse were in the millions of dollars. One study estimated that the social cost to the District of heroin addiction was $205,800,000 a year. The study calculated that the average addict spent between $25 and $40 a day on heroin.[30]

The study also looked at how addicts financed their addiction.

Nixon's Other War

As described in Chapter Four, in response to the nation's growing heroin addiction problem and the hysteria about rising crime rates, Nixon declared his "war against drugs." As his successors would do, Nixon used the District of Columbia as a test area for his anti-drug program. During his first term, Nixon decided that to win re-election he would have to show progress in addressing the crisis of crime, a crisis that was exaggerated to facilitate the campaign theme of restoring law and order to the nation, particularly the inner cities. His administration used statistics from the District of Columbia to argue that the federal government could solve the drug problem in the rest of the country.[31]

In February 1969, Nixon asked Attorney General John Mitchell to focus federal anti-drug efforts on heroin use. Mitchell's mission was to stem the flow of illegal narcotics into the District from New York and Baltimore. Nixon also promised that a substantial number of federal narcotics agents would be transferred to the District.[32] Egil Krogh, Jr., whose official title was Nixon's Deputy Counsel but in reality acted as John Ehrlichman's personal assistant, pressed city officials for more streetlights, more police patrols, and other measures that would stem the tide of District crime. Yet drug-related crime continued to climb, reaching an all-time high in November 1969.[33]

Robert DuPont suggested to Krogh that Nixon focus on reducing crime by attempting to rid the streets of narcotics addicts through methadone maintenance. DuPont suggested creating a "filing station" type of distribution where addicts could line up and daily receive their dose of methadone.[34] He was able to convince Krogh to use false statistics to prove that District crime rates had fallen.[35]

A Free-Market Drug Industry

Heroin use declined in the mid-Seventies. This had less to do with the anti-drug efforts of Nixon and more to do with the destruction of the French Connection and the end of the Vietnam War, both of which affected the availability of heroin and other drugs. Soon, other drugs, especially amphetamines, began to hit the streets. Two of the most popular amphetamines were methamphetamine and phenatrazine, known as BAM.[36]

In the early to mid-Eighties, new and purer heroin supplies began to arrive via New York from the Golden Crescent area of the Middle East. Afghan Gold replaced Mexican Mud—the Mexican heroin that dominated Washington in the Seventies—and street purity rose dramatically. In 1978, the average street purity was about 1.8 percent. By the mid-Eighties, it had risen to about 7 percent.[37] Washington came to have one of the most serious heroin problems in the country. The year 1980 saw eighty-two overdose deaths. By mid-1985, the number had risen to 185 annually.[38] Other cities that were much larger than the District saw many fewer deaths: Chicago with fifty-three, Detroit with ninety-one, and Philadelphia with sixty-five.[39] The problem became so bad at one point that, with nine people dying in one weekend, then-Assistant Police Chief Issac Fulwood went on the eleven o'clock news with a "consumer" alert to warn addicts not to purchase drugs that particular night.[40]

Several dozen open-air drug markets operated during this time. In addition to the 14th Street area, markets opened up and ran for nearly twenty-four hours on Martin Luther King Avenue in Southeast Washington, on H Street NE, and in other parts of Northwest. Brand names such as Rattlesnake, Goldenboy, Black Tape, Murder One, and Direct Hit designated both the type and quality of the heroin as well as which particular group was selling it.[41] As would happen a few years later with crack, heroin dealers descended from New York to muscle their way into the District's market. This "free-market" competition led to unprecedented violence in the city and set the stage for the crack invasion.

At that time, the city had between 12,000 and 16,000 heroin addicts, although one narcotics officer thought that the actual number was closer to 25,000.[42] Three-quarters of these addicts were Black.[43] The city's treatment centers, however, were seeing only about 3,400 addicts monthly.[44]

In a nutshell, the city's most effective response to the drug crisis was to create an elite squad of top narcotics and homicide officers whose mission was to halt the drug killings. Known on the street by the name "Copperjack," from the type of ammunition popular with street killers at the time, the squad was one of three special task forces created to address Washington's drug scene. The other two were the DEA-MPD Task Force that went after smuggling operations and major dealers, and the STP (Stop Trafficking and Pushing) "jump squad" that targetted street-level dealers.[45]

Reagan's benign neglect and the arrival of crack would create new conditions that would propel the drug problems in the nation's capital to unforseen heights.

In the following decades, the drug problem would actually escalate within the nation's capital, wreaking unexpected havoc on the Black community. Rather than address the roots of the problem—joblessness, poverty, racism, and social alienation—government officials focused only on the most flagrant symptoms of addiction and trafficking, while perpetuating some of the most racist stereotypes of the modern era. The next chapter details the events that shaped those years, highlighting policy initiatives as well as community activism and response.

Chapter 9

THE DRUG CRISIS IN WASHINGTON, D.C. PART II

The Barry Saga

On the night of January 18, 1990, Mayor Marion Barry placed a phone call to an old friend and reputed lover, Rasheeda Moore. Barry wanted to visit Moore at her hotel room at the Vista Hotel in Washington, making it clear that his interest in seeing her was primarily sexual. In response to an invitation from Moore, Barry hesitated at first, pointing out there might be "too many nosy Rosies" at the hotel.

When he arrived, Moore offered Barry alcohol and crack cocaine in a pipe. After some prodding, Barry took the pipe and smoked the crack. From their concealed hiding place, where the entire event was being filmed on videotape, FBI agents burst forth and placed Barry under arrest. The mayor of the capital city in one of the most powerful nations in the world, a capital city also awash in drug-related homicides, had been filmed smoking crack. Television stations in Washington and around the nation interrupted their regular programming to inform startled viewers of the news. ABC news reporter Sam Donaldson found the story significant enough to interrupt his broadcast from Red Square in Moscow. The arrest and trial of Marion Barry, and the eventual public airing of the FBI "sting" videotape, became a topic of heated discussion around the world.

In the late 1980s, following one mayoral scandal after another and the simultaneous public perception that the drug crisis had gotten out of hand, Mayor Barry became the target of major media scrutiny. For most of the year preceding the mayor's arrest, the dominant news outlets in the Washington metropolitan area had been relentlessly attacking him, the theme being whether or not allegations of drug use by Barry could be substantiated. At the center of the story was the mayor's relationship with Charles Lewis, a close friend and former employee of the District of Columbia government. In December 1988, a maid at a downtown hotel had complained to the management that

Lewis had offered her cocaine in exchange for sex. Two city detectives on the way to investigate were called off when it was discovered that the mayor was present in the room. Both Barry and Lewis denied any wrongdoing, but Lewis was subsequently arrested in the Virgin Islands while attempting to arrange a crack cocaine sale to an undercover agent. Lewis went on to become one of the leading prosecution witnesses in Barry's 1990 trial.

The Charles Lewis uproar was just one in a long line of personal and political scandals that rocked the Barry administration. During Barry's second term in office, 1982-1986, a number of Barry's close advisors had been charged and convicted of wrongdoing. The most publicized of these was the conviction in 1985 of Ivanhoe Donaldson, the mayor's top political advisor, on charges of embezzlement of public funds originally earmarked for welfare programs. One woman, Karen Johnson, went to jail after refusing to testify about her relationship and possible drug use with the mayor before a Grand Jury investigation.

For his part, Barry denied being a user of drugs and spent a good deal of time touring local schools and giving anti-drug speeches or leading anti-drug marches. While many Blacks were embarrassed by Barry's behavior, many others were skeptical of the political intention behind predominantly White press coverage. This skepticism was increased by racist cartoons of Barry in local publications such as *Regardies*.[1]

The mayor's arrest, however, qualitatively changed the political situation in the District of Columbia. It was no longer possible for Barry to deny drug use. Indeed, during the trial in the Summer of 1990, Barry's own attorney, R. Kenneth Mundy, acknowledged that Barry had used cocaine. But Barry and his allies launched a public relations effort to convince the public, particularly the Black public, that his case represented a classic entrapment paradigm. On the other hand, federal government officials and the media, local as well as national, went to great lengths to convince the public that the investigation and subsequent "sting" of Barry was "fair" and not racially motivated.

Barry's strategy paid off. Memories of subjugation at the hands of insensitive federal officials were still fresh in the minds of many District residents. Some District residents recalled the words of President Nixon's former attorney general, John Mitchell, who compared the workings of the District government to the "Amos and Andy" show. It was also clear that the judge in the Barry case, Thomas Penfield Jackson, and the prosecutor, Jay Stephens, were appointees of President Ronald Reagan, not to mention the FBI. The local Black press pointed to the innumerable federal investigations of Black elected officials, the long and sordid history of government involvement in harassing or even encouraging the assassination of prominent Black reformists or revolutionaries, such as Malcolm X, Dr. Martin Luther King, and the Black Panthers. The majority of Blacks in the District of Columbia agreed with the view that the Barry "sting" was racially motivated.

This view was held by many Blacks at the national level as well. NAACP leader Benjamin Hooks, for example, denounced the "sting" as racist, and was one of a number of national Black leaders to rally to Barry's defense. Marion Barry was, after all, no ordinary Black leader. He was the first of a generation of prominent civil rights activists to get elected to the office of mayor in one of the most important U.S. cities.

In August 1990, Barry's jury reflected the split opinion of the community and was hung on twelve of the fourteen charges against Barry. He was found innocent of one charge and was convicted of one count of cocaine possession. On the twelve charges that hung the jury, most votes where evenly split.

While many, if not most, Blacks were pleased that the mayor was not incarcerated for a substance abuse problem, this did not mean that he was to be seen as a positive role model. Neither the predominantly Black jury nor the majority of Blacks in the District believed Barry to be literally innocent of drug use. One journalist noted that "some of the bitterest remarks I heard were from Blacks who thought the jury was far too easy on a man they saw as a junkie womanizer who has just brought disgrace to their city."[2]

Nor was this previously sympathetic majority moved by Barry's nationalist rhetoric into believing he had future as a political leader in the District of Colombia. Barry's decisive defeat for an at-large city council seat in the Fall of 1990 was one indicator that the confidence in Barry's ability to deliver meaningful change was eroding. This sentiment was also shared beyond the borders of the District of Columbia. Black newspapers in other cities criticized Barry for his failure to exercise positive leadership and for willfully deceiving his constituency.[3]

But beyond Barry's personal problems lay a much deeper dilemma for the city and for progressive movements. This dilemma had largely been ignored by the local Black press, which focused almost exclusively on the misdoings of the federal government, but little on the actual record of Barry. He had just spent many months on a public relations campaign relying on the rhetoric of racial solidarity. But beyond the calls for solidarity, there was no program for renewal in the Black community, no innovative ideas for employment, housing, education or the drug crisis. That Barry was harassed by the federal government is beyond question. But the larger question is whether Barry's strategy had much to offer the city as a way of lessening poverty and despair.

Does D.C. Stand for Dodge City?

Drug-related violence and shootouts became so prevalent in the District of Columbia during the Eighties that one local go-go band recorded a song stating that D.C. did not stand for Dodge City. First PCP, then crack cocaine swept hundreds of local youths and adults into a new and much more deadly era of drug culture and economy.

"Crack seemed to overwhelm the city in 1987. Washington provided a lucrative market for crack which sold much cheaper than it did in New York," comments Judge Reggie Walton, a former attorney and judge in the District of Columbia and now coordinator of state and local outreach for the national drug control policy office.[4] Judge Walton indicates that much of the trade and traffic in the District is organized through "groups" and notes that Mafia-style organizations have never had much of a presence in the city. Yet the front pages of the city newspapers abound with stories of gangland-like killings in the District.[5]

These stories tell of bloody rivalry for control of the drug traffic in various District neighborhoods. A large portion of the city's drug trafficking transpires through these gang organizations. Investigators report that Black gangs such as the "Enforcers" and the "5 N 0 Crew" have their roots in neighborhood street crime and are often solidified in prison.

As in other parts of the nation, children are often the victims of drug-related violence. Doctors and officials at the District's public D.C. General Hospital report injuries among children as young as eight years old who have been recruited to play a part in the distribution of illegal drugs.

Crammed into the sixty-three square miles that make up the District of Columbia are dozens of open-air drug markets to feed the District's estimated 20,000 cocaine addicts. Random killings and planned executions associated with the struggles for control of these markets have led to record homicide rates in the District. In 1989, 434 people were killed and, in spite of declining drug use, the numbers were higher in 1990.[6]

The District's criminal justice system has aggressively pursued drug dealers and users, from arrests to prosecution to incarceration. Ninety-nine percent of those charged with a drug offense in the District between 1985 and 1987 were Black. The ratio of drug convictions to the general population is higher in the District than in other major cities. In 1986, the District with 627,000 residents reported 3,140 drug trafficking convictions and Manhattan, with a population of 1.8 million, reported

3,085 convictions.[7] In 1989, 67 percent of adult arrestees tested positive either for heroin, cocaine, or PCP. Figures from local hospitals suggest that anywhere from 20 percent to 40 percent of the mothers of newborn infants test positive for drugs.[8] Yet in spite of all these figures, the city's cocaine trade, while in comparative decline, continues to thrive.

About one in every five persons in the District is poor and lives below the poverty line, and the majority of poor people also happen to be Black, comprising approximately 62 percent of the total population.[9] Lack of employment or educational skills, discrimination, and inadequate means for self-help make this poverty chronic.

The District of Columbia shoulders the burden of the region's social problems, yet the District itself is not a poor region; some of the surrounding counties in suburban Maryland and northern Virginia are among the wealthiest in the nation. The inequitable distribution of wealth and power explains why the drug epidemic has hit poor and minority communities the hardest, even though drug use is spread throughout the entire metropolitan Washington, D.C., area.

Measuring the extent of the metropolitan area's drug problem is not simple. Richard Broughton, an intelligence official in the Washington, D.C., regional office of the Drug Enforcement Administration, states that measuring the size of the trade is "like asking how many gallons of water are in the ocean. We know how many square miles there are but we're not sure how deep it is." Broughton estimates that the cocaine trade is a $24 million-a-day business in the District and the surrounding suburban counties of Maryland and Virginia.[10]

Estimates of drug usage and trafficking in the District come from several statistical indicators. These include drug overdose reports, emergency room drug mentions, arrestee urinalysis test results, arrests, prosecutions, and convictions for drug offenses, drug treatment admissions, and surveys of drug use in high school populations. Together these indicators capture an element of the drug problem but are by no means a complete description.

The District has traditionally had a higher-than-average use of PCP, although that use has declined markedly beginning in 1989. For example, a 1988 study showed that of those receiving drug treatment in the District, over 25 percent describe PCP as their drug of choice, as opposed to only 4 percent in the rest of the nation.[11] Data collected from the Drug Abuse Warning Network (DAWN) show that for the years from 1981 to 1987, most emergency room mentions were for PCP.[12] The number of adult arrestees testing positive for PCP use declined to 17 percent in 1989.[13]

Data from twenty-six of the largest metropolitan areas shows the District to be one of the five cities showing the greatest heroin and cocaine use. Between the third quarter of 1986 and the same quarter of 1987, emergency room mentions involving cocaine doubled, reflected by cocaine increases of 109 percent from 7,645 in 1985 to 15,999 in 1987.[14] Urinalysis data reveals that by November 1987, three out of every four arrestees tested positive for one illicit substance, excluding marijuana, with half testing positive for cocaine.[15]

Heroin overdoses accounted for the largest percentage of overdose deaths between 1985 to 1988. The increase in overdose deaths for this period is accounted for by the increasing use of cocaine. In 1985, cocaine accounted for 5 percent of overdose deaths, a figure which had risen to 13 percent by 1988.[16] This medically related data was confirmed by telephone surveys of District residents. A total of approximately 37 percent of the cross section surveyed said they know someone who regularly uses drugs.[17]

The most visible response to the drug problem has been increased law enforcement. A 1990 Rand Corporation study found that a shocking one-quarter of the city's young Black males may be involved with drug selling at some point prior to their thirtieth birthday. One-sixth of the District's Black males who were eighteen years old in 1985 were charged with drug selling before they turned twenty-one. More than one in four young District males aged eighteen to twenty-nine was criminally charged between 1985 and 1987 and half of this group had at least one drug charge already on record.[18]

The prioritization of enforcement over the last few years has resulted not only in large arrest figures, but also in increased numbers of prosecutions and convictions. By 1986, over half of all felony prosecutions and convictions in the District involved drug charges and over one-third of all prison commitments were for drug convictions.[19]

Prior to 1988, the District of Columbia led the nation's largest cities (those with a population of greater than 500,000) in per capita drug arrests, averaging 1,000 arrests per 100,000 population annually.

New York City has the most addicts numerically, with about 434,000, but the District has the highest per capita addict rate when compared to other states (32.9 addicts per 1,000).[20] In Washington, D.C. eighty-five percent of those testing positive for drugs in 1988 were thirty-one years of age or younger. Men accounted for 82 percent of all positive tests for drugs in 1985, and Blacks accounted for 92 percent of positive drug tests, with Whites accounting for 7 percent.[21]

White suburban residents contribute significantly to the drug trade in the District. According to the Rand Corporation, 42 percent of those arrested on possession charges between 1985 and 1987 were nonresidents, and 30 percent of those were White. Twenty-one percent of the individuals charged with selling drugs were nonresidents, and of those, 10 percent were White.[22]

Like other regions of significant drug traffic, the drug trade in the District has generated a new industry of professional money launderers. These individuals, for the most part, are "respectable" White professionals with no criminal record. In the District, for example, one drug ring's profits were laundered through three Northwest apartment buildings owned and operated by a group of Washington businessmen. A First American Bank branch on Capitol Hill routinely processed as much as $60,000 in cash at a time.[23]

Health Crisis in the City

In the District of Columbia, there exists a growing crisis in the health care delivery system which is driven in large measure by the drug epidemic. There are about 100,000 individuals in the District who are or will be chemically dependent, and about 20 percent of these will seek treatment in District facilities. There are also estimated to be about 110,000 individuals lacking health insurance in the District. These individuals tend to make visits to the emergency rooms of area hospitals as a substitute for seeing an expensive private doctor. By the Spring of 1990, officials of at least three of the leading hospitals in the District were announcing personnel layoffs and the curtailing of services due to the expense of maintaining services for which the patients could not pay.

Inner-city health care has also been affected by the drug crisis giving rise to what one writer refers to as a "bio-underclass," a generation of physically damaged cocaine babies.[24] In the District, an estimated 15 percent of newborn babies have been exposed to crack cocaine while in the womb. Crack contributes heavily to the high infant mortality rate in the District. In 1987, 199 babies died and in 1988, 244 babies died as a result of fetal dependency syndrome.[25]

It is noteworthy that perhaps one-third of the city's crack addicts are low-income Black women. Increased crack use among female addicts, according to medical officials, is the real cause of the sharp increase in infant mortality rates. It is also significant to note that many drug treatment programs deny entry to women who are pregnant.

The drug crisis in the District cannot be discussed without mentioning the AIDS epidemic. As of November 1989, the District reported 1,889 AIDS cases, of whom 1,162 had died. An important trend to note is that the number of cases in the Black community continue to rise while the number in White communities have begun to decline. In 1986, Blacks accounted for 42 percent of all AIDS cases. As of 1989, this figure had risen to 58 percent.[26] This trend results partly from the differing lifestyles, incomes, and access to health care that Black gay men and White gay men receive. The "safe sex" message has been marketed more effectively to White gay men. And White gay men tend to be more open about their lifestyle, making the task of outreach easier.

Another important figure indicates that 69 percent of women AIDS patients contracted the disease from IV drug use—56 percent were IV drug users themselves and 13 percent were the partners of IV drug users. Of the total twenty-eight pediatric AIDS cases in 1989, twenty-two babies were born to IV drug users or women partnered with IV drug users.[27] Sadly enough, many of these women were simply unaware that they had contracted the AIDS virus.

While District health officials have concentrated on the AIDS problem, other sexually transmitted diseases (STDs) have also increased dramatically. In the case of the female addicts and STDs, trading sex for crack is a standard practice in the crack houses, and this multiple-partner sex is usually unprotected by the use of condoms. Syphilis cases in the District nearly quadrupled from 1985 to 1990, affecting men and women equally.

The District's Black Youth in Crisis

In the District, the infant mortality rate stands at 20.3 per 1,000 births. The drop-out rate is 40 percent in the public schools. Official unemployment is low, about 5 percent overall, and 16 percent in the Black community. Among Black and Latino poor youth, the unemployment rate is somewhere around 25 percent, lower than some major cities, but still at depression levels.[28] Consequently, the drug economy has increasingly become the principal cash-generating activity in the poor neighborhoods of the District. Rent payments, car purchases, and the provision of food and clothing for many families is completely tied to the drug trade. In the findings of a recent Rand Corporation study:

> Drug selling is clearly an important career choice and major economic activity for many Black males living in poverty in the District of Columbia. In recent years, the percentages of young Black males charged with drug selling before their 21st birthday have been alarming.... We estimated the total net earnings from street drug markets at approximately $350 million in 1988. The figure compares with total earnings from property crime—for the entire metropolitan Washington area—of $140 million to $225 million, much of which came from shoplifting. It is useful to note that Black males aged 18-40 in the District had an estimated legal

income of $1.2 billion in 1988; we estimate that $300 million in street drug earnings went to that same demographic group.[29]

Surprisingly, the Rand Report found the median yearly earnings of an adult resident dealing drugs daily at the street level to be only $24,000 net.[30] The Rand study estimates that 24,000 District residents were active street sellers in 1987, with about 14,000 "regular" drug sellers. A regular drug seller, one who sells more than one day per week, faces an annual 1.4 percent risk of being killed, a 7 percent chance of being seriously injured, and a 22 percent chance of being imprisoned. Yet such risks have failed to act as a deterrent for the substantial numbers of young males participating in the trade even on an occasional basis.

The District, lacking in traditional industry and bolstered by the huge government presence, has sometimes been described as "recession-proof." But the new jobs created in the metropolitan region require a relatively high level of education, while the quality of education in the public schools has not kept pace. Graduates of the District's schools are about two years behind the national norm in math and English skills.[31] It is therefore not surprising that some industries in the region, especially those needing a skilled workforce, are experiencing a labor shortage.

The Reign of Rayful Edmond

At the time of his arrest in 1989 at age twenty-four, Rayful Edmond III, was the most renowned and notorious drug kingpin in the history of Washington, D.C.. He reigned in some circles as a local hero who shared his riches with friends and relatives and neighbors, until his arrest on drug charges.

On December 6, 1989, Edmond was convicted of running a criminal conspiracy in the traffic of drugs, specifically of bringing hundreds of kilograms of cocaine into the Washington area, making many millions of dollars, and running one of the most significant drug trafficking operations on the East Coast. Edmond was sentenced to life without parole.

Edmond, reportedly a personable young man, advertised his success with clothes and cars. He routinely lavished gifts on his associates and sometimes on strangers or neighbors who were down and out. The owner of one fashionable store in the posh Georgetown section of the District recalled Mr. Edmond spending $1,500 to $2,000 in cash almost every two to three weeks on himself and several teenaged associates. Another store owner remembers Mr. Edmond spending $20,000 on a single shopping spree. He purchased automobiles for his associates and reportedly owned several dozen of the most expensive models.[32] Edmond gained a reputation for being 'above the law' through his innovative ability to avoid prosecution.

At his peak in the Summer of 1988, Edmond controlled a city organization generating sales of more than $2 million a week and employing more than 150 people—runners, enforcers, lieutenants, members of the Edmond family, and friends.

The police believed that Edmond's 150-member gang was responsible for more than thirty District homicides over a three year period. The slayings linked Edmond to a complex list of victims and murder suspects who subsequently became victims themselves. The motives for the deaths ranged from drug debts to attempts to control neighborhoods known to be Edmond's turf.

Edmond's activities seem to be a natural outgrowth of his family life. Federal investigators report his father gave him his first kilogram of cocaine, and his mother told a confidante in a tape-recorded conversation that Edmond was young "when she first started him out in the drug business."[33] The Edmond trial brought to light how drugs reached the street. Edmond's couriers brought brick cocaine from the West Coast to a suburban Virginia apartment, and from there into various safe houses in the District. For Edmond's organization, the cocaine came from members of Los Angeles street gangs, from Crips, and from contacts on the West Coast with the Colombian drug cartels. The cartels supply the gangs with the cocaine powder and the gangs cook it into crack and distribute it to cities throughout the United States.

The Edmond case is significant for a number of reasons. In part, it explains why for many individuals Edmond represents hope for the future. How easily inner-city youths can be attracted to a business which, while illegal and extremely risky, still pays higher dividends than would otherwise be possible, and provides access to the "finer things" in life that many of these working-class youth know they could otherwise never aspire to. It also clearly traces the relationship between the drug cartels in Colombia and American inner-city youth gangs.

In a direct way, Edmond and his organization fit the model of the Reagan era: aggressive individualism and luxury consumption. Edmond was a capitalist whose business represented one of the largest employers of Black youth and the largest Black business in the Washington area.

The arrest, trial and conviction of Rayful Edmond did not reduce the prevalence of drug dealing in Edmond's former Northeast Washington territory. Law enforcement officials say that the drug activity there was quickly divided up by more than a dozen smaller dealers. The supposed anti-drug message from these officials came down in the words of U.S. Attorney Jay Stephens, "if you are sentenced to life without parole, you die in prison."[34]

Finally, the Edmond case highlights a facet of the drug trade not receiving much notice or comment in the media or elsewhere: Despite Edmonds unlawful and harmful activities, he achieved a professional-like quality which was rooted in his desire to establish a nationwide network of Black drug dealers and money launderers.

Decline or Denial?

In April 1990, District drug czar Sterling Tucker joined national drug czar William Bennett in a press conference, where they announced "encouraging" signs about the decline of the drug epidemic in the District. Mr. Tucker suggested the decline was related in part to the District's job programs for young people: "The job programs have to be responsible for keeping some [youth] off drugs."[35] Several months after this statement was made, the Rand Corporation released its study showing that most drug dealers were also otherwise employed.[36]

This optimism was based primarily on the fact that the levels of drug use found in arrestees had been declining for about a year. Thus, the District's Office of Criminal Justice Plans and Analysis, for the year 1989, found that the percent of the District's adult arrestee population testing positive for drug use declined for the first time since the advent of drug testing, decreasing from 72 percent to 67 percent. PCP use also decreased from 33 percent in 1988 to 17 percent in 1989, and the percent of juveniles testing positive for drugs declined from 31 percent in 1988 to 24 percent in 1989. This decline is significant and, as of 1990, represents the convergence of a number of factors. One is international: It is believed that the drug cartels in Colombia are withholding drug shipments to drive prices higher. The cartels have also been involved in an intense struggle with the Colombian government. The other factors are domestic: The media campaign has perhaps had some deterrent effect, as has the experience of communities which have suffered the brunt of the epidemic. The open-air drug markets, while not eliminated, have been severely disrupted.[37]

A decline in demand and availability of drugs should not lead to complacency or an underestimation of the drug epidemic. The District of Columbia has committed more money and personnel than ever before to stopping the flow of drugs into the city. Yet law enforcement officials admit that the city's cocaine trade continues to thrive even if demand for the drug is somewhat less. The estimated 20,000 crack addicts in the District represent a hard-core demand for the drug. The

District is lacking in sufficient treatment facilities, with only 600 inpatient beds and 4,000 outpatient slots. One should also keep in mind that the many individuals now in jail as a result of the war on drugs are individuals who may still have a substance abuse problem when they emerge from incarceration.

Washington and the War on Drugs

On April 11, 1989, flanked by Attorney General Richard Thornburgh and Housing and Urban Development Secretary Jack Kemp, Drug Czar William J. Bennett, unveiled anti-drug plans for the nation's capital that he promised would make the District a test case in the war against drugs. Bennett told reporters that the District's drug problem was "as bad as it gets."[38] Citing a city "out of control," Bennett unveiled an "emergency" $80 million plan to attack the city's drug problems, with less than $1 million of this plan designated for treatment and education. Law enforcement was the main center of the plan. The plan called for the building of a new federal prison, and a new jail in the Washington area, the creation of a federal anti-drug task force to pursue "high-level traffickers," the eviction of suspected drug dealers from public housing projects and additional federal prosecutors, drug agents, and military analysts.

In discussing his plan, Bennett commented that "what should change is the right people going to jail." Bennett described the law enforcement aspects of his plan as an approach to deal with the immediate drug infestation, stating that the District government had failed to serve its citizens. Bennett indicated that the District was an embarrassment, and that criminals were subverting the public good.

The theme of blaming the District government for the drug epidemic was one of the most visible aspects of the federal government's approach during Bennett's term as national drug czar. The press conference was held without the participation of the District government officials, who weren't even invited.

The federal officials indicated that the major deficiency in the District's drug war was a lack of sufficient prison space to incarcerate the guilty. The theory behind the Bennett emphasis on law enforcement was that if enough drug dealers were removed, then the drug problem would ease because the drug kingpins would eventually run out of people willing to sell.

At the press conference, Bennett and Thornburgh also stressed that the war against drugs, in a long-term sense, is a war of values. Citizens play the key role in this larger battle through their constructive anger against drugs. The short-term need, then, is for prison space and the long-term need is for a change in values through citizen involvement.

By the end of 1989, even police officials in the District were openly critical of the Bennett approach. Chief of Police Isaac Fulwood charged that Bennett had basically spent "too much time talking and doing nothing," other than spouting rhetoric blaming District officials for the drug epidemic. Specifically, Fulwood charged that the federal government's plan for the District had underemphasized treatment for drug users and that the concentration on enforcement had done nothing to solve the crisis, noting that the District police had arrested 42,000 people, with no impact on crime. Instead, he stated that the anti-drug plans should focus on drug treatment and education.[39] Jesse Jackson, recognizing the lack of meaningful federal/local cooperation, led a delegation of local officials to the White House to press top-level Bush administration officials to undertake a regional anti-drug effort. Jackson emphasized a coordinated effort focusing on both public safety and treatment for drug users, rather than a plan focusing on crime alone.

A year after the launching the drug war in the District of Columbia, many Bush administration officials concluded that the effort to make the nation's capital a "test case" had failed, a difficult pronouncement to make, given that the drug war in the District was the first major initiative of Bennett. Federal officials attempted to blame the city for the failure and pointed to the arrest of Barry on cocaine charges as evidence of the lack of an anti-drug effort by local officials. The specific charge, put forth by anonymous officials prior to the April press conference, was that the District had money available under the Bennett anti-drug plan that had not been spent. The bulk of this money was funds for additional jail space that was never built. The construction, however, was blocked because community groups opposed such a facility in their neighborhood and not because of any intransigence on the part of District officials.

Senate conservatives have remained active in the war of words on the District. In May 1990, Senators blasted District officials for having a "permissive attitude" toward drugs and violence. Senator Gramm (R-Tex) argued, for example, that the District should be devoting a larger proportion of its resources to the criminal justice system, establishing minimum mandatory sentences, and adopting the death penalty.[40]

The stated goal of the Bennett drug war—to eliminate the drug trade in the District—has been a failure. There was an increase in drug arrests and convictions, and evictions of poor residents from federally subsidized housing projects, and more police agents were hired. The homicide rate in 1990 was even higher than in the previous record-breaking year. But a more damning statistic is that the availability of drugs in the nation's capital has not declined significantly and that the flow of drugs into the capital has continued unabated. Moreover, as a recent Rand Corporation study demonstrates, simply locking up people won't solve the problem because most drug dealers are not intimidated by the prospect of being incarcerated. The problem is not getting criminals off the streets—the District has had one of the highest incarceration rates for young Black men—but keeping others from taking their places.[41]

Bennett generated a climate of national public opinion which blames the government of the District of Columbia and its officials for a problem which is far more the responsibility of federal policy and officials. He also asserted the prerogatives of federal power over the District to make clear who really rules the District, and to send a message about the lack of feasibility of further political empowerment at the local level through statehood.

On April 13, 1990, Bennett appeared at a press conference with Sterling Tucker, to review the status of the District and federal anti-drug campaigns. A much subdued Bennett downplayed that the District was any kind of a "test case" in the war against drugs and made a point of noting the cooperation between District and federal officials.

Bennett declared Washington, D.C., a limited success. First of all, Bennett declared the federal government had done everything it "said it would." Military prosecutors were, for example, detailed to assist in federal drug cases in the District, along with various teams of law enforcement agents. He cited other achievements such as the eviction of 249 residents of crack houses and the addition of twenty-five FBI agents to the Metropolitan Washington Field Office to address drug cases. Bennett's "limited success" claim used the same statistic quoted by Sterling Tucker, that of declining drug use levels among arrestees in the District in 1989. But Bennett could not hide from the ongoing record murder rate, stating that "last year's murder rate was a bitter disappointment to all concerned."[42]

The most striking aspect of the Bennett drug plan was the fanfare surrounding the overt "bashing" of the District of Columbia, naming it a kind of "Sodom and Gommorrah and failure of liberal philosophy."

When Bennett stepped down as national drug czar on November 8, 1990, he blamed the failure to make good on his promise to defeat the District's drug problem on Mayor Barry. As a parting shot at the District and Barry, he sarcastically quipped that Barry "had a different interest in the topic [of cocaine] than mine."[43]

The District's Drug Czar

With the announcement in April 1989 by William Bennett that the Bush administration planned to make the District the national focus of a "drug war," the District of Columbia government responded in kind. Mayor Barry established a "Drug Control Policy" office, in response to the pervasive and unparalleled drug epidemic gripping the District, with the primary responsibility being "coordinating city-wide initiatives for drug interdiction, intervention, treatment and educational efforts."[44] The announced policy of the office was "zero tolerance" for dealers as well as users.

Barry announced the appointment of Sterling Tucker to head the office. Like many other prominent District politicians, Tucker came from outside Washington. Tucker came to the District in 1956 to head the local branch of the Urban League. In the 1950s, the NAACP and the Urban League were the major Black activist organizations. He worked closely with business leaders and government officials. Tucker's methods "were respectable and professional. White business leaders and government leaders by the early 1960s looked to him as a primary spokesman for the Black community."[45] Tucker was appointed to the city council by President Lyndon Johnson in 1967, and was elected as the first chairman of the council in 1974. He was defeated in the race for Mayor by Marion Barry in 1978.

Barry's appointment of Tucker to the position of drug czar was seen as an attempt by Barry to address his negative image by giving the highly visible position of local drug czar to an individual like Tucker, who retains substantial credibility, especially among the Black middle class. It was also apparent that not many individuals could be found to take the position in what was increasingly appearing to be a corrupt administration.[46]

A year after his appointment, Tucker released a series of relatively optimistic, if guarded, assessments of the war against drugs in the District. Tucker praised a number of law enforcement campaigns launched by the District in the year after the creation of his office in April 1989. "Reclaiming Our Streets," involving fourteen agencies of the District government, is a program that facilitates arrests, the towing of abandoned vehicles, and the boarding up of crack houses, as well as providing help to families and assisting with job and social service referrals. The "Not on My Block" program, described by Tucker as an outgrowth of the "Reclaiming Our Streets" program, encourages citizens to sign up on a block-by-block basis to participate in the same activities of the "Reclaiming Our Streets" efforts.

Tucker also praised joint law enforcement work undertaken by the District's Metropolitan Police Department and the U.S. Drug Enforcement Agency Task Force in making arrests, seizing drugs, vehicles and weapons, and recovering stolen property. The District Drug Czar reported that the District in 1989 had seized over $25 million in vehicles, illegal drugs, real estate property, weapons, and other assets. In his statement, however, Tucker was obliged to admit that there were no "significant changes in crime rates at this time."[47]

Although Tucker touted community involvement in anti-drug efforts, many of the community groups listed in the "Reclaiming Our Streets" or "Not on My Block" projects were short-lived. As Washington Post columnist Courtland Milloy commented: "Fed-up citizens with orange hats and walkie-talkies keep most of the alleyways and side streets clear, but at best they're just moving the drug trade around, not making the impact Tucker believes them to be."[48] Boasting about the closing down of crack houses, he adds, has little effect when the District's Alcohol and Drug Abuse Services Administration (ADASA) cannot provide figures for how many addicts have been helped to recovery.

These projects are not unique to the District of Columbia. Cities such as Philadelphia and Jacksonville, Florida, have with some success targeted multi-faceted anti-drug efforts in a given neighborhood.[49] However, these community groups are motivated by positive response and, even if they are short-lived (sometimes precisely because they succeed in moving out the drug traffic) they are useful in promoting a sense of community solidarity and a message of disapproval for drugs. Most of the community groups were not, however, initiated by the Office of Drug Control Policy—rather, they were spontaneous efforts. And some community anti-drug activists were openly critical of Tucker for appearing to claim credit for the formation of the groups. Leroy Thorpe, founder and president of Citizens Organized Patrol Efforts of Greater Washington, D.C. (COPE), criticized Tucker's work as "ineffective."[50]

Tucker's main activity was to assemble a high-level committee of local judges; law-enforcement officials; education, health, and family experts; and private citizens to make recommendations for a comprehensive approach to the drug problem. The committee's reports were very uneven. However, they did recognize that much of what must be done does not require new legislation but, rather, more effective implementation of current laws and better utilization of resources.

One questionable recommendation is that the driver's licenses and business and professional licenses of people convicted of drug offenses, including conviction for possession, should be revoked. This revocation would cover everyone from plumbers and cab drivers to attorneys. It seems dubious that removing someone's ability to earn a living will help solve the drug epidemic.

The panels functioned with a number of progressive assumptions, noting, for example, that viable employment options need to be expanded in order to win the minds and hearts of our children, our youth, and our families. Enemies in the drug war are seen as, among other things, lack of knowledge about the corrosive effects of drugs, lack of successful role models for young people in the inner city, and the lure of a "big money" lifestyle.

The reports are also replete with many suggestions for increasing staff and funding for existing support programs for women and children, and calling for new programs. For example, the recommendations concerning "pregnant substance abusers and their unborn children" call for increased Medicaid eligibility and social welfare support; the creation of a referral network for resources available to patients, institutions, and agencies; and staffing for a women's service clinic, which would focus on health and psychological treatment. Some of these are federal programs, such as Medicaid, over which the District government has little or no control.

Yet by the panels' own admission, the District has woefully inadequate treatment availability (with an estimated 17,000 intravenous drug users, ADASA has about 4,000 treatment slots), and it is difficult to speak of drug abstinence before such treatment facilities exist. The reports appear more in the nature of a "wish list" for an ideal society—or for the mayoral administration of Sharon Pratt Dixon which took office in January 1990—rather than a concrete battle plan for the immediate problem at hand. What became evident along the way was that some of the recommendations, such as treatment on demand, would become watered down to meet fiscal limitations.[51]

One other city official played a prominent role for several years in the anti-drug battle. Reed Tuckson, a medical doctor and commissioner of public health in the late 1980s until he resigned in frustration at the difficulties of working with the city administration, was one of a number of top-level city officials who departed the Barry administration as the former mayor's scandals mounted during the late 1980s.

The energetic Tuckson gained a national reputation for his work in attacking the health aspects of the drug crisis, and for treating the drug crisis as a health issue. Tuckson advocated the concept that the drug war should really be treated as a public health issue.

Tuckson was an energetic critic of the city for its policy of spending relatively less money fighting social problems such as AIDS and more money on law enforcement. He earned a great deal of respect in the District for his efforts because, in the words of one District official, "it was obvious to people that he cared deeply about the problems."[52] As the city's main body charged with addressing the drug problem, ADASA provides assessment, counseling, treatment inpatient and outpatient services, and prevention assistance. Most ADASA patients have no means to pay for the services rendered. It is the primary source of treatment of those from the criminal justice system. The philosophy of ADASA is to provide patients with the services and resources that will motivate them to arrest and keep in remission their substance dependence, and to develop a positive lifestyle. According to ADASA's Kwesi Rollins, although treatment workers function under many kind of treatment theories, the traditional "12 step" program in substance abuse is central to all of these theories.[53]

Data from ADASA from 1984 to 1988 show that ADASA admissions are predominantly Black men, with about 30 percent being Black women. Referrals from the criminal justice system account for about half of all the ADASA admissions. These individuals do not appear to have the same commitment to recovery as the voluntary admissions, and, in addition, there are a great many addicts who have not become desperate enough to seek treatment.[54]

Treatment workers at ADASA have found that addicts who come to the city's twenty-two treatment centers are plagued with a variety of circumstances "that might represent both the cause and effect of their addictions. Homelessness, joblessness, poor health, unstable family relationships and unsuccesful attempts at being drug-free are but a few of these."[55]

The Community Fights Back

Washington, D.C., neighborhoods, in common with other U.S. urban centers, have long experienced crime problems. There were anti-drug marches in the decades of the 1960s and 1970s. But nothing has compared to the present drug-dealing, muggings, assaults, and homicides. Although media attention has focused on areas with the heaviest drug trafficking and violence, that violence has also impacted many other areas of the city.

These problems have generated a number of different anti-drug efforts from community groups. One of the best known efforts has been organized by the Nation of Islam's Muslim Patrols. The group was dubbed "The Dopebusters" by a local Black newspaper.

The Dopebusters, the local affiliation of Minister Louis Farrakhan's Nation of Islam, opened a mosque several blocks from the Mayfair Mansions apartment complex in Washington, which along with a neighboring complex, the Paradise Manor, numbers about 7,000 residents. The complex of apartments used to be a residence for the city's aspiring Black middle class forty years ago. In the 1960s and 1970s, the upwardly mobile began to integrate other areas of the District. Several years ago, the area became one of the worst drug and crime-infested areas of the District.

Armed with walkie-talkies and dressed in their customary suits and bow ties, the Muslims began patrolling the buildings and ridding them of drugs and drug dealers. These patrols were conducted on a twenty-four-hour basis.

The Dopebusters are led by Dr. Abdul Alim Muhammad, a physician who also operates a medical clinic in the Paradise Manor complex, including drug counseling services. Muhammad holds the position once held by Malcolm X and Louis Farrakhan, that of national spokesman for the Nation of Islam.

The initial campaign of the Muslims created a big stir in the area media when Gary Hankins, the White leader of one of the police unions, and others questioned whether the Muslims constituted a kind of "paramilitary force" handling functions that ought to be addressed by the police. Questions arose especially when the patrols had a scuffle with suspected dealers.

Controversy was greatly heightened when the city council passed a resolution honoring the anti-drug work of the Dopebusters which, in one clause of one sentence, also spoke favorably of the political vision of the Nation of Islam. The controversy was sparked by public protests from a number of prominent organizations, most notably some of the city's mainstream Jewish groups. These protests were blanket critiques of the city council for passing a resolution addressing an activity of the Nation of Islam. They did not address the anti-drug work of the Muslim group nor actually proffer much of a critique of the Nation, other than to note concern over past anti-Semitic rhetoric.

The work of the Dopebusters is of interest for what it tells us about strategies to fight the drug crisis. The Dopebusters have demonstrated the importance of a multi-tiered approach to tackling the drug problem. In addition to the physical patrols mounted by the Muslims, the Muslims undertake a wide range of other activities as well, including the conveyance of a sense of worth and a sense of values. They also assist the elderly with chores, escort children to school, operate a full-service medical clinic which includes a drug-treatment component and counseling for the apartment-complex-residents.[56]

Dr. Muhammad points out that the Muslims rid the complex of drugs and crime without spending a single penny. He says: "Maybe the federal government should look at programs that are working like ours. ...I believe that a solution to this national drug problem is in our midst. The answer may be in the least expected place."[57] Dr. Muhammad, subsequent to the successful Dopebusters campaign, ran an unsuccessful race for Congress in nearby Prince Georges County, Maryland, a district that is 50 percent Black, and is represented by White Democratic Party liberal Steny Hoyer. The race was significant since it represented the first entry in electoral politics by the Nation of Islam.

Average citizens are taking up the drug battles in the District as they are across the nation, often spontaneously, sometimes in cooperation with police. The Fairlawn Coalition in Southeast Washington, for example, is one of several neighborhoods in the District to mount nightly citizen anti-drug patrols over the past few years. The Fairlawn Coalition patrols have succeeded in scaling down the open-air drug markets that have plagued the neighborhood. The Coalition relies on foot patrols of groups of citizens who are unarmed, their only weapon being that of nonviolent confrontation. They quietly stare dealers away. The Fairlawn Coalition activists have been threatened, and some have been hit by eggs and rocks, but police officials feel the activity is generally safe when people work in groups. District Police Chief Issac Fulwood states that: "As a general rule, retaliation does not happen....The drug dealer is not as brave as we've made him out to be. We've given him too much credit. He's a bad-ass guy when he catches you in the dark. He's not as bad when you shine the light on him."[58]

Similarly, citizens in the historic Shaw neighborhood of Northwest Washington have begun an anti-drug crusade—Citizens Organized Patrol Efforts (COPE). COPE organized its first anti-drug march in the District on December 11, 1988. During the 1950s, the Shaw neighborhood was a residential and meeting place for much of the District's Black middle class. But by the late 1960s, with the breakdown in segregation and the dislocation caused by the riots following the assassination of Dr. Martin Luther King, Jr., much of this presence left the neighborhood. The neighborhood anti-drug patrol in Shaw grew out of monthly marches and anti-drug rallies. Organizers shut down a number of crack houses and drove the open-air drug market out of the Shaw neighborhood.

These types of citizen patrols have effectively rid neighborhood sectors of blatant street dealing. These programs are typical of efforts around the country. They involve neighbors writing down license plate numbers of drivers buying drugs, telling police of alleged drug dealers, tearing down abandoned buildings that were used as crack houses, as well as the creation of an anti-drug program including education, treatment, neighborhood patrols, youth activities, parental skills training, and counseling. A lot of these tactics involve time-tested family values, stressing family, education, personal achievement, and sometimes church involvement.

Washington officials, the District's former drug czar Sterling Tucker, and the police have called for increased citizen involvement in the war against drugs. For conservatives like former national drug czar William Bennett, this type of citizen involvement is seen as an adequate substitute to institutionalizing more just and progressive government policies.

One problem with these and the many other "neighborhood watch" programs is that they disband, often within months of forming. In addition, they can only move dealers from one location to another, rather than eliminating the dealing altogether. Only a small number of citizen patrols are actually formed, and residents are frequently inhibited by fear, the lack of swift police response, and the difficulty in providing logistical support to groups that do form.

Under the city's Neighborhood Watch program, the Police Department organizes a city block when a substantial number of residents sign a petition agreeing to take part. Police meet with the group, give them basic information and training on how to identify drug activity and transactions, as well as numbers to call when activity is spotted. Many of these residents subsequently report the activity to police. The head of the District's Police Department community relations division estimates that about one-half of the blocks listed as organized Neighborhood Watch programs are, in fact, inactive.[59]

Community relations police officers do not have sufficient staff to go on meeting with groups. Also, residents participating in the anti-drug tips often complain that: their calls—reporting tips on routine drug activity—are treated as non-emergency and hence pushed down the priority list by police dispatchers. One Neighborhood Watch coordinator complained: that "You call police because you need them, and nine times out of ten, you need them right away. Very seldom does it happen that way...Some people quit calling."[60]

Impact of Barry's Arrest and Trial

The ten-week Marion Barry trial on drug and perjury charges transfixed Washington during the Summer of 1990 and heightened racial tensions in the city. Its larger importance lies in showing Barry as representative of leaders increasingly unable to deliver empowerment and improvement in the lives of Black Americans.

Sentiment in the District about Barry's arrest in January 1990 and his subsequent trial and conviction, along with the role of the federal government in bringing Barry to trial, was split. The verdict seemed to reflect the community's own entangled sentiments over the Barry trial. Strong disapproval of the federal government's prosecution was expressed amongst most Blacks and a minority of Whites. The trial from this point of view was seen as a graphic example of entrapment and selective prosecution of Black elected officials. On the other hand, most people, Blacks as well as Whites, felt that Barry should not continue to hold public office.

Reverend Jesse Jackson called the trial part of "an ugly pattern of White judicial leadership attacking Black political leadership." NAACP Executive Director Benjamin Hooks sharply criticized the "selective prosecution of Black officials." Hooks stated that the feeling of disparate scrutiny goes back at least thirty years to the days of Representative Adam Clayton Powell (D-N.Y.): "Even if…the government spent only $4 million on this investigation, that figure seems excessive in the pursuit of recreational drug abuse, which is the essence of the government's case.…America would make a grave mistake, and a sad one, to assume that Black America will stand idly by and let James Crow, Esquire, continue his grandfather's legacy in a more subtle and crafty way."[61]

Hook's comments were typical of the approach of many, including much of the local Black press and establishment, who chose to focus only on the role of the federal government. These individuals tended to excuse the behavior of Marion Barry, and even contributed to his political strategy by lending credibility to exaggerated rumors such as the cost of Barry's trial. Federal officials were cagey about the costs, which primarily served to fuel suspicions—some put it at under several million dollars. But Barry supporters in the local Black media set the figure at about $40 million, a figure that even Barry's attorney R. Kenneth Mundy rejected as grossly exaggerated after the verdict.

By contrast, other Black leaders were critical of the role of the federal government but were also willing to critically examine the contributions of the ex-Mayor to the larger goals of Black empowerment. Roger Wilkins, a history professor at George Mason University in Virginia, and a senior fellow at the Institute of Policy Studies, noted that: "We must have standards in the Black community. This is a racist society, and it will be for a long time to come. That people make racist attacks on certain Black people does not absolve those who have been attacked of behaving decently and keeping their human commitments."

Wilkins pointed out that the Black Power movement of the 1960s was aimed at service to the community. In an implicit reference to the former mayor, he wrote: "The Civil Rights Movement...didn't mean sleazy networking by Black politicians and their circling sharks. It meant lifetimes devoted to nurturing Black people, developing strong institutions and struggling to change the prevailing values of the society."[62]

Ultimately Barry's own defense to the prosecution—a public relations effort—seemed to have brought a good deal of success. Barry suggested in an interview with *The Washington Post* that the government tried to "kill him" by letting him in the Vista sting operation ingest a potent amount of the crack drug.[63] Prosecutors in the Barry trial found themselves having to deny allegations that the FBI had an assault force of FBI agents roaming the country targeting Black elected officials. Barry's defense attorney had charged that the lead FBI agent in the Barry sting operation moves around the country in sting operations against Black elected officials, that several women friends of Barry's had been offered money to participate in a sting operation, and that several FBI women agents had refused to participate as well.[64]

Actually, Barry had no alternative other than to go to trial, because the prosecuting U.S. attorney, Jay Stephens, refused to plea bargain on a felony perjury charge. This was the felony charge which could have put Barry in jail and prevented him from holding public office. Attempts by Barry to plea bargain on misdemeanor charges in return for the dropping of the more serious charges fell on deaf ears.

Washington's Contradiction Heightened

Whites were overwhelmingly critical of Barry. *The Washington Post,* which called for Barry to resign, was regarded by some Blacks as a collaborator with a powerful federal establishment bent on destroying Black political power in the District. *The Post* declared that "the mayor of Washington has been convicted on a drug charge. The trial should be remembered, not forgotten, for the record it established. It was a useful—even essential—examination of evidence that the mayor was involved with illegal drugs."[65]

Howard University sociologist Joyce Ladner noted that on the day the videotape of Barry smoking crack was shown, Blacks were visibly upset or sad, whereas at least some Whites seemed gleeful. Tensions were increased by the initial attempt, of presiding Judge Thomas Penfield Jackson to keep Nation of Islam leader Louis Farrakhan and maverick Black priest George Stallings out of the courtroom under the argument they would "intimidate" the jurors. Jackson was prompted by a higher court to reverse this attempt, while Farrakhan described the judge's attempt to ban him as part of the double standard historically imposed upon Blacks in the USA.[66]

There was also a weariness about the trial in the metropolitan Washington region. Many residents wanted to put the trial behind them, and opinion remained divided, frequently by race, over the propriety of the jury's actions. Only about 52 percent said they were satisfied with the outcome; 45 percent thought the prosecution was racially motivated; 31 percent thought Barry should do time in jail. Others, such as columnist Roger Wilkins and Howard University sociologist Alvin Thornton, argued that the controversy had diverted public opinion from issues of long-term concern to the Black community—education and health care.[67]

Not surprisingly, Barry's judicial "victory" was assailed by the press and by public opinion in South America. Colombians expressed outrage over the Barry verdict while they were putting their lives on the line in the battle against the drug cartels.[68]

Most did not literally believe Barry to be innocent of the charges. The majority Black jury, for example, did not believe Barry to be innocent of drug use. But Barry's guilt or innocence did not become the issue in the trial. Among Blacks, many blamed him for the negative consequences of the trial. At one extreme, Vernon Jordan claimed that cries of racism were misguided and that any public official would have been treated the same as Marion Barry. At the other was Nation of Islam activist Abdul Alim Muhammad, who described the news media covering the trial as "no better than some gang of rednecked, tobacco-chewing Ku Klux Klan members."[69]

Perhaps one of the most remarkable aspects of the Barry trial was the transformation that Black opinion underwent during the trial. Immediately after the arrest of Barry in January 1990, a substantial number of Blacks were angry with the Mayor. That anger persisted and was manifested again when Barry ran for city council against the desires of about 70 percent of the electorate and subsequently received only about 20 percent of the vote in that election. But during the trial, the real issue became not Barry but the conduct of the federal government and the historical legacy of Black oppression.

For many Whites, Black support of Barry during the trial seemed inexplicable. *The Washington Post* posed the following question: " What is going on here? The mayor of the nation's capital, which also happens to be an American drug capital, is facing multiple drug-related charges. Yet he can walk into the D.C. Convention center and nearly upstage Nelson Mandela. What is the Marion Barry mystique? ...when Barry appears at Black churches and rallies in D.C., he receives a hero's welcome, and many Black leaders nationwide rally to his cause."[70]

The trial and the accompanying question of whether Barry would run for re-election as mayor created a certain disarray in local politics—along with his final decision to run again for political office in the at-large city council election, a decision that put him at odds with long-time council progressive Hilda Mason, co-chair of the 2,500-member independent Statehood Party. The arrest and trial of Barry also created paralysis within the government, complicated by a budget deficit estimated at approximately $90 million.

Marion Barry was a product of the Civil Rights movement. Born in Mississippi, Barry attended Fisk University in Memphis and went on to become one of the leaders of the Student Non-violent Coordinating Committee, one of the most dynamic and militant youth movements in American history. The goals of that movement, an end to legalized segregation and the granting of the voting franchise to Black people, were largely achieved. The strategy of that movement—to pressure the Democratic Party, government establishment, and corporations into granting concessions—was effective in achieving those goals. Barry gained political office in the late 1960s on the wave of popular sentiment in support of the goals of the Civil Rights movement.

In building support during the trial, Barry allied himself with nationalist leaders such as Louis Farrakhan and Rev. George Stallings, and relied on a nationalistic rhetoric of racial solidarity. Barry's manipulation of this symbolism helped to enlist the sympathies of many Blacks in the city, and helped to distract attention from the fact that only a few months before, Barry was calling for a crackdown on drug users and holding himself forth as a model for young children.

The problem with Barry's approach was that behind the rhetoric there was no progressive program of any sort, no qualitative resolution to the crises of Black poverty, education, drugs, inequality, and unemployment. While his initial election in 1978 shook up the city's old power structure with Black activism, he also built strong ties to White real estate developers over the years, using his zoning and taxing powers to achieve dramatic downtown redevelopment. These ties were believed to be a factor in Barry's opposition to rent control in 1985 and his spotty record in support of such core economic issues as housing reform and expanded higher education. It became a truism in the District that Barry over the years had become less and less interested in a civil rights agenda. It seemed ultimately to many that Marion Barry's main agenda was simply staying in power.

Whereas Barry had consistently expressed during the trial concern about the well-being of his family and the need to take more time for his family and personal life (his wife, Effi Barry, admitted in an interview that Barry had not had dinner with his family in his twelve years in office more than a half-dozen times) there was little in his announcement after the trial or in his decision to run again for public office in the Fall of 1990 that seemed to take these factors into account. Nor was there a great sense from Barry that he had much to regret concerning the long ordeal that he had a central role in creating for the city. Speaking to a crowd of cheering followers the day after the verdict, Barry asked for forgiveness for any hurt "he may have caused." Even after the results of the September 1990 Democratic Party primary, where Barry opponent Sharon Pratt Dixon routed her rivals in a victory seen as part of an anti-Barry backlash, Barry seemed determined to press forward with his political career.

Barry's main strategy in the Fall 1990 general election for an at-large city council seat was to seek support by portraying himself as the victim of federal government discrimination. Barry blamed racism for his defeat in that election.[71]

In addition to raising questions about the strategy to prevent or discourage drug usage—should casual users of cocaine be imprisoned?—Barry's long trial also damaged the city's credibility with Congress. Barry's problems gave ammunition to the enemies of statehood.

The trial also brought into the spotlight some of the glaring inequities created by lack of statehood. The fact that the District's judicial process is dominated by federal appointees was brought into focus by the trial. All District judges are appointed by the President and all felonies are prosecuted by the office of the U.S. Attorney General. One Black paper in the District editorialized: "Why does the District have to have an outside political appointee, who does not reflect the thinking nor the race of the predominant culture of the District, to render justice in this city?"[72]

Lessons from the District's Drug Wars

The experience of the District of Columbia with regard to the drug wars is significant for the nation from a number of vantage points: as a Black-majority city and center of Black political power; as the nation's capital and hence a major urban, administrative, and political center; as a center of democracy whose citizens lack national voting representation; and as the experiment for the federal government's anti-drug policies.

Even though drugs are used throughout various class and racial strata, it is clear that the crack epidemic in the Washington, D.C., region has disproportionately impacted upon the poor and minority communities of the District. The 400-plus murders, the hundreds of addicted and abandoned crack babies in the public hospitals, the 20,000 cocaine addicts in a city with a maximum of 5,000 treatment spots, an incarceration rate exceeding that of any state, are some of the indicators of this crisis. Less in immediate evidence but no less important is the destruction that the crisis has wreaked on the extended-family structure.

This disproportionate impact is a national theme. The battle against drugs has, in spite of Mr. Bennett's description of the typical drug user as being White and middle-class, become centered in Black communities around the nation. In an interview with the authors of this book in Washington, D.C., on October 4, 1990, national drug czar assistant Reggie Walton was asked to explain this discrepancy. Mr. Walton replied that it was easier for police to spot and apprehend dealers operating on street corners in the poorer Black neighborhoods of the District than it was to infiltrate the parties and social events where drugs are used in the more fashionable and predominantly White neighborhoods.[73]

The drug epidemic in the District has also allowed the enemies of Black and progressive empowerment an opening to blame Blacks for the social ills that beset all urban communities. The drug-related scandals plaguing former Mayor Marion Barry allowed conservatives and others to set back the drive for statehood, to disparage the fledgling Home Rule in the city, and to deepen racial and class schisms in the city.

The experience of the District as a "model" for the national anti-drug policies of President Bush demonstrates the absolute futility of a strategy which relies exclusively on law enforcement. In spite of an increase in arrests, convictions, and incarceration, the drug crisis continues. Drug-driven homicides continue at record levels, and the presence of drugs in the District remains. Decline in the use of drugs could be explained by a number of factors other than increased enforcement. Chief of Police Fulwood has added his voice to a growing consensus around the nation that the drug war cannot be won by the police and the prisons, and that emphasis must be placed on the social and economic roots of the problem. But these voices have not been heard by the Bush administration.

The federal emphasis on enforcement seems all the more misplaced when viewed in the context of the criminalization of District youth and the concomitant attacks on civil liberties. The city council passed a number of laws aimed at curbing the drug trade by emphasizing mandatory minimum sentences for drug offenses and youth curfews in declared drug zones. Similar actions have been taken elsewhere in the nation, as in Atlanta where police have set up roadblocks at the entrance to the city's housing projects.[74]

At the same time, white-collar launderers of drugs, such as local bank officials not held accountable for accepting thousands of dollars in drug monies, go unconvicted. By not investing more in the "front end" of society, such as by creating better schools and more employment opportunities, it is evident that our national policies are creating a whole generation of "throw away" youth. This loss of human resources is a national tragedy, especially at a time when the United States needs all the resources it can muster to remain competitive economically.

The drug policy office in the District, established for a variety of reasons, including the poor image of the city under Mayor Marion Barry, generated a number of local studies emphasizing these root causes. However, these reports lacked any proposals about how costly new programs, such as treatment on demand, might be paid for. When the Dixon administration assumed power in January 1991, the District's drug office was eliminated and merged into the mayor's staff. Urban administrations require some kind of office or focus on the drug problem, if only to coordinate regional anti-drug efforts. The lack of such an office in Atlanta brought criticism to that city's anti-drug efforts.[75]

A real war on drugs emphasizing the social and economic roots will cost a lot of money. This is no secret to officials on the front lines of the anti-drug struggle. In Los Angeles, for example, where it is estimated that fully one-half of the nation's cocaine comes from, these officials have been waging a public campaign to enable the city to gain access to special federal aid monies.[76]

Much of this federal money can only come from the sources where we as a nation waste money on a monumental scale, such as the military. But we must do better in our cities as well, even with our constricted resources. Community health workers in San Francisco have helped reduce the AIDS rate even for those intravenous drug users who decline to seek governmental or private aid. These workers pass out bottles of bleach to sterilize needles, distribute condoms, and simply talk with street people about the dangers of AIDS.[77]

Some people argue that the District government, with a city workforce of 50,000 in a city with a total population of about 600,000, is a bloated bureaucracy. There is some truth to these concerns. In the case of the public school system, for example (by no means the most inefficient government agency), expenditures on administration versus instruction are higher than that of eight of nine comparable urban school districts.[78] Cutting this bloat should result in better services and free up more resources.

The major source of funding from the anti-drug war must come from elsewhere. The federal government should, on a formula basis, pay the District a fair amount for the services (water, sewage, police, fire, roads, etc.) that it renders on the 50 percent of District land that is federally occupied. Suburban commuters who utilize these same services should also be willing to pay a commuter tax. Lawyers, accountants, and other professionals, some of whom have been able to earn six-figure incomes in the District, should be willing to return some of their gains to the city that made their riches possible, in the form of a professional tax. It has been estimated that funding from the above sources could generate more than $1 billion in new District resources.[79]

Residents of the District of Columbia pay some of the highest per capita taxes in the nation (among states, only Wyoming and Alaska pay more). Additional resources for the drug war ought not to come from these hard-working, over-taxed citizens. Yet the District's fiscal policies are intimately linked to policies that favor the wealthy. A 1988 study showed a gross underassessment of commercial properties in the District of Columbia, a phenomenon made possible by inequitable tax formulas and by wealthy developers hiring law firms to overwhelm the city's tax assessing bureaucracy with legal complaints.[80]

The challenge to local progressives seeking to fund a real war on drugs is to raise the fairness and equity question with respect to taxation. Cries for austerity in a time of economic recession, such as the District and the nation are experiencing at the time of the writing of this book, have a class and race bias when the cuts focus mainly or exclusively on eliminating the jobs of government workers. Anti-drug programs and promises will cost money—the question is who will pay for them.

The Future for the District

Since the early days of Home Rule, politics in the District had been dominated by Marion Barry. With Barry's departure from the mayor's office, a new scramble began for control of the city. Two key political and progressive institutions in the city, churches and labor unions, found themselves divided about the mayoral and other candidates. In the 1990 elections in the District, incumbent candidates fared very badly. Marion Barry gave up his seat of mayor in an unsuccessful bid for city council, and congressional delegate of nineteen years Walter Fauntroy and city council chairman David Clarke each lost in their bid's to capture the mayor's seat.

The winner of the 1990 mayoral race was Sharon Pratt Dixon. Dixon was not the political novice portrayed in the media. A former treasurer of the national Democratic Party, she had consistently been in last place during the election but won on the strength of an anti-Barry vote and a promise to make significant changes in local government. The other leading post in District politics, the non-voting delegate seat vacated by Walter Fauntroy, was captured by Eleanor Holmes Norton, a former civil rights activist and chair of the Equal Employment Opportunity Commission under President Carter. Jesse Jackson meanwhile won election to his first elected seat when he captured one of the newly created elected statehood lobbying positions popularly referred to as "shadow senators." Although the position was not thought to be a politically weighty one, Jackson would bring his considerable talents and energies to bear on behalf of statehood and other issues.

With regard to the drug issue, Dixon, Norton, and Jackson all ran with a similar position on the drug issue: the drug problem cannot be "arrested away" and the drug war needs to shift from enforcement and address the root causes. Mayor Dixon in particular, in charge of the city's $3.2 billion budget, faced considerable challenges about how to fund a progressive war on drugs in the face of shrinking city revenues and a relatively stagnated federal payment. Promising to govern and actually governing were two different tasks. Her challenge is similar to that facing elected officials in urban centers around the country: how to reconcile campaign promises such as "treatment on demand" with the actual fiscal difficulties of the city.

Part III

A Different Path

White House and sometimes of members of Congress. In a world only a few years shy of the twenty-first century, where potential peaceful cooperation exists between West and East for the first time since World War II, the drug-dealing allies of the United States deserve no support and must be exposed and punished. Given the CIA's legacy of duplicity and deceit, it may be time to think of abolishing the agency all together or, minimally, redefining its mission in today's world.

Local communities have an important role in ending the drug problem. Protestors who demand more law enforcement should also demand community-based treatment centers and alternative sentencing for first-time drug offenders. Activists engaged in exposing the exploitative economic and political role of the United States internationally should organize at the community level. This will help community groups develop the basis with which to pressure their elected officials to support economic and political reform in the Third World—the best chance for ending the supply of illegal drugs to the United States.

Many progressive activists, who have supported calls for economic democracy and an end to the racist assaults of the drug war, have been peripheral to the day-to-day drug issues that local communities are attempting to address. Progressives need to combine their vision of broad social reform with concrete programs and organizational vehicles for change at the local level. The two perspectives are not mutually exclusive.

Numerous community-based groups are desperately seeking skilled (and unskilled) volunteers to bring fresh insights into the issues they face. These groups already have defined specific objectives in the communities where they can potentially have a great impact. Networking among these groups through meetings, conferences, and newsletters are only some of the ways that progressives external to the community could contribute their skills and resources. The following recommendations are synthesized from the views of activists, professionals, and concerned individuals who are fighting to end drug trafficking and abuse while also building a just and equitable world.

Supply-Side Options

To stop importation of illegal drugs into the United States, egalitarian economic development, social opportunity, and political reform must be created in the Third World. Until the peasants and workers in countries that export to the United States are given a real alternative to illegal crop production, no amount of eradication or interdiction will be even moderately successful. The have-nots of the Third World must be given the resources to go (and grow) in a new direction. A number of suggestions have been put forth by the international community that, if adopted, would have an immediate impact on drug trafficking.

Purchase Coca Leaves and Opium Crops

Peru's foreign minister at the United Nations, Guillermo Larco-Cox, made a three-part proposal to deal with the drug problem in the developing world. He suggested that first the West decriminalize drugs to eliminate the illegal trade. Second, he proposed that farmers be given an alternative to growing coca leaves and opium. Finally, he recommended that the United States purchase the illegal crops.[1]

The Interethnic Association for the Development of the Peruvian Forest (AIDESEP), made up of eighteen Indian organizations, also recommends that the United States purchase coca leaves at a higher price than dealers as tradeoff for the billions that the United States already gives in aid and anti-drug funds. They say that surplus funds can be used to develop alternative crops, build the nation's infrastructure, provide security for farm regions, increase basic social services to rural areas, and expand educational opportunities. The Association estimates that such a program would cost about $3 billion for both Peru and Bolivia.[2]

The United States, which already spends billions on fruitless interdiction and eradication efforts, could purchase crops directly from the farmers in the drug producing countries that grow them. Although some drug growing areas are inaccessible due to civil war or other factors, in many nations growing coca leaves or opium is legal and farmers are organized into cooperatives or unions. The problem is that the overwhelming amount of these crops are diverted to the illegal market.

There is a precedent for AIDESEP's proposed action. In March 1970, the United States paid Turkey $3 million to stop growing opium and shift to other crops. Within a year, Turkey reported that its opium growing provinces had dropped from twenty-one to four. Later, however, the actual acreage under opium production increased by 5,000 acres. At the time, the United States also gave Turkey about $100 million in military and economic aid. In June 1971, an agreement was reached where the United States would pay Turkey $100 million dollars over a three-year period, beginning in 1973, to encourage farmers not to grow opium. The figure was later reduced to $35 million.[3]

End Fruitless Eradication Efforts

Efforts to end eradication have failed miserably. As the House Committee on Government Operations concluded, a new direction is needed on the part of the United States in ending drug trafficking in

Bolivia and Peru. Instead of getting rid of drugs, U.S. policies have promoted corruption, thievery, lack of enthusiasm, peasant resistance, diversion of funds to anti-guerilla activities, and murder.

Aerial sprays and biological weapons used to eliminate the coca fields threaten the environment and people of the area more than the production of coca leaves. This lesson should have been learned in the Nixon era. The Nixon administration supported the biological development of a "screw worm" that would devour poppy crops.[4] The Department of Agriculture's Stoneville, Mississippi, laboratories actually created several mutations of weevils in an effort to create this creature. Poppy crops were planted in Louisiana and Arizona to test the bug. Only when it became clear that the screw worm was not "host-specific," that is, it was not limited to eating poppy fields, was the idea dropped.[5]

Amazingly, the Bush administration revisited this idea in 1990. The Department of Agriculture was attempting to develop coca-eating caterpillars that would devour the coca leaf crops of Peru and Bolivia. The idea was to study the Malumbia moth, which eats coca leaves in its caterpillar state, and to develop a more voracious and ravenous variety of it. President Bush had requested $6.5 million dollars for this dubious effort. Needless to say, the governments of Peru and Bolivia rejected the idea.[6]

End "Zero Tolerance" Interdiction

> I would say interdiction has probably improved tenfold. Unfortunately, production has grown twentyfold.
>
> —Former Customs Commissioner William Von Raab[7]

Interdiction has not worked. Billions of dollars have been wasted in a fruitless effort to stop drugs from entering the United States. In Fiscal Year 1988, interdiction cost about $1.04 billion in federal dollars alone.[8] According to the Coast Guard, despite spending about $1 billion annually, only 5 to 7 percent of heroin and cocaine entering the United States is seized.[9] In 1988, the U.S. Navy/Coast Guard, sailing for a combined 2,347 ship-days at a cost of $40 million, caught a mere seventeen ships and eighty smugglers.[10]

Florida has an 8,246-mile coastline that is virtually impossible to guard. The United States has 60,000 square miles of ocean on its coastline and contiguous territorial waters which, in effect, can not be protected short of a massive war-ready armada on twenty-four hour alert.[11] Federal efforts along this line, such as Operations Intercept and Alliance that attempted to search every vehicle crossing the Mexican border, have seized few drugs from professional smugglers and caused unacceptable and unpopular delays.

Traffickers have demonstrated an amazing capacity to evade enforcement tactics. When the Coast Guard increased its efforts to stop the big boats that smuggled marijuana into southern Florida, for example, traffickers switched to using the larger boats as "mother ships" that would load the drugs onto smaller, faster, and less conspicuous boats. The average seizure fell from an average 9 tons in 1978 to 4.6 tons in 1986.[12] Drugs can be smuggled into the United States in countless ways. Drugs have been smuggled in roses, frozen food pulp, lumber, and in just about any commodity that is imported to the United States[13]

A statistical model built by researchers at the Rand Corporation concluded that "improved interdiction will have little impact on U.S. cocaine consumption." Increased seizures would not force such an exorbitant rise in domestic prices for cocaine that consumers would be discouraged from buying. Dealer-created increases were noted in 1990 as dealers attempted to persuade consumers that the drug war was affecting their supplies, thereby forcing an increase in price. The hustle did not last long, as other dealers realized that they could undersell the holdouts and still make a large profit.[14] Clearly, interdiction functions more as a lucrative part of the drug industry rather than as a succesful method of detterence.

Provide Stronger Oversight and Penalties on Chemical Exports

In the Anti-Drug Abuse Act of 1988, measures were included that addressed the problem of precursor chemicals being diverted from the legal market to the illegal drug market. Enforcement continues to be lax, however, and there appears to be little reduction in access to these chemicals by illegal drug manufacturers. The government should impose higher penalties and greater regulation of export for these chemicals.

End the Criminalization of Inner-City Youth

On the domestic side, the administration's war on drugs, which has consisted mainly of attempts to stop the street trafficking of crack cocaine, quickly emerged as a war aimed at the Black community. Like the targets of previous U.S. wars and "police actions," the Black community has been invaded, had its civil rights overthrown, been the victim of bias and sensationalistic media coverage, and seen its youth beaten and gunned down in the name of police protection. It's time to call an end to the war. It's time for an unconditional peace that preserves the dignity of the community, allows for real development, and saves its young people.

Most immediately, the mass criminalization of Black youth, particularly Black males, must be ended. Mandatory sentencing, which has been shown to discriminate against minority, inner-city small dealers, has to be repealed. The association of mass numbers of Black youth with the criminal justice system has the potential to destroy a whole generation of young Blacks and ruin the lives of tens of thousands of individuals and families.

Along these lines, local communities can develop and implement alternative sentencing options for nonviolent youth offenders. Incarcerating young teenagers with hardened career criminals is unjustified and serves only to further alienate those who can be saved from a life as repeat offenders. Alternative sentencing options could include community service, day-reporting centers, intensive short-term incarceration, and residential probation.[15] Wealthy and influential White law-breakers, such as Reagan-era criminals Oliver North and Mike Deaver, have just such options available to them. The reluctance to grant these same alternatives to inner-city offenders due to lack of economic or family stability must be fought.

The Greater Washington Americans for Democratic Action has suggested establishing neighborhood judicial councils. The councils would handle minor offenses and civil disputes and would be comprised of community people. In these cases, the local prosecutorial power would be waived, with restitution and rehabilitation done at the community level.[16]

Ceasing the drug war also means stopping unconstitutional law enforcement procedures. Youth curfews, massive police invasions, warrantless searches, long pre-trial incarcerations, excessive fines, identification systems for entering public housing areas, illegal property seizures, and pre-conviction evictions of tenants accused of drug trafficking—these actions typify the "war powers" authority of the government that American citizens must act against.

The issue of youth violence and crime is being addressed by a number of programs nationally. Some of the successful prevention models include:

- the Boston Youth Program, which held a ten-session curriculum on anger and violence that provided information, discussion, and role playing to promote alternatives to violence;

- Peer Dynamics, sponsored by the Nebraska Commission on Drugs, which trained students in how to work with each other to build self-esteem and communication skills;
- the Paramount Plan, named for the city of Paramount in Los Angeles County, a gang prevention model aimed at fifth and sixth graders, whose main activities included neighborhood parents' meetings and creating an anti-gang curriculum;
- House of Umoja (also called the Philadelphia Plan), a gang prevention program that garnered peace pledges from youth gangs;
- the Gang Violence Reduction Project in East Los Angeles, developed by the California Youth Authority in 1978, that promoted gang peace treaties and provided positive alternatives;
- Community Youth Gang Services Corporation of Los Angeles which does gang violence prevention[17]

Establishing New Approaches to Policing and Law Enforcement

Realistically, law enforcement must play a role in ending the drug crisis. Neighborhoods and streets must be made secure, and the central responsibility for that falls on the shoulders of local police. Enlightened approaches to law enforcement are being implemented. The National Organization of Black Law Enforcement Executives (NOBLE) has developed a model community-based policing program known nationally as the Community-Oriented Policing System (COPS).[18] Starting in Houston, Texas, and Newark, New Jersey, the program and its variations have expanded to a number of other cities such as New York City; Madison, Wisconsin; Newport News, Virginia; and Washington, D.C.—where it is called Community Empowerment Policing—community activists find it works.

The COPS approach emphasizes police cooperation and partnership with community groups and is focused on prevention rather than on reaction to crime. Neighborhood-level input on strategies and community issues is sought by local police. In turn, the police more actively direct people to other city services and departments that can prevent or resolve problems. Some of the tactics employed include improved street lighting, removal of abandoned cars, and working with individuals to better protect their homes against burglary. One of the strongest components of the program is early and constructive intervention with at-risk youth.

NOBLE's Executive Director, Elsie Scott, believes that the COP strategy "could have a very positive impact" on the drug problem because the thrust is to empower the community. She cautions, however, that the program needs time to seed and that changes won't happen overnight.[19] In addition to innovative law enforcement approaches, the application of justice needs major reform. One area that is being given attention is the development of sentencing alternatives to relieve prison overcrowding and reduce the human and material costs of incarceration. By September 1990, more than forty states were under orders to relieve overcrowding in all or part of their prison systems.

Among the alternative sentencing options (also known as intermediate sanctions) being tried are intensive probation, community service, tailor-made programs, home confinement, and electronic monitoring. Although the full impact of these efforts have yet to be fully studied, early indications are encouraging. They have been found to be less expensive, and as or more effective as traditional probation and parole programs. In a study released by the Government Accounting Office in September 1990, those individuals in intermediate sanction programs committed fewer crimes than regular parolees.[20]

Demand-Side Options

From community activists to police chiefs to heads of state, success in the battle against illegal drugs will be minimal until the U.S. demand for drugs is curbed. For the Bush administration, this has meant punitive measures against users. William Bennett's quests to punish users were so extreme that even Bush rejected some of his original recommendations. One idea that was discarded was Bennett's proposal that federal highway funds be denied to states that refuse to suspend the drivers' licenses of casual users.[21] Despite evidence that casual use was declining, the administration implored states to "prosecute vigorously all misdemeanor drug offenses."

Rather than treat drug use as another component of law enforcement, it's time to recognize drug abuse as a health crisis similar to that of smoking or drunk driving. Karen Bass, formerly a clinical instructor at the University of Southern California School of Medicine and Executive Director of the Community Coalition for Substance Abuse Prevention and Treatment, says that if there is going to be a drug war it "should be lead by the Surgeon General as opposed to the Attorney General."[22] She has been active in mobilizing health professionals to become more involved at the community level in the battle against drugs. In West Germany, Holland, England, and other nations with severe drug abuse problems, even limited application of a health-oriented approach to the situation has found some success.

Provide Accessible, Quality Treatment

Among anti-drug advocates, it has become almost ritualistic to argue that scarce federal funds for anti-drug efforts ought to be shifted from fruitless and dangerous law enforcement to the expansion of treatment and education programs. And understandably so. Even NIDA has concluded that treatment must be expanded, recruitment must be extended, and the quality of treatment must be enhanced.[23] On the surface, this seems to be the best hope for curbing and eventually eliminating drug abuse. All treatment is not equal, however, and there is even debate over whether treatment is needed at all for certain drug addictions. It's important to look at the philosophy of treatment, the actual practice of treatment, and finally the politics of treatment.

A number of Black treatment experts, such as Ron Clark of Washington's Rap, Inc., argue that a Black perspective must be central to treatment programs that address principally Black patients.[24] Rather than using a "race neutral" approach, which invariably infuses the cultural and social standards of Whites, an African-American treatment perspective incorporates the sensitivities and respect that are the foundations for Black addicts coming to grips with the source of their problem: low self-esteem that leads to destructive, compulsive, and addictive behavior. For Blacks, as Clark argues, low self-esteem is bred into them by the racism that permeates U.S. society at both the collective and individual levels.

A pamphlet distributed by the Institute on Black Chemical Abuse makes note of a number of characteristics of Blacks who do not become substance abusers. These characteristics should serve as goals to be included in the operation of any treatment program whose main participants are Black. Such a program should focus on:

- helping participants develop a "realistic" perception of the "American dream" and notions of self-worth not tied to the possession of material goods;
- the development of problem-solving skills rather than problem-denial and problem-avoidance skills;
- providing positive role models—physical, emotional, intellectual, and career-wise—through study and direct contact;
- providing the experience of success in as many areas as possible;
- assisting participants in identifying their links with the larger social group that they belong to, i.e., race, class, community, and other sectors of society;

- developing achievable short-range goals; providing access to sources of help—financial, emotional, spiritual, etc.—and effective ways to utilize social resources;
- projecting an unglamorized picture of drugs, their effects, and drug lifestyles; and developing non-normative standards to judge one's self by.[25]

While these principles could apply to many of the individuals who enter drug treatment programs, they are particularly relevant to many Black addicts. Applying these principles would also be a helpful way of intervening with problems such as alcoholism and depression.

A number of treatment modalities are available for treating drug addiction. These include detoxification, methadone maintenance, therapy, medicinal blockers, the twelve-step method used by Alcoholics Anonymous, and acupuncture. Program practices and standards vary tremendously, and little progress has been made on developing the criteria by which to measure what constitutes a successful and valuable treatment approach.

There are currently an estimated 500,000 to 900,000 heroin addicts in the United States, and approximately 650 methadone maintenance programs servicing only 100,000 individuals.[26] These statistics force progressives concerned with drug treatment options to seriously address and consider both the hazards and advantages of methadone treatment.

Where treatment has been available, generally it has worked. The Treatment Outcome Prospective Study (TOPS) looked at 10,000 individuals from 1979 to 1981 in ten cities in thirty-seven programs. The TOPS study concluded that three to five years after treatment less than 20 percent of those who used hard drugs—cocaine and heroin—went back to using regularly. Among the 80 percent who stayed clean, crime involvement was reduced by one-third to one-half and most found full-time jobs.[27]

One study estimates that for every dollar spent on treatment services, $11.54 is saved in social costs. That amount includes imprisonment. While it costs roughly $50,000 annually per inmate to incarcerate, treatment expenses are much more modest and beneficial in the long run. Outpatient methadone treatment costs an average $3,000 per person while non-hospital residential treatment is about $14,600.[28]

The effects of methadone addiction, however, are negative and controversial. One 1974 DEA report, "Methadone: A Review of Current Information," stated that methadone deaths outnumbered heroin overdoses five to one.[29] In New York, the study reported that more methadone addicts were arrested than heroin addicts.[30] Other studies have shown that methadone addicts are as frequently arrested and unemployed as heroin addicts.

Drs. Vincent Dole and Marie Nyswander, who developed methadone maintenance as a heroin treatment modality, believed that heroin caused a permanent metabolic change in the nervous system, providing no basis for an addict to ever withdraw.[31] Unlike other early methadone experimenters, they consciously and deliberately used methadone for addicting, not detoxing, heroin addicts.

It is also significant to note that evidence exists which suggests that in some cases, heroin addiction can be overcome without any treatment at all. Some researchers have estimated that more than 90 percent of the 80,000 soldiers in Vietnam who were addicted to heroin were able to overcome that addiction without treatment once they returned to the United States. The implication is obvious: relieved of the stress of war and easy access to drugs, a soldier's reintegration into a receptive family lifestyle and the creation of a hopeful future can reduce the need for heroin to the point where its addiction could be conquered.[32]

The situation with cocaine treatment is even worse. The majority of current treatment centers were geared toward men's heroin addiction or alcoholism. Most of the federally funded research being done on cocaine addiction is a search for a methadone-like narcotic. Researchers have been experimenting with anti-convulsant drugs such as carbamazepine, which is used to treat epileptics. Other researchers have tried anti-depressants such as desipramine, imipramine, and amantadine. Ibogaine, a West African plant with intoxicating properties, has been brought to the lab for testing. Research on these substances continues, though not at the level of funding that it should.[33] What is needed is an aggressive demand for more radical and experimental approaches to medicinal treatment.

Let us remember that Bennett has not been a strong advocate for treatment or a cheerleader for its effectiveness. On one occasion, he referred to those who see treatment as key to solving the drug crisis as wild-eyed optimists.[34] In a white paper, he wrote: "The majority of drug users…don't need drug treatment. What is crucial is that they stop using drugs." In arguing against the notion of treatment on demand, he writes that 90 percent of those in treatment do not seek it on their own let alone "demand it."[35] From Bennett's point of view, treatment on demand is costly and unbalanced, while criminal justice-compelled treatment is the best approach.

Perhaps Bennett's most insightful observation is that those who have something to lose (a job, a family, or a house) do better in treatment than those with nothing to lose.[36] However, the implication of this insight is apparently lost. No aspect of Bennett's drug program addresses providing those with nothing to lose, with something.

According to the March 1990 issue of *Governing,* acupuncture appears to hold some promise in the efforts to treat drug addiction. Acupuncture has been used to treat drug and alcohol addiction in New York at the Lincoln Hospital Substance Abuse Division since 1974.[37]

The major problems in using acupuncture are lack of resources necessary to establish programs, to train individuals in its use, and to fund further research in the field. Of all treatments used, acupuncture is the least expensive. The National Acupuncture Detoxification Association estimates that the complete cost of setting up and operating a program is roughly $5,000. A low estimate of the cost of implementing a methadone maintenance program is $3,200.[38]

Many communities, Black and White, have been resistant to accepting treatment centers into their area. Fears of decreased property values, more crime, and the influx of addicts into the neighborhood has provoked numerous "not-on-my-block" movements. Progressive legislators have attempted to overcome this reluctance by suggesting incentives such as tax breaks, increased police patrols, homestead exemptions, reduced assessments, and community involvement on the boards of directors of these centers. These new incentives would also be made available to areas where established centers exist. Community leaders must be won over to the concept of treatment centers and not fall victim to the prejudiced notion that treatment centers will breed more problems than they solve.[39]

Institute National Clean Needle Exchange Programs

Efforts to provide addicts with clean needles as a step in reducing the spread of AIDS have met with stiff opposition from the administration, certain government officials, and some sectors of local communities. When Health and Human Services Secretary Louis Sullivan was first appointed, he ran into an administration buzzsaw for suggesting that he might support the concept of clean needle exchanges. He soon changed his opinion.[40]

Despite this resistance, several public and private agencies have initiated needle exchange programs that apparently are meeting with success. In New York, a pilot needle exchange program was begun in 1988.[41] According to Jose Paris, a supervising public health official and member of AFSCME Local 768: "The AIDS epidemic has really changed what the whole approach to drug addiction has to be about." Paris, an ex-addict, went on to say: "We're no longer just dealing with the deadly disease of addiction, but with many thousands of people dying because they're sharing needles."[42]

Half of New York's addicts have been exposed to AIDS. Yet, at best, treatment programs exist for only 40,000—less than 10 percent.[43] Clean needle programs also exist in the cities of Boulder, Colorado; Portland, Oregon; and Seattle, Washington, among others. In Boulder, sixty out of an estimated 850 addicts are registered for the program. In Portland, 300 out of 7,500 are in such programs, and in Seattle, 800 out of an estimated 10,000 to 15,000 addicts. In all of these cities, health officials estimated that a range of only 3 to 6 percent of addicts in the city test positive for HIV, the virus that leads to AIDS.[44]

Many other nations have instituted clean needle programs with great success. In Hong Kong, needles are legal and widely available and there are no reported cases of AIDS.[45] In Canada it is estimated that between one-third and one-fourth of Vancouver's drug addicts are registered in the clean needle program.[46] In Zurich, Switzerland, over 6,000 clean needles a day are distributed, and Swiss police keep hard drug use restricted to certain areas where a federally funded health center is run.[47]

Declare a Public Health Emergency

In the United States, two separate medical nations are developing. In one, individuals may enjoy access to the latest health care technology, health care coverage, health literature, and a safe environment. In the other, death rates and health problems are comparable to, if not worse than, those in the developing world.

AIDS continues to be a deadly killer. By the end of 1989, 100,000 AIDS cases and more than 50,000 deaths had occurred in the United States. More than 1,300 of these AIDS cases were pediatric. By 1992, the United States will have over 365,000 cases and 263,000 deaths. The fastest growing group with AIDS is intravenous, or IV, drug users. In New York in 1988, IV drug users with AIDS exceeded the gay and bisexual population with AIDS for the first time. Eighty percent of all heterosexual cases of HIV infection in the city were attributed to IV drug use. New York City, which has the nation's largest group of IV drug users, is experiencing the greatest rise in AIDS transmission through drug abuse. AIDS is the leading cause of death for New York City men between the ages of thirty and fifty-nine, of young girls and women aged one to nine and thirty to thirty-nine, and the leading cause of death in New York state prisons. In 77 percent of the pediatric AIDS cases in the city, at least one parent is an IV drug user. There are about 50,000 women in New York City of childbearing age who are IV drug users and another 100,000 at risk who have partners who are users. A nine-month study done by Dr. Joyce Wallace of Manhattan concluded that 33.7 percent of the city's prostitutes were infected with the AIDS virus.[48]

The crisis is one not only of physical health, but of mental health as well. Depression and stress are at an all-time high. We need a national health care system that provides health services to the millions of people now denied access to even the most basic health requirements. In addition, community-based health centers that would address both physical and mental health problems should be established.

Launch a Massive Nationwide Literacy Program

About 25 million people in the United States are functional illiterates.[49] For this group of invisible citizens located in urban and rural areas across the land and in prisons, job-training programs and educational opportunities are out of reach. Growing numbers of people lack basic reading and writing skills. For the thousands of individuals who cannot fill out forms to receive needed social services, illiteracy is a life-threatening handicap.

While Barbara Bush has made increased literacy one of her prime projects, she has mainly advocated building volunteer-based groups as the chief means of attacking the problem. Like most conservative "one-person-at-a-time" approaches to social problems, hers falls far short of the need. Existing community-based literacy projects need financial support, and new programs need to be implemented. We need to push for literacy action now.

Until there exist functional and accessible literacy programs, many of those who attempt to overcome their substance abuse will become frustrated at their lack of opportunity due to illiteracy. Without the possibility of finding non-menial work, many will relapse into their former habits. Literacy education at the community level can play an important role in the training and development of community.

Legalization and Decriminalization

Debates over legalization and decriminalization polarize quickly. Those who oppose legalization and decriminalization tend to dismiss out of hand any discussion on the subject as though merely bringing up the topic is a surrender to the drug lords. William Bennett has stated that those who call for legalization have put up the flag of surrender.[50]

Equally problematic have been advocates of legalization who have called irresponsibly either for the immediate legalization of all drugs or have seen the issue as one solely of individual freedom. The latter view, held by some conservatives, essentially says "let the chips fall where they may." Their goal is reestablishment of some social order that they believe has broken down due to the prohibition-driven violence of the drug crisis. Conservatives such as former Secretary of State George

Shultz and columnist William F. Buckley fall into this category. Schultz wrote in a letter to Bennett:

> Every friend of freedom, and I know you are one, must be revolted as I am by the prospect of turning the United States into an armed camp, by the vision of jails filled with casual drug users and of an army of enforcers empowered to invade the liberty of citizens on slight evidence. A country in which shooting down unidentified planes "on suspicion" can be seriously considered as a drug war tactic is not the kind of United States that either you or I want to hand on to future generations.
>
> It seems to me we're not really going to get anywhere until we can take the criminality out of the drug business and the incentives for criminality out of it.... We need at least to consider and examine forms of controlled legalization of drugs.[51]

Those who argue for the purity of individual rights, including libertarians and many progressives, believe that everyone should have the right to buy the drug of their choice without government interference other than for health regulation. Inherent in this argument is the assumption of social equalities that do not exist. The consequences of drug abuse do not befall groups of people regardless of race, and neither does the capacity to make informed choices about the safety and use of different drugs.

Legalization of some drugs, by all indications, would resolve some of the biggest problems of the current drug crisis and drug war. The violence and homicides associated with drug prohibition would virtually disappear. So would much of the arrest and incarceration of tens of thousands of people who are sent to jail on simple possession charges. The overwhelming number of homicides associated with drugs have to do with drug transactions or territorial battles and not with drug use per se. There would very likely be a reduction in property and street crimes committed for drugs because legal drugs would be much cheaper.

Legalization of drugs alone, however, would leave untouched the issues that give rise to drug abuse and their destructive impact on poor and minority communities. Issues of economic development, employment opportunities, access to medical services for addiction, as well as the despair brought on by homelessness and poverty are not addressed by the legalization option. In addition, the marketing of drugs to the poor and to people of color would, unless severely restricted, likely increase. There is no indication that substance abuse in these communities would diminish particularly, since drug use goes up with decreased productivity, increased social violence, or increased property loss. Once those issues are resolved, it's doubtful that the media or various levels of government will be pressured to make the drug problem a priority.

Perhaps the real question concerning legalization and decriminalization is whether a particular drug, legal or illegal, can be used responsibly. For those drugs—such as alcohol— for which it is determined that the majority of people in society can use responsibly, legalization is a prudent and rational step if strict regulation and education and treatment services are available and accessible. In this context, the decriminalization for use and possession of small amounts of marijuana seems not only logical, but an essential step in mitigating the harm of the drug war.

Millions of Americans, and many more millions around the world, use marijuana. Studies, including a number of exhaustive federal ones, indicate that marijuana use in moderation can be no more harmful than beer. Marijuana has been shown to be no more a gateway to hard drugs than milk. It's the criminalization of marijuana that brings its users in contact and in association with traffickers and users of more addictive and toxic drugs. The position taken by the National Organization for the Reform of Marijuana Laws (NORML), which calls for marijuana legalization, is that excessive use of marijuana can be harmful. Marijuana smoking does present some obvious health risks, such as lung damage for long-term, heavy users. Marijuana has a very low acute toxicity and is virtually impossible to overdose on. In the short term, the dangers of marijuana are similar to those of any drug or intoxicant that impairs one's senses, i.e., accident potential due to impaired memory, problems concentrating, and problems with limited peripheral vision.[52] Furthermore, marijuana has been decriminalized in some parts of the United States. In Alaska, up until November 1990, possession of small amounts of marijuana were legal. In Ann Arbor, Michigan, possession of a small amount for personal use can be fined for $100.[53]

For those drugs that are harmful and deadly, such as crack cocaine and ice, their use should be treated as a priority health issue and attacked in the way that the American Cancer Society has addressed the problem of tobacco addiction. The purchase of illegal crops, as suggested earlier, would go a long way in stopping some of these drugs from entering the country. Large dealers should be dealt with severely, and laws already on the books to do that should be applied.

No policy options should lose sight of the fundamental goal of drug reform: community stability, just development, and the good health of individuals and society. This must be primary in considering the legalization of any specific drug as a tactical option. As long as economic and racial inequities exist, abuse will continue whether drugs are legal or illegal.

Distinct from the government's approach, each drug should be analyzed for it particular physical and psychological impact on individuals as well as its social and economic consequences. In addition, how a drug is produced, marketed, and distributed and who benefits financially from its sale are also critical considerations. One question concerning any move toward legalization is the issues of who would profit and how those profits would be disbursed. Whatever private enterprises developed would have to be heavily taxed and those taxes used to establish treatment and prevention programs for addicts.

Given the toxic character of tobacco, we should find new ways to halt the spread of smoking. Cigarette prohibition would surely create an underground market that would probably cause more problems than would be solved. Yet, community leaders could learn from the successful efforts of Canada's anti-smoking movement. Canada targeted the tobacco companies, which they portrayed as murderers, as opposed to smokers, who are often seen as self-selected victims. In response to the "smokers' rights" groups organized by the companies, the anti-smoking forces formed RODDS, which stood for Relatives of Dead and Dying Smokers. After waging a massive public relations campaign exposing the complicity of the tobacco companies in the thousands of deaths caused by smoking and disclosing the ties between the companies and politicians, two of the strongest anti-smoking laws in the world passed the Canadian Parliament. The Tobacco Products Control Act and the Non-Smokers' Rights Act contain provisions that would severely curtail the power of the tobacco industry if implemented in the United States.[54]

Under Canadian law, tobacco ads are banned from newspapers and magazines as well as television and radio. U.S. newspapers often claim freedom of the press in defending their taking cigarette ads, yet they hypocritically and routinely reject as "obscene" advertisements from groups like Planned Parenthood. In Canada, brand-name promotion in sports and the arts is restricted. This prevents the kind of subtle and deceptive promotion that comes from events like the Kool Jazz Festival and Virginia Slims Tennis Tournament or strategically placed billboards in baseball stadiums that show up on televised games. In the United States, twenty-two of twenty-four stadiums have cigarette billboards.[55]

In Canada, distribution of free cigarette samples, which serve the purpose of recruiting new and young smokers, is prohibited. In addition, there are stronger warnings on cigarette packs, health information must be included, and warnings on billboards must be moved to the top and be no less than 20 percent of the overall size. As a result, a number of tobacco companies have decided not to use billboards at all.[56]

Who Pays the Cost of Ending the Drug Crisis?

Citizens should not be misled by the arguments from politicians that funds are not available for the programs necessary to end the drug crisis. The U.S. budget has been bloated with military spending since the end of World War II. According to a report by the Jobs With Peace Campaign, for every dollar paid in income taxes fifty cents goes to the military, while only one cent goes toward housing, three cents toward education, and two cents toward food and nutrition.[57] During the 1980s, military spending increased 46 percent while housing *decreased* by 77 percent, health care services by 49 percent, employment and job training 48 percent, mass transit 33 percent, child nutrition 19 percent, and education 7 percent.[58]

Comparisons of military spending to potential social spending are stunning. Military spending compared to meeting America's housing need is a good example of this misplaced priority. One harpoon missile costs about $940,000. This same amount of money could build four duplex houses ($400,000), renovate ten units of abandoned housing ($450,000), and weatherize twenty-two homes ($90,000). Since 1980, the military budget has doubled from $140 billion to $300 billion while housing programs were cut from $32 billion to less than $10 billion.[59]

The Congressional Black Caucus (CBC) was the main voice in Congress opposing Reagan's military buildup in the 1980s and has produced an annual alternative budget since the first year of Reagan's term in 1980. The CBC budget has supported and called for the expansion of social programs, advocated cuts in defense, and proposed a progressive restructuring of the tax burden. CBC's Fiscal Year 1990 budget proposed increases in education, health, housing, employment training, and anti-drug funding. It also recommended a 5 percent reduction in the military budget and a 5 percent reduction in active forces.[60] Under the CBC budget, tax surcharges would be imposed on the top 5 percent income bracket and the top 10 percent of corporations. The CBC budget would remove the so-called tax "bubble" in income rates that allows the wealthy to pay a lower income tax than many of those in the middle class.[61] The Bush administration has continually attacked the principle of progressive tax rates for the rich.[62]

The potential of a "peace dividend" has also excited social reformers. The end of the Cold War pulls the rug out from the argument that a military buildup must continue to meet the so-called Soviet threat. The savings to come from cutting weapon development and troop deployments, estimated to be in the billions, can be used for social programs in the United States that have been suffering from lack of funds in recent years. Conservatives in Congress and in the administration have made it clear, however, that they would prefer to direct any windfalls either to reducing the deficit—which they caused—or investing in the new "democracies" of Eastern Europe.

The war in the Persian Gulf has reopened questions about cutting military spending. Military threats, such as the one perceived to exist from Iraq's Sadaam Hussein, do not require the level of Cold War military spending that has occurred previously. More important, a foreign policy that assumes negotiations as the principal means of resolving international conflict argues against unchecked military buildup.

A number of activists have called for a "Marshall Plan" for saving the cities. They argue that the inner cities of America's major metropolitan areas are in a state of economic emergency that requires massive government resources if they are to be saved. Long-time activist and former Executive Director of the National Rainbow Coalition Ron Daniels views the idea of a Marshall Plan for Black America as a means of "reparations" for the hundreds of years of underdevelopment of the Black community by the U.S. government. The National Urban League calls for an Urban Marshall Plan for the Black inner cities that would cost at least $50 billion. The money would fund programs such as a national health plan, a fund for building affordable housing, the support and extension of set-asides for small Black businesses, job training, and energy assistance projects.

The Need for Political and Economic Power

> The curse of poverty has no justification in our age. It is socially as cruel and blind as the practice of cannibalism at the dawn of civilization…. The time has come for us to civilize ourselves by the total, direct and immediate abolition of poverty.
>
> —Martin Luther King, Jr.

In the long run, economic development, social equality, and the elimination of poverty are the "magic bullets" to end drug trafficking and abuse in poor communities and communities of color. The income gap in the United States between Whites and Blacks grew during the Eighties. The gap between rich and poor also greatly expanded during that period.

The concentration of wealth into the hands of so few reflects the growing class divisions of U.S. society. According to the Center on Budget and Policy Priorities: "The richest 2.5 million people [about 1 percent of the population] now have nearly as much income as the 100 million Americans with the lowest income." That is an incredible and telling division between the rich and the poor in America.[63] In 1990, the income share of the richest fifth of Americans was the highest ever recorded while the share of the lowest fifth was at the lowest point since 1954.[64]

The problem of youth employment is a manifestation of the generally bleak employment opportunities facing inner-city and rural residents. The deindustrialization of the cities has created as much economic hardship as the continued destruction of America's farms. The Black community, both urban and rural, is affected more harshly and has fewer chances of recovery than the White population.

In Black America, the top priority of elected officials, community activists, and political leaders has to be economic development for the masses of Blacks who have not benefitted from the gains of the past. Formidable public and private resources must be called into action to conquer the current situation. Job training programs will have to be expanded to prepare participants for careers, not just jobs. At the same time, meaningful and fairly compensated employment must be created as a partnership of community, government, and the private sector.

Rev. Jesse Jackson has promoted the slogan "Investment in America." He advocates using the nation's pension funds to rebuild the nation's economic base in inner cities and rural areas. He calls for investment in five areas: reinvestment in the country's infrastructure; retraining workers; reindustrialization of America's productive capacity; research for commercial development; and recovery from a military to a peace-time economy. To manage the financial aspects of this process, Jackson advocates the creation of a privately administered American Investment Bank.

In the process of economic recovery, private sector initiatives must be supported by public policy commitment. It is unrealistic to expect profit-compulsive businesses to see the value of investing in drug treatment programs and economic development that will take years to bear fruit. The few enlightened companies that expend the resources necessary for this type of activity will be overshadowed by the large number of corporations whose greed and abandonment of the cities in the first place contributed to their decline. Chief among the possibilities of government-sponsored programs is the rebuilding of the infrastructure of the cities and the building of housing for low-income and homeless people.

A radical redistribution of wealth and an examination of the prejudices of the capitalist economic system must be at the core of a movement led by people of color and working people for fundamental economic reform. The dissolution of socialist governments has led many Western leaders to brag once again about the enduring virtues and benefits of capitalism. Any call for government to play a role in creating economic parity among its citizens is viewed as socialism-in-disguise and dismissed. The economic and social plight in the Black community, however, is not the result of socialism, but of capitalism at its most developed stage. While economic parity alone will not end either individual or institutional racism, it is the foundation on which to build the movement for an egalitarian society. None of these suggestions are remotely possible without increased political and economic power on the part of those most dispossessed in our society, particularly communities of color. It is not enough to simply call for reforms in the current approach to the drug crisis. Strategies for increased and responsive political power and economic development must come from those communities most in need.

In the Black community, leadership must be held more accountable than ever before. From the Congressional Black Caucus to local elected officials to national and local Black organizations, leaders must be challenged to represent our needs. For too long, there has been a gap between these groups and individuals and the Black community as a whole. We need to develop new methods and structures for dialogue and accountability.

At the same time, new leadership, new organizations, and new strategies must be brought forth. The young generation must not dwell on the rhetoric and achievements of Black leaders past, but must develop new progressive ideas and approaches for the future of Black America, for the entire nation and for the world.

In addition to the Black community, whose stake in ending drug trafficking, drug abuse, and the excesses of the drug war seems obvious, other communities must join in this battle. There are many more White users and addicts than in the Black communities and other communities of color. They too are the victims of the drug crisis and the drug war. The drug war of the administration has become the vehicle for attacks on people around the world and here at home. The erosion of civil liberties will not and cannot stop at the border of the Black community.

Conclusion

Dooney Wilson is the son of a crack addict in the Washington, D.C., area. On several occasions, the seven-year-old watched his mother get arrested. This young Black male, a child of the Reagan era, also witnessed numerous addicts overdose. When asked by a *Washington Post* reporter how these shattering experiences would affect his life, Dooney replied, "I don't want to sell drugs, but I'll probably have to."[65]

This book is about what former Washington, D.C., Congressman Walter Fauntroy calls Dooney's message—a message that says the least of us must be provided with opportunities and hope if we are to save the society that we live in. This book is an effort to dissect Dooney's message by examining all dimensions of the drug problem as well as the possibilities of its solutions. Dooney's dreams, and those of millions of others, don't have to be nightmares. The dreams of a good life, of security, of being included in society need not only belong to or be realizable for just the elite of the world.

As we embark on the 1990s, the "drug crisis" is already disappearing as a key issue among politicians and in the media. The Bush administration is making claims of "turning the corner" and "seeing the light at the end of the tunnel," which is merely to say that it can point to a decline in use among certain privileged groups who have been persuaded by the hype or frightened by the prospect of going to jail.

In the Black and poor communities of the inner cities, however, the horror continues. The drug crisis can be beaten, but the will and the commitment must equal the rhetoric and fervor thus far shown. The need is not as much for great leaders as it is for ordinary people to audaciously and passionately grapple with the great issues of our time in human history.

To paraphrase C.L.R. James, the brilliant and late Caribbean writer, the choice before us as a people and a nation is clear: Either we descend into barbarism or we rise to greatness. There is still time for us to make that choice.

Afterword

Concluding Comments by
Jesse L. Jackson

When the history of the Nineties is written, future generations will note the scourge of drug abuse and crime as a major deterrent to the development of our nation economically, socially, and politically.

Pipe Dream Blues has reminded us all too well of the gory details of this drug phenomena. Its pages of painful and haunting documentation of our government's role in the illegal drug trade reveals that the "Wars on Drugs" have often been as corrupt as the drug culture itself.

Through it all we must ask the question, have the social problems inherent in our society driven drug abuse throughout the generations or have drugs driven us to the problems of crime, homelessness, suicide, and infant mortality? Only the next generation will be able to tell.

For years I have called upon our young people to be sane, sober, and sensitive in their responsibility to shape our nation's future. I have concentrated my efforts on junior and high school students—even grade school children—who are faced with the drug option before many of them can even read. I never cease to be amazed by the number of young people who stand up and come forward when I call upon them to choose hope over dope. No fewer than 60 percent of all school assemblies stand when I ask if they know someone who is dead, in jail, or has contemplated suicide because of drugs.

For too long, politicians and the media have attempted to paint a picture of drugs and its accompanying crime as a Black-Caribbean-Hispanic sub-culture phenomena that has just now infiltrated the White community. The truth is that the drug suppliers, the distribution network, the financial-retail institutions and even our judicial system are in some strange way linked with this marriage between racism and drugs. Until this chain of corruption is weeded out and put to an end, we may never rid ourselves of the crisis.

By taking a hard and unabashful look at this deadly cycle of drugs, crime, and racism, *Pipe Dream Blues* has given to us a new testament by which we should re-evaluate the modern day "war on drugs." We must now ask the hard questions.

Denial, we are told, is one of the earliest signs of addiction. Could it be that our nation's political, judicial, and economic system has in its own way become addicted on the drug culture? Or is it a malignant cancer that can only be treated, but never cured?

We knew as we marched from Selma to Montgomery in 1965 that we would not win our liberation exclusively through obtaining the right to vote. However, the right to vote was a very important step in the long drive to win social, political, and economic power. Our nation's love affair and marriage with racism continued even after the Supreme Court granted it an official divorce. It follows that the divorce between the drug culture and these institutions will not end easily either.

Finally, we must also recognize that the wave of crime taking place in our society does have a cause. It has been wrought because of a callous neglect of our urban centers by the federal government. Throughout the 1980s, the Reagan and Bush administrations cut aid to urban American by 75 percent. The Reagan and Bush legacy has led the country to the largest banking scandal since the Great Depression and the greatest national debt in the history of our nation.

We must fashion the new war on drugs with a renewed war on poverty, a war on illiteracy, a war on racism and economic exploitation. When we can make serious progress towards ending these scourges on our society, then we will not only solve the drug crisis, but we will also save our nation from an even greater threat: self-destruction.

Keep Hope Alive.

ENDNOTES

INTRODUCTION

1. Sam Meddis, "Whites, Not Blacks, at the Core of the Drug Crisis," *USA Today,* 20 December 1989.

2. Randolph N. Stone, Esq. "The War on Drugs: The Wrong Enemy and the Wrong Battlefield," *National Bar Association Magazine,* December 1989, p. 18.

Chapter 1

1. Sally Reed and R. Craig Sautter, "Children of Poverty," *Kappan Special Report,* June 1990, p. 3.

2. Ibid.

3. Ibid, p. 4.

4. Ibid.

5. Tim Wise, "Being Poor Isn't Enough," *Dollars & Sense,* September 1990, pp. 10-11.

6. Ibid.

7. Lynn Duke, "Whites' Racial Stereotypes Persist," *Washington Post,* 9 January 1991, p. A4.

8. Alexander Cockburn, "From Andes to Inner Cities, Cocaine Is a Good Career Choice," *The Wall Street Journal,* 7 September 1989, p. A15.

9. Ibid, Reed and Sautter, p. 5.

10. *The Lost Decade,* Democractic National Committee, November 1989, pp. 32-34.

11. *Hate Violence and White Supremacy,* Klanwatch Intelligence Report No. 47, December 1989.

12. Evan Stark, "The Myth of Black Violence," *New York Times,* 18 July 1990, p. A21.

13. Ibid.

14. Ibid.

15. Ibid.

16. "Young Black Men Most Likely to Be Jailed," *Washington Afro-American,* 10 March 1990, p. A1.

17. Howard Snyder, "Growth in Minority Detentions Attributed to Drug Law Violators," *Juvenile Justice Bulletin,* Office of Justice Programs, U.S. Department of Justice, March 1990, pp. 1-2.

18. "Questions Answered About Drug Use Among African-American Youth," *Fact Sheet,* The Washington Area Council on Alcoholism and Drug Abuse.

19. Don Colburn, "The Risky Lives of Young Black Men," *Washington Post Health,* 18 December 1990, p. 7.

Chapter 2

1. Ron Harris, "Blacks Feel Brunt of Drug War," *Los Angeles Times,* 22 April 1990, p. A1.

2. Maxine Waters, "Drugs, Democrats, & Priorities," *Nation,* 24 July 1989, p. 142.

3. Katherine McFate, "Black Males and the Drug Trade: New Entrepreneurs or New Illusions," *Focus,* May 1990, p. 5.

4. Arnold S. Trebach, "Can Prohibition Be Enforced in Washington?" *The Truth Seeker,* Sept/Oct 1989, p. 22.

5. Vivian Rouson Gossett, *Alcohol and Drug Abuse in Black America,* Institute on Black Chemical Abuse, Minneapolis, MN, 1988, p. 2.

6. Edward M. Brecher and the Editors of Consumer Reports, *Licit and Illicit Drugs,* Little, Brown, Boston, 1972, p. 398.

7. Eric Williams, *Capitalism and Slavery,* Andre Deutsch Limited, London, 1964, p. 37; Henry Hobhouse, *Seeds of Change,* Harper & Row, New York, 1985, pp. 116-117.

8. Ibid; Williams, pp. 78-79.

9. Ibid, p. 80.

10. Ibid, p. 79.

11. Jerome E. Brooks, *The Mighty Leaf,* Little, Brown, Boston 1952, p. 105.

12. Ibid.

13. Eugene D. Genovese, *Roll Jordan Roll: The World the Slaves Made,* Vintage Books, New York 1986.

14. Denise Herd, "We Cannot Stagger to Freedom: A History of Blacks and Alcohol in American Politics," *Yearbook of Substance Use and Abuse, Vol. 3,* Human Science Press, New York, 1983.

15. Jack Herer, *The Emperor Wears No Clothes,* Queen of Clubs Publishing, Van Nuys, CA, 1990, p. 65.

16. Ibid, p. 1.

17. Ibid,

18. Ibid,

19. Kenneth M. Stamp, *The Peculiar Institution,* Vintage Books, New York, 1956, p. 49.

20. "Native Americans Declare War on Alcohol," *The Newsletter,* Fall 1988, p. 11.

21. Patrick Anderson, *High in America,* Viking Press, New York, 1981, p. 48.

22. Alvin Moscow, *Merchants of Heroin,* The Dial Press, New York, 1968, p. xiv; David Musto, "The History of Legislative Control Over Opium, Cocaine, and Their Derivatives," *Dealing With Drugs,* Pacific Research Institute, San Francisco, 1987, p. 62.

23. Ibid; Brecher, pp. 17-19.

24. John Helmer, *Drugs and Minority Oppression,* Seabury Press, New York, 1975, pp. 18-33.

25. *Great Decisions 1989,* New York: Foreign Policy Associates.

26. Karl Marx, *Capital,* Vol. 1, New World Paperbacks, New York, p. 398.

27. Ibid; Brecher, p. 4.

28. Daniel Kagan, "How America Lost Its First Drug War," 20 November 1989 *Insight,* p. 10.

29. Ibid.

30. "Miscellanea: Pioneers in the Cocaine Trade," *The Forensic Drug Abuse Advisor,* September 1989, p. 7.

31. Ibid; Kagan, p. 10.

32. Ibid; Brecher, p. 271.

33. *Drug Trafficking in the Washington Metropolitan Area,* Oversight Hearing, Subcommittee on Fiscal Affairs and Health, Committee on the District of Columbia, 99th Congress, 17 April 1985, p. 314.

34. Ibid; Kagan, p. 11.

35. Ibid; Kagan, p. 12.

36. Ibid; Kagan, p. 13.

37. *Opium Problem: Message From the President,* 61st Congrss, 21 February 1910, p. 50.

38. Ibid; Kagan, p. 13.

39. Ibid; Brecher, p. 18.

40. Edward Hunting Williams, "Negro Cocaine 'Fiends' Are a New Southern Menace," *New York Times,* 8 February 1914, sec. 5, p. 12.

41. Ibid; Herer, p. 68.

42. John Hope Franklin, *From Slavery to Freedom,* Vintage, New York, 1969, pp. 439-440.

43. Ibid, p. 474.

44. Ibid, p. 480.

45. Ibid, p. 479.

46. Ibid; Gossett, p.4.

47. Ibid; Gossett, P.4

48. W.E.B. Dubois, "Drunkenness," October 1928, *Crisis,* No. 35, p. 348.

49. Ibid; Gossett, p. 4.

50. Ibid; Herer, p. 65.

51. Ibid, p. 66.

52. Liner notes from album *Pot, Spoon, Pipe and Jug,* Stash Records, Tenafly, NJ.

53. Ibid; Herer, pp. 67-68.

54. Ibid, p. 23.

55. Ibid.

56. "New Billion-Dollar Crop," *Popular Mechanics,* February 1938, pp. 238-239.

57. Ibid; Herer, p. 23.

58. Ibid.

59. Oversight Hearing, p. 316.

60. Ibid; Herer, p. 25.

61. Ibid, p. 26.

62. Ibid, p. 66.

63. Ibid, p. 27; Brecher, pp. 36-37.

64. Norman Riley, "The Crack Boom is Really an Echo," *Crisis,* March 1989, p. 27.

65. Newsday Editors, *The Heroin Trail,* Signet, New York, 1973, p. 199.

66. Ibid.

67. Stephen Fox, *Blood and Power,* Penguin Books, New York, 1989, pp. 25-26, 163-165.

68. Ibid; Riley, p. 27.

69. Malcolm X, *The Autobiography of Malcolm X,* Ballantine Books, New York, 1965, p. 99.

70. Ibid, pp. 259-261

71. Francis A.J. Janni, *Black Mafia,* Pocket Books, New York, 1975, pp. 101-102.

72. Ibid; Newsday Editors, p. 196.

73. Hank Messick, *Of Grass and Snow,* Prentice-Hall, Englewood, CA, 1979, p.15.

74. Ibid, pp. 24-35.

75. Newsday Editors, pp. 194-195.

76. Jefferson Morley, "The Kid Who Sold Crack to the President," *City Paper,* 15 December 1989, p. 31.

77. Ibid, Messick, pp. 36-37.

78. Michael Covino, "How the 69th Mob Maximized Earnings in East Oakland," *California Magazine,* November 1985, p. 87.

79. Ibid; Messick, p. 148.

80. Congressmen Morgan Murphy and Robert Steele, *The World Heroin Problem,* U.S. Government Printing Office, 1971.

81. *Washington Star,* 4 May 1980.

82. Ibid; Anderson, p. 54.

83. Gene Marine, *The Black Panthers,* Signet Books, New York, 1969, pp. 45-46.

84. Tom Brune, and James Ylisela, Jr., "The Making of Jeff Fort," *Chicago,* November 1988, pp. 208-210.

85. Nelson George, *Stop the Violence,* National Urban League publication, Pantheon, New York, 1990, p. 44.

86. "Prisoners in 1988," *Bureau of Justice Statistics Bulletin,* April 1989, U.S. Department of Justice.

87. "Profile of State Prison Inmates 1986," *Bureau of Justice Statisitics,* January 1988, Special Report, U.S. Department of Justice.

88. Ibid.

89. Sharon LaFraniere, "U.S. Has Most Prisoners Per Capita in the World," *Washington Post,* 5 January 1991, p. A3.

90. "Young Black Men Most Likely to Be Jailed," *Washington Afro-American,* 10 March 1990, p. A1.

91. Ibid.

92. Ibid; McFate, p. 5.

93. Raymond M. Brown, "NACDL, the Black Community, and the War on Drugs," *The Champion ,* November 1990, pp. 18-20.

94. Ron Harris, "Blacks Feel Brunt of Drug War," *Los Angeles Times,* 22 April 1990, p. A26

95. Ibid.

96. "Drug Use Down Report Says," *USA Today,* 20 December 1990, p. 6A.

97. Ibid.

98. *Intricate Web,* General Board of Global Ministries, The United Methodist Church, 1990, p. 5.

99. Jack Kelley and Sam Vincent Meddis, "Critics Say Bias Spurs Police Focus on Blacks," *USA Today,* 20 December 1990, p. 6A.

100. Letter from Jim Murphy, Director of New York State Coalition for Criminal Justice, *City Sun,* 27 September to 3 October 1990.

101. Gerry Fitzgerald, "Dispatches From the Drug War, *Common Cause,* January/February 1990, p.16.

102. Ibid.

103. Harris, p. A26.

104. Michael Hasty, "Drug War Targets Civil Liberties," *Washington Peace Letter,* September 1989, p. 4.

105. Harris, p. A27.

106. Ibid., p. A26.

107. Ibid.

108. Ibid.

109. Ibid.

110. Ibid.

111. Ibid; Gossett, p. 13.

112. National Research Council, *Common Destiny,* National Academy Press, Washington, D.C., 1989, p. 302.

113. Ibid, p. 8.

114. Ibid.

115. Press Release, U.S. Department of Commerce, Bureau of Census, 31 August 1988.

116. Ibid.

117. Walter L. Updegrave, "Race and Money," *Money,* December 1989, p. 154.

118. Ibid, p. 152.

119. Ibid, p. 170.

120. Ibid.

121. *Common Destiny,* pp. 335-337.

122. *Drug Trafficking: A Report to the President,* U.S. Department of Justice, 3 August 1989, p. 33.

123. Carlos Sanchez, "A Fifth of Poor in Study Involved With Drugs," *Washington Post,* 28 July 1989.

124. Paul Choitz, "McBoycott Against Unfair Wages," *In These Times,* 21 March 1990.

125. "Drug Economy in Black America is Between $16 Billion and $20 Billion, *Ebony,* August 1989, p. 108.

126. Patrick Welsh, "Young, Black, Male and Trapped," *Washington Post,* 24 September 1989, p. B4.

127. David R. Gergen, "Drugs and White America," *U.S. News & World Report,* 18 September 1989, p. 79.

128. Ibid; Stone, p. 18.

129. Ibid; Stone, P. 18.

130. George Curry, "Urban League Declares War on Drug Pushers," *Chicago Tribune,* 7 August 1989, p. 1.

131. Ibid.

132. Khali Abdegeo, "Wings of Hope," *SCLC National Magazine,* March/April 1990, p. 40.

133. Ibid.

134. Ibid.

135. Ibid, p. 41.

136. Gary Kamiya, "The Crack Epidemic: The Season of Hard Choices," *Crisis,* March 1989, p. 32.

137. Cecil Williams, Conference Welcoming Statement, April 1989.

138. Ibid.

139. Ibid.

140. Walter W. Morrison, "An Interview with Mayor Kurt L. Schmoke, Baltimore," *Crisis,* March 1989, p. 31.

141. Ibid.

142. Congressman George Crockett, "A 'Helping Hand' —Not Jail—for Drug Use," *The Detroit News,* 11 February 1990.

Chapter 3

1. Barbara Ommolade, "The Real Lives of Black Single Mothers," *Village Voice,* 15 July 1986.

2. Data provided by Congressional Research Services, July 1990.

3. Scott Armstrong, "U.S. Women's Prisons Overflow," *Christian Science Monitor,* 24 July 1990, pp. 1-2.

4. Ibid.

5. Report on Washington, D.C. television program *22:20,* May 1990.

6. Bill Gordon, "Crack's Incredible Cost to San Francisco," *San Francisco Chronicle Reprint,* 21 February 1989, p. 1.

7. Charles Rangel, "Born Hooked: Confronting the Impact of Perinatal Substance Abuse," Congressional Hearing Statement, Select Committee on Children, Youth, and Families, U.S. House of Representatives, 27 April 1989.

8. "The High Risk of Cocaine, Other Drugs," *ADAMHA News,* November/December 1989, p. 3.

9. Ron Harris, "Blacks Feel Brunt of Drug War," *Los Angeles Times,* 22 April 1990, p. A26.

10. Lynn M. Paltrow, Kary Moss, Judy Crockett, ACLU Testimony, House Subcommittee on Health and the Environment, 30 April 1990, p. 4.

11. Ibid; Paltrow, p. 6.

12. Stacie Alexander Fallon, "Drug Abuse Claims Babies of Addicts," *State Government News,* June 1990, p. 10.

13. Ibid; Paltrow et al., pp. 34-43.

14. Susan LaCroix, "Jailing Mothers for Drug Abuse," *Nation,* 1 May 1989, p. 585.

15. Ibid.

16. Jean Davidson, "Drug Babies Push Issue of Fetal Rights," *Los Angeles Times,* 25 April 1989, p. 3.

17. Ibid.

18. Ibid.

19. "Woman Convicted in Drug-Related Abuse of Unborn Son," *AP Wire,* 23 May 1990.

20. Ibid; Paltrow et al., p. 6.

21. Ibid; LaCroix, p. 585.

22. Louise Bishop, "Should Pregnant Women be Held Criminally Liable for Substance Abuse?" *State Government News,* June 1990, p. 22.

23. Ibid.

24. Ibid; Paltrow et al., p. 25.

25. Ibid; LaCroix, p. 586.

26. Ibid, p. 588.

27. Ibid; Paltrow et al., p. 8.

28. Ibid; Fallon, pp. 9-10.

29. Ibid; Paltrow et al., p. 26.

30. Ibid; Fallon, p. 10.

31. Ibid.

32. Cheri Collins, "When Parents Pay for Their Children's Mistakes," *State Government News,* June 1990, p. 20.

33. Ibid.

34. Ibid.

35. Michael Isikoff, "Crack Holds Many Inner-City Women in Its Grip," *Washington Post,* 20 August 1989, p. A18.

36. Gina Kolata, "In Cities, Poor Families Are Dying of Crack," *New York Times,* 11 August 1989, p. A10.

37. Juliet Ucelli and Dennis O'Neil, "The Cost of Drugs," *Forward Motion,* May 1990, p.5.

38. Ibid; Isikoff, p. A18.

39. Ibid.

40. Ibid; Fallon, p. 9; Catherine Foster, "Fetal Endangerment Cases Increase," *Christian Science Monitor,* 10 October 1989, p. 8.

41. Constance Garcia-Barrio, "Cocaine's Youngest Victims," *American Visions,* p. 16.

42. Indices: A Statiscal Index to District of Columbia Services, The District of Columbia Government, Office of Policy, p. 202.

43. Howard W. French, "For Pregnant Addicts, a Clinic of Hope," *New York Times,* 28 September 1989, p. B2.

44. Earl Ofari Hutchinson, *Crime, Drugs and African Americans,* Impact Publications, Inglewood, CA, 1990, p. 8.

45. Bill Gordon, "Crack's Incredible Cost to S.F.," *San Francisco Chronicle,* 21 February 1989, p. 4.

46. Ibid; Garcia-Barrio, p. 16.

47. Ibid; "The High Risk of Cocaine, Other Drugs," p. 3.

48. "HHS Releases Report on Crack Babies," *Focus,* National Council on Disability, Spring 1990, p. 1.

49. Ibid; Garcia-Barrio, p. 16.

50. Ibid; "The High Risk of Cocaine, Other Drugs," p. 3.

51. Ibid; Garcia-Barrio, p. 16.

52. "Study Examines Impact of Cocaine Exposed Babies on Welfare System," *The Drug Bulletin,* D.C. Office of Criminal Justice, May 1990.

53. Ibid, p. 1.

54. Ibid.

55. Ibid; "HHS Releases Report on Crack Babies," p. 1.

56. Nancy Gibbs, "Do You Want to Die," *Time,* May 1990, p. 59.

57. Ibid, p. 64.

58. Ibid.

59. Ibid.

60. Ibid; Rangel, p. 4.

61. Ibid, p. 6.

Chapter 4

1. "Pete Stark's Drug Test," *Washington Post,* 4 October 1989, p. A25.

2. Richard Cohen, "…And Keith Jackson's Trial," *Washington Post,* 19 December 1989, p. A23.

3. Lewis Lapham, "A Political Opiate," *Harpers Magazine,* December 1989, p. 43.

4. Barbara Gellman, "Mistrial Declared in Cocaine Arrest Near White House," *Washington Post,* December 22 1989, p. F5.

5. Jefferson Morley, "The Kid Who Sold Crack to the President," *City Paper,* 15 December 1989, p. 31.

6. David Hoffman, "George Bush: Promises to Keep," *Washington Post,* 20 December 1989, p. A25.

7. Richard L. Berke, "Democratic Reply on Drugs: Commit Another $2.2 Billion," *New York Times,* 13 September 1989.

8. *Treatment Works,* National Association of State Alcohol and Drug Abuse Directors, Washington, D.C., March 1990, p.v.

9. Ibid, p. iv.

10. *Great Decisions 1989,* Foreign Policy Association, New York, 1989, p. 85.

11. "National Drug Strategy Legislative Package Unveiled," *Monthly Narcotics Report,* Select Committee on Narcotics Abuse and Control, U.S. House of Representatives, May 1990.

12. Al Giordana, "Who Drafted the Press?," *Washington Journalism Review,* January/February 1990, pp. 23-24; Morris J. Blachman and Kenneth E. Sharpe, "The War on Drugs: American Democracy Under Assault," *World Policy Journal,* Winter 1989-90.

13. Terry Mitchell, "Boot Camp: Are They Coming for You?," *High Times,* March 1990, pp. 51-52.

14. Matthew Reiss, "Gulag for Drug Users: 'You Are Now the Property of…,'" *In These Times,* 20 December 1989.

15. Edward Jay Epstein, *Agency of Fear,* Putnam, New York, 1977.

16. Gerry Fitzgerald, "Dispatches from the Drug War," *Common Cause,* January/February 1990, p. 15.

17. Ibid, p. 17.

18. Ibid, p. 15.

19. "Nation's Richest Harvest: $41 Billion Just for Pot," *Omaha World Herald,* 14 September 1989, p. 39.

20. Ibid; Epstein.

21. Lee Feinstein, "Fighting the Next War," *Mother Jones,* July/August 1990, pp. 34-35.

22. Ibid.

23. Ibid; Berke.

24. "In One Pocket—Out The Other," *DSG Special Report 101-17,* Democratic Study Group, U.S. House of Representatives, 1990, p. 1.

25. Ibid.

26. Ibid.

27. Ibid.

28. Ibid.

29. John Dillan, "Bush Prepares to Launch Damage-Control Strategy," *Christian Science Monitor,* 5 September 1990, p. 1.

30. "Crackmire," *The New Republic,* 11 September 1989, p. 7.

31. Jacob Sullum, "Bill Bennett's Blinders," *Reason,* March 1990, p. 21.

32. Michael Isicoff, "Sharp-Tongued Intellectual Faces a Different Enemy," *Washington Post,* 13 January 1989, p. A17.

33. Ibid; Sullum, p. 22.

34. Ibid.

35. Mark Green and Gail MacColl, *Reagan's Reign of Error,* Pantheon, New York, p. 89; "Bennett: Drug Czar!?" *SCAR News,* Summer 1989, p. 12.

36. Ibid.

37. *The Lost Decade,* Democratic National Committee, November 1989, p. 11.

38. Ibid, p. 12.

39. "Rhetoric vs. Resources: 'Just Saying No' to Funds for Anti-Drug Efforts During the Reagan-Bush Administration," *DSG Special Report* No. 101-16, Democratic Study Group, U.S. House of Representatives, 2 September 1989, p. 12.

40. Ibid; Giordana, p. 21.

41. Michael Isikoff, "Bennett Exits Drug War With Potshots," *Washington Post,* 9 November 1990, p. A11.

42. Michael Isikoff, "Martinez Chosen Drug Policy Director," *Washington Post,* 1 December 1990, p. A4.

43. Ibid.

44. Jeff Goldberg, "How Our Heads of State Got High," *High Times,* April 1980.

45. Ibid.

46. "Drug Wars Past and Present," *Washington Post,* 5 September 1990.

47. Ibid.

48. Ibid.

49. Ibid., "Rhetoric vs. Resources: 'Just Saying No' to Funds for Anti-Drug Efforts During the Reagan-Bush Administration."

50. Gordon Witkin, "Inside the High-flying Pot Industry," *U.S. News & World Report,* 6 November 1989, p. 27.

51. *The Lost Decade,* Democratic National Committee, Washington, D.C., November 1989, p. 8.

52. Ibid.

53. Michael Isikoff, "From Justice Dept. to Drug Defendant," *Washington Post,* 23 August 1990, p. A17.

54. Barry Molefsky, "Economics of Drug Trafficking," *The Drug Problem,* CRS Review, November/December 1989, p. 9.

55. Select Committee on Narcotics Abuse and Control Report, U.S. House of Representatives, March 1989, p. 1.

56. *Drugs, Law Enforcement and Foreign Policy,* A Report of the Subcommittee on Narcotics, Terrorism and International Operations, U.S. Senate, 13 April, 1989, p. 25.

57. Select Committee on Narcotics Abuse Report.

58. "Does This War Make Sense?" *The Economist,* 21 January 1989, p. 35.

59. Michael Hedges, "Drug Czar Claims Gains," *Washington Times,* 6 September 1990, p. A1.

60. *Hard-Core Cocaine Addiction: Measuring—and Fighting—the Epidemic,* Staff Report, Senate Judiciary Committee, 10 May 1990; *Drug Use in America: Is the Epidemic Really Over?* Staff Study, 19 December 1990.

61. Ibid, Giordana.

62. Ibid, p. 23.

63. "Partnership for a Truth-Free America," *High Times,* September 1990, p. 10.

64. Lewis H. Lapham, "A Political Opiate," *Harper's,* December 1989, p. 45.

65. Martin A. Lee and Norman Solomon, *Unreliable Sources,* Lyle Stuart, New York, 1990, pp. 162-165.

66. Ibid; "Solitary for Quayle's Accuser," *New York Times,* 20 December 1988, p. 166.

67. Robert Lopez, "The Cold Hard Facts About Ice," *Business Today,* Fall 1989, p. 9.

68. Michael A. Lerner, "The Fire of 'Ice,'" *Newsweek,* 27 November 1989, pp. 37-38.

69. "Crack vs. Crank," *The Forensic Drug Abuse Advisor,* September 1989, p. 4.

70. Ibid; Lerner, p. 40.

71. Ibid, pp. 38-39.

72. Ibid; Lopez, p. 9.

73. Ibid; Lerner, p. 40.

74. Tom Sellers, "The Big Chill: A New 'Ice Age' Drug Horror Looms for the 1990s," *Prevention Research Review,* Winter 1990, pp. 9-11.

75. Ibid, p. 10.

76. Ibid; Lopez, p. 10.

77. Ibid; Sellers, p. 12.

Chapter 5

1. Michael Stone, "Coke Inc.: Inside the Big Business of Drugs," *New York,* 16 July 1990, pp. 26, 28.

2. "The General and the Cocaleros," *The Economist,* 9 December 1989, p. 40.

3. James Cook, "The Paradox of Anti-Drug Enforcement," *Forbes,* 13 November 1989, p. 110.

4. James Petras, "Drug-War Rhetoric Conceals Cartel's Capital Ties," *In These Times,* 15 November 1989, p. 16.

5. Ibid.

6. Christopher Marquis, "Peru Rejects $36 Million for Drug War," *Miami Herald,* 14 September 1990, p. A1.

7. "The World's Billionaires," *Forbes,* 24 July 1989, p. 123; Douglas Farah, "Drug Lord's Surrender a Victory for Columbia," *Washington Post,* 18 January 1991, p. A14.

8. Douglas Farah, "Cali's Quiet Cartel Becomes No. 1," *Washington Post,* 17 October 1990, p. A18.

9. "Cocaine's 'Dirty 300,'" *Newsweek,* 13 November 1989, p. 40.

10. Stephen J. Hedges, "The Dragon Lady's Revenge," *U.S. News & World Report,* 2 July 1990, p. 23.

11. Henrik Kruger, *The Great Heroin Coup,* South End Press, Boston, 1980. p. 177.

12. Gerald L. Posner, *Warlords of Crime,* Penguin Books, New York, 1988, p. xv.

13. Jill Walker, "Los Angeles Isn't Alone in Problems With Gangs," *Washington Post,* 3 July 1990, p. A10.

14. *Drug Trafficking: A Report to the President,* Office of the Attorney General, Department of Justice, Washington D.C., 1989, p. 33.

15. Ibid; Walker.

16. Katherine McFate, "Black Males and the Drug Trade," *Focus,* May 1990, pp. 5-6.

17. Carl S. Taylor, *Dangerous Society,* Michigan State University Press, East Lansing, MI, 1989, p. 99.

18. Hariette Survovell, "Posse Power," *Penthouse,* November 1989, p. 72.

19. Ibid; McFate.

20. Ibid.

21. *Money Laundering: A Banker's Guide to Avoiding Problems,* Office of the Comptroller of the Currency, Washington, D.C., December 1989, p. 2.

22. Jefferson Morley, "Contradictions of Cocaine Capitalism," *Nation,* 2 October 1989, p. 346; Stephen Labaton, "The Cost of Drug Abuse: $60 Billion a Year," *New York Times,* 3 December 1989, p. D6.

23. Ibid; *Drug Trafficking,* p. 37.

24. Stephen Brookes, "Drug Money Soils Cleanest Hands," *Insight,* 21 August 1989, p. 15.

25. Ibid; Morley, pp. 342-343.

26. Ibid, p. 344.

27. Peter Brewton, "S&L Probe Has Possible CIA Links," *Houston Post,* 4 February 1990, p. A1.

28. Margaret Carlson, "It's a Family Affair," *Time,* 23 July 1990, p. 23.

29. Rick Emrich, "S&Ls Funded Covert Operation," *Convergence,* Fall 1990, pp. 7-9; Ibid; Brewton.

30. Ibid.

31. Ibid.

32. Albert B. Crenshaw, "When Cash Talks, Some Merchants Are Listening," *Washington Post,* 21 September 1990, p. F1.

33. Ibid.

34. Michael Isikoff, "Their Man in Washington," *Washington Post National Weekly Edition,* 9 October 1989, p.10.

35. Steve Waidmen and Mark Miller, "The Drug Lawyers," *Newsweek,* 13 November 1989, p. 41.

36. Ibid.

37. Nicholas C. McBride, "US Chemicals Used to Process Illicit Drugs, *Christain Science Monitor,* 27 July 1988, p.3.

38. Ibid, p.6.

39. *Beyond Law Enforcement: Narcotics and Development,* The Panos Institute, February 1990, p. 3.

40. Buenaventura, Marcelo, *Victims of the Drug Trade,* unpublished paper, 1990.

41. Jack Herer, *The Emperor Wears No Clothes,* HEMP Publishing, Van Nuys, CA, 1990, p. 83.

42. Milton Moskowitz, Michael Katz, and Robert Levering, *Everybody's Business,* Harper & Row, San Francisco, 1980, pp. 227-228.

43. Ibid.

44. Carol Stevens, "These Will Make You Feel Better," *The Washingtonian,* April 1990.

45. Ibid; Herer, p. 28.

46. John Summa, "Eli Lilly," *Multinational Monitor,* June 1988.

47. Ibid.

48. Jo Ann Kawell, "The Magic Bullet," *NACLA Report on the Americas,* March 1989, pp. 18-19.

49. "Questions Answered About Prescription Drug Abuse," *Fact Sheet,* Washington Area Council on Alcoholism and Drug Abuse, p. 2.

50. Ibid.

51. Ibid; Stevens,

52. Ibid.

53. Ibid.

54. *The Politics of Drugs: Who Suffers, Who Deals, Who Profits,* Workers' World Library, December 1988, pp. 11-12.

55. Intricate Web, General Board of Ministries, The United Methodist Church, 1990, p. 12.

56. "An Uproar Over Billboards in Poor Areas," *New York Times,* 1 May 1989, p. D10.

57. Ibid.

58. Ibid.

59. Ken Smikle, "Post No Bills," *Emerge,* June 1990, pp. 25-26.

60. Ibid.

61. Ibid.

62. Ibid; Herer.

63. Ibid; *Intricate Web,* p. 12.

64. Jason DeParle, "Warning: Sports Stars May be Hazardous to Your Health," *The Washington Monthly,* September 1989.

65. Ibid; Herer.

66. "Native Americans Declare War on Alcohol," *Minority Newsletter,* Fall 1988 p. 11.

67. John Burgess, "Exports Fire Up Tobacco Industry," *Washington Post,* 16 December 1990, p. H1.

68. Blanchard Randall, IV, "Drug Testing for Illegal Substances," The Library of Congress, Congressional Research Service, 20 January 1987.

69. "Around the Nation," *The Counselor,* May/June 1990, p. 12.

70. WRC television special report on hair testing, Washington, D.C., June 1990.

71. "Relief by Mail," *The Economist*, 2 December 1989, p. 35.

72. "NY Educator Claims Link in Black Skin and Drugs," *Jet*, 10 April 1989, p. 37; "Scientist Reveals Blacks Who Fail Marijuana Tests Could Prove Drug Free," *Jet*, 19 May 1986, p. 10.

73. Ibid; McFate, p. 2.

Chapter 6

1. Louis Kraar, "The Drug Trade," *Fortune*, 20 June 1988, p. 27.

2. Frances Moore Lappé, Rachel Schuman, and Kevin Danaker, *Betraying the National Interest*, Grove Press, 1987, p.12.

3. Frederic Clairmonte and John Cavanagh, "Playing for High Stakes," *The National Reporter*, Spring 1987, p. 31.

4. Ibid, p. 31.

5. Kathy McAfee, "Why the Third World Goes Hungry," *Commonweal*, 15 June 1990, p. 380.

6. Merrill Collett, *The Cocaine Connection*, Foreign Policy Association Headline Series, 1989, p. 64.

7. Ibid; Clairmonte and Cavanagh, pp. 31.

8. *Economist*, 24 September 1988.

9. Ibid; Clairmonte and Cavanagh, p. 31.

10. Ibid; Collett, p. 65.

11. Ibid; Clairmonte and Cavanagh, p. 32.

12. Ibid; Collett, p. 65.

13. William Branigin, "Crack, LA-Style Gangs Trouble Torpid Belize," *Washington Post*, 19 September 1989.

14. Ibid.

15. Stuart Auervach, "Columbia Assails US Coffee Policy, *Washington Post*, 13 September 1990, p. C1.

16. Ibid.

17. Ibid.

18. Diane R. Bartz, "Colombia Takes Hit as Coffee Price Plunges," *In These Times*, 11 October 89, p. 5.

19. Ibid; Lappé, p. 27.

20. John Dillan, "Andeans Hooked on Drug Money," *Christian Science Monitor*, 7 March 90, p. A1.

21. *Intricate Web*, General Board of Global Ministries, The United Methodist Church, 1990, p. 41.

22. Ibid; Dillan.

23. Ibid, *Intricate Web,* p.9.

24. *Intricate Web,* p. 44.

25. *Beyond Law Enforcement: Narcotics and Development,* The Panos Institute, February 1990, p. 3.

26. Ibid, p. 6.

27. Joann Kawell, "Does The Pope Do Dope?" *NACLA,* March 1989, pp. 28-29.

28. William Branigin, "Trial in Camarena Case Shows DEA Anger at CIA," *Washington Post,* 16 July 1990, p. 1.

29. Alfred McCoy, *The Politics of Heroin in Southeast Asia,* Harper and Row, New York, 1972, p. 14.

30. Henrik Kruger, *The Great Heroin Coup,* South End Press, Boston, 1980, p. 3.

31. Ibid; Kruger, p. 14.

32. Brian Freemantle, *The Fix,* Tom Doherty Associates, Inc., New York, 1985, p. 32.

33. Hank Messick, *Of Grass and Snow,* p. 13.; Kruger, p. 33.

34. Ibid; Kruger, p. 33.

35. Ibid, p. 14.

36. Ibid, p. 89.

37. David Truong, "Running Drugs & Secret Wars," *Covert Action Information Bulletin,* No. 28, p. 2.

38. Ibid; Kruger, p. 130.

39. Ibid, p. 136.

40. Alfred W. McCoy, "Golden Triangle: Southeast Asia & the Failure of International Drug Interdiction," 1890-1990, unpublished paper, University of Wisconsin, Madison, 11-13 May 1990.

41. Robert J. Michaels, "The Market for Heroin Before and After Legalization," *Dealing With Drugs,* Pacific Research Institute, San Francisco, 1987, p. 313.

42. Ibid; Truong, p. 4.

43. Ibid.

44. Ibid; Kruger, pp. 123-124.

45. "The Contra-Drug Connection," *The Christic Institute,* November 1987, p. 6.

46. William Vornberger, "Afghan Rebels and Drugs," *Covert Action Information Bulletin,* No. 28, pp. 11-12.

47. Ibid; Vornberger, p. 11.

48. Ibid, p. 1.

49. David L. Westrate, *Heroin Trafficking in Southeast Asia, Southwest Asia and the Middle East,* presentation to the House Select Committee on Narcotics Abuse and Control, 1 August 1989, p. 8.

50. Ibid; Vornberger, p. 12.

51. Ibid, p. 12; William Roy Surrett, *The International Narcotics Trade: An Overview of Its Dimensions, Production Sources, and Organizations,* Congressional Research Services, 3 October 1988, p. 8.

52. James Rupert and Steve Coll, "U.S. Declines to Probe Afghan Drug Probe," *Washington Post,* 13 May 1990, p. A29.

53. Ibid.

54. Ibid.

55. Ralph Cwerman, "Lebanon's Valley of Drugs," *Washington Post,* 18 November 1990, p. C1-C2.

56. Ibid.

57. Frank Snepp and Jonathan King, "George Bush: Spymaster General," *Penthouse,* January 1991, p. 52.

58. The Christic Institute has waged a national campaign to expose the drug trafficking activities of the contras. See their Special Report, *The Contra-Drug Connection.*

59. Jonathan Marshall, "Drugs & U S Foreign Policy," *Dealing With Drugs,* Pacific Research Institute, 1987, p. 166.

60. "The Drug Cartel: Beating the Rap," *The Washington Spectator,* 15 August 1989, p. 2.

61. "Oliver North & Co. Banned From Costa Rica," *Extra!* October/November 1989, p. 1.

62. Ibid.

63. Oliver North, "Waging War: A Community-based Frontal Assault on Society's Ultimate Fatal Attraction," *New Dimensions,* February 1990, p. 76.

64. Ibid; *Great Decision 1989,* pp. 86-87.

65. *Drugs, Law Enforcement and Foreign Policy,* a report of the Subcommittee on Narcotics, Terrorism and International Operations, U.S. Senate, 13 April 1989, p. 241.

66. Ibid, pp. 216-217.

67. Ibid, p. 230.

68. Ibid, p. 239.

69. Elaine Shannon, *Desperados,* Penguin Books, New York, 1988, p. 491; Joel Bleifuss, "In Short," *In These Times,* 10 to 16 January 90, p. 4.

70. Ibid, Snepp and King, p. 86.

71. Ibid, *Drugs, Law Enforcement and Foreign Policy,* a report of the Subcommittee on Narcotics, Terrorism and International Operations, pp. 246-247.

72. Ibid, p. 223.

73. Ibid, p. 240.

74. Ibid, p. 241.

75. Ibid, p. 241.

76. Ibid, pp. 238-239.

77. Jonathan Alter, "For Bush, the Best of a Bad Bargain," *Newsweek,* 1 January 1990, p. 23.

78. Ibid, *Drugs, Law Enforcement and Foreign Policy,* a report of the Subcommittee on Narcotics, Terrorism and International Operations, p. 245.

79. Ibid, pp. 253-254.

80. Ibid, pp. 250-251.

81. Ibid, p. 238.

82. Ibid; Alter, p. 23.

83. "Censored News: Drug Links of Panama's New Rulers," *Extra!* January/February 1990, p. 5.

84. Ibid.

85. Ibid.

86. Jane Hunter, *The Israeli Connection: Israeli Involvement in Paramilitary Training in Colombia,* Arab American Institute, Washington, D.C., 1989, pp. 2-5.

87. Ibid.

88. Jane Hunter, "Arms Sold to Cocaine Cartel Through Antigua and Barbuda," *Israeli Foreign Affairs,* May 1990, pp. 1, 4-6.

89. Ibid.

90. Mort Rosenblum, "Hidden Agendas," *Vanity Fair,* March 1990, p. 116.

91. Ibid, p. 106.

92. Ibid, p. 102.

93. Ibid, p. 114.

94. Ibid, p. 116.

95. Ibid, p. 114.

96. Ibid, p. 114.

97. Ibid, p. 116.

98. Ibid, p. 118.

99. Ibid; William Branigin, "Trial in Camarena Case Shows DEA Anger at CIA," *Washington Post,* 16 July 1990, p. 1.

100. Ibid.

101. Ibid.

102. Ibid.

103. "CIA Used Drug Ranch in Training, Report Says," *Washington Post,* 5 July 1990.

104. Ibid.

105. Gen. A. M. Kotlyarov, "Drug Abuse Control in the USSR," *The Police Chief,* August 1990, pp. 22-26.

106. Ibid.

107. Ibid.

108. Jack Herer, *The Emperor Wears No Clothes,* Queen of Clubs Publishing, Van Nuys, CA, 1990, p. 57.

109. Ibid, p. 57-60.

110. Ibid; Kotlyarov, p. 22.

111. Ibid.

112. Karen Wald, "Drug/Corruption Scandal Shakes Cuba," *Frontline,* 28 August 1989, p. 1.

113. *End of the Cuban Connection,* José Marti Publishing House, Havana, Cuba, 1989, p. 314.

114. "Does Black Africa Have a Drug Abuse Problem?" *Capital Spotlight,* 26 July 1990, p. 9.

115. Ibid.

116. Memorandum of Understanding Between the Federal Military Government of the Federal Republic of Nigeria and the Government of the United States of America, Lagos, Nigeria, 21 March 1990.

117. Yvonne Roberts, "To the Slaughter," *New Statesman & Society,* 13 October 1989, pp. 10-11.

118. "The United Nations and Illicit Narcotics Control," *Emmes Executive Memo,* April 1990.

119. Ibid.

120. "The Cartagena Summit," Columbia News Report, Government of Columbia, Spring 1990, pp. 1-4.

121. Ibid.

122. See Jo Ann Kawell, "Going to the Source," *NACLA,* March 1989 for details on the impact of U.S. drug policies in Peru.

123. "In Short," *In These Times,* 11 to 17 October 1989, p. 5.

124. Ibid; Marshall, p. 154.

125. Ibid, p. 150.

126. Julio Godoy and Barbara Schulte, "Fighting Mythical Traffic," *Third World,* p. 55.

127. Gerald L. Posner, *Warlords of Crime,* Penguin Books, New York, 1988, p. 184.

128. Lance Gay, "Is There a Dutch Lesson on Drugs?" *Washington Times,* 23 January 1990, p. A11.

129. Ibid.

Chapter 7

1. Constance Green, *The Secret City: A History of Race Relations in the Nation's Capital,* University Press, Princeton, NJ, 1967, p. vii.

2. Neil Spitzer, "A Secret City," *Wilson Quarterly,* New Year's 1989, p. 102.

3. Ibid, p. 109.

4. Sam Smith, *Captive Capital, Indiana University Press* Bloomington, IN, 1974.

5. Walda Katz Fishman, Jerome Scott, Ralph C. Gomes, and Robert Newby, "The Politics of Race and Class in City Hall," *Research in Urban Sociology, Volume I,* Jai Press, 1989, pp. 135-137.

6. *Indices: A Statistical Index to District of Columbia Services, The District of Columbia Government, Office of Policy* July 1990, p. 187.

7. Ibid; Spitzer, p. 112.

8. David Shribman and Joe Davidson, "Many in Washington Now Find Drug War Isn't a Distant Affair," *Wall Street Journal,* 14 April 1989, p. A8.

9. Associates for Renewal in Education, *City of Magnificent Intentions,* Intac, Washington, D.C., 1983, p. 162.

10. Ibid; Spitzer, p. 103.

11. Ibid; Smith, p. 167.

12. Jeremiah O'Leary, "When Good Ol' Boys Ran the City, It Wasn't the Good Old Days," *Washington Times,* 14 July 1989, p. B4.

13. Ibid, Smith, p. 245.

14. Ibid, Associates for Renewal in Education, p. 518.

15. Brian Kelley, "Home Rule," *Regardies,* May 1989, p. 60.

16. *Washington Post,* 28 November 1989, p. A1.

17. Ibid; Kelley, p. 61.

18. Dennis Desmond interview with Acie Byrd, Washington, D.C., 18 October 1990.

19. Dennis Desmond interview with Josephine Butler, Washington, D.C., 16 October 1990.

20. Ibid; Dennis Desmond interview with Acie Byrd.

Chapter 8

1. Edward Jay Epstein, *Agency of Fear*, G.P. Putnam's Sons, New York, 1977, p. 73.

2. D.F. Musto, "The History of Legislative Control Over Opium, Cocaine and Their Derivatives," *Dealing With Drugs*, Pacific Research Institute, San Francisco, 1987, p. 45.

3. Ibid, p. 55

4. Clarence Lusane interview with Marcellus Boston, Washington, D.C., April 1990.

5. Thomas Bell, "Once the 'Queen' of Washington's Underworld, Odessa Madre Dies Penniless," *Washington Post*, 8 March 1990.

6. Courtland Milloy, "The Life and Times of the Queen of Washington's Underworld," *Washington Post Magazine*, 23 September 1980.

7. Ibid; "Queen of D.C. Underworld Dies," *Capital Spotlight*, 1 March 1990.

8. Ibid; Milloy.

9. Ibid.

10. Ibid, Bell.

11. Ibid.

12. Clarence Lusane interview with Napoleon "Nap" Turner, Washington, D.C., 8 August 1990 and 12 September 1990.

13. Clarence Lusane interview with Joseph Wright, Washington, D.C., 8 January 1990.

14. Clarence Lusane interview with Marcellus Boston, Washington, D.C., 6 April 1990; Harry Jaffe and Bob Rast, "Mobbed Up," *Regardies*, November 1989, p. 112.

15. *The Extent of the Drug Problem in the National Capital*, 1969 Congressional Hearings, p. 20.

16. Sterling Tucker, "Drugs: Everywhere All the Time," *Washington Star*, 11 July 1971.

17. Clarence Lusane interview with Metropolitan Police "undercover" officer, Washington, D.C., 18 April 1990.

18. Ibid; *The Extent of the Problem*, p. 20.

19. Mike Folks and Jim Keary, "Edmond Linked to Mob Family," *Washington Times*, 20 November 1989.

20. Robert DuPont and Richard N. Katon, "Development of a Heroin-Addiction Treatment Program," *JAMA*, 24 May 1971, p. 1320.

21. Robert DuPont and Richard N. Katon, "Physicians and the Heroin Addiction Epidemic," *Modern Medicine*, 28 June 71.

22. Ibid; *The Extent of the Problem*, p. 11.

23. Clarence Lusane interview with Joseph Wright, Wahsington, D.C., 7 January 1990; Washington Area Council on Alcoholism and Drug abuse (ACADA) Summary "Easter v. D.C. No. 19365," 1989.

24. Ibid; DuPont and Katon, "Development of a Heroin-Addiction Treatment Program," p. 1321.

25. Ibid.

26. Ibid; *The Extent of the Problem,* p. 28.

27. *Washington Star,* 9 November 1969; Clarence Lusane interview with Metropolitian Police "undercover" officer, Washington, D.C. 18 April 1990.

28. Ibid; *Washington Star* 9 November 1969.

29. Clarence Lusane Interview with Ron Clark, Washington, D.C., 12 July 1990.

30. John Holahan, *The Economics of Drug Addiction and Control in Washington, D.C.: A Model for Estimation of Costs and Benefits of Rehabilitation,* A Special Report by the Office of Planning and Research, Washington, D.C., November 1970.

31. Ibid; Epstein, p. 71.

32. *Washington Post,* 23 February 1969

33. Ibid, Epstein, p. 73.

34. Ibid, p. 77.

35. Ibid, p. 126.

36. James Grady, "D.C.'s Heroin War," *City Paper,* 24 to 30 June 1983.

37. Courtland Milloy and Linda Wheeler, "Washington's Other Industry: Heroin—The Traffic Is Heavy and Wide Open," *Washington Post National Weekly Edition,* 8 April 1985.

38. Ibid.

39. Ibid.

40. Ibid.

41. Ibid; Grady.

42. Ibid; Milloy and Wheeler.

43. Ibid.

44. Ibid; Grady.

45. Ibid.

Chapter 9

1. "Oliphant's Washington," *Regardies,* May 1989, p. 31.

2. William Raspberry, "The Verdict for Barry and the Verdict for the City," *Washington Post ,* 12 August 1989, p. C1.

3. See, for example, Michael V. O'Neal, "The Barry Bust and Our Leaders," *Big Red News* , 27 January 1990, p. 3.

4. Dennis Desmond and Clarence Lusane interview with Judge Reggie Walton, Washington, D.C., 4 October 1990.

5. Tracie Reddick, "Gangland Killings in D.C. Emulate Capone-Era Style," *Washington Times* , 31 August 1989, p. A1.

6. Some criminologists and police officers attribute the violence to a gang struggle over a shrinking drug market. Gabriel Escobar, "D.C. Homicides, at 436, Set 3rd Straight Record," *Washington Post* , 24 November 1990, p. A1.

7. *Drug Abuse and Crime* , Office of Criminal Justice Plans and Analysis, District of Columbia government, December 1989, p. 24.

8. Ibid.

9. Statistical Index for 1989, Government of the District of Columbia, p. 231.

10. Lynne Duke, "Drugs Are a Shadowy Force in D.C. Area's Economy," *Washington Post* , 19 July 1989, p. A1.

11. Peter Reuter, John Haaga, Patrick Murphy, and Amy Praskac, *Drug Use and Drug Problems in the Washington Metropolitan Area* , Rand Study, Santa Monica, CA, July 1988, p. v.

12. Ibid, Drug Abuse and Crime, p. 6.

13. *Drug Abuse and Crime—1989 Statistical Year-End Update* , Office of Criminal Justice Plans and Analysis, District of Columbia Government, December 1989, p. 1.

14. Ibid, *Drug Abuse and Crime* , p. 6.

15. Ibid; Reuter, Haaga, Murphy, and Praskac, p. vi.

16. Ibid; *Drug Abuse and Crime* , pp. 5-6.

17. Ibid, p. 5.

18. Peter Reuter, Robert MaCoun, and Patrick Murphy, *Summary of Money from Crime: The Economics of Drug Dealing in Washington, D.C.* , Greater Washington Research Center, Washington, D.C., 1990, p. 2.

19. Ibid; Reuter, Haaga, Murphy, and Praskac, p. vi.

20. "N.Y., D.C. Tops for Cocaine Addiction," *USA Today* , 10 May 1990, p. 7A.

21. Ibid; *Drug Abuse and Crime* , p. 14.

22. Ibid; Reuter, MaCoun, and Murphy, p. 4.

23. Ibid; Duke, p. A1.

24. Charles Krauthammer, "Children of Cocaine," *Washington Post* , 30 July 1989.

25. Ibid, p. A1.

26. Reed Tuckson, Commissioner of Public Health, D.C. Government, testimony before the D.C. Committee on Human Services, 29 November 1989.

27. Ibid.

28. Ibid, Statistical Index for 1989, p. 187.

29. Ibid; Reuter, MacCoun, and Murphy, pp. 16-17.

30. Ibid, p. 3.

31. *Our Children, Our Future—Revitalizing the District of Columbia Public Schools, D.C. Committee on Public Education,* 1989, p. 41.

32. Joe Davidson, "How a 24-Year Old Reigned as a Local Hero Until His Arrest," *Wall Street Journal,* 13 November 1989, p. 1.

33. Elsa Walsh, "Rayful Edmond: A Mystery Worth Solving," *Washington Post,* 17 December 1989, p. B7.

34. Nancy Lewis, "Conviction Called 'Clear Message' to Youths," *Washington Post,* 7 December 1989, p. A20.

35. Sterling Tucker, "Press Statement" D.C. Government Office of Drug Control Policy, 13 April 1990.

36. Ibid; Reuter, MacCoun, and Murphy, p. v.

37. Dennis Desmond interviews with Steve Rickman, Office of Criminal Justice Plans and Analysis; and Richard Broughton, Northern Virginia Crack Task Force, Drug Enforcement Agency, 31 July 1990.

38. "The District's Year Under William Bennett's Plan, *Washington Post,* 13 April 1990, p. B4.

39. Sari Horwitz, "U.S. Anti-Drug Effort Called Wrong for D.C.," *Washington Post,* 16 December 1989. p. A1.

40. John E. Smith, "District's 'Attitude' on Drugs Criticized," *Washington Times,* 17 May 1990, p. B1.

41. District of Columbia Police Chief Issac Fulwood has been one of the critics of a strategy that relies almost exclusively on law enforcement.

42. Virginia Governor Douglas Wilder has also been critical of the enforcement emphasis of the federal government.

43. More to the point was that Bennett had become bored as the drug issue became less central to the news media and to federal policy makers. Neil A. Lewis, "Quitting, Bennett Blames Others for Work Undone," *New York Times,* 9 November 1990, p. A19.

44. Statement of the Executive Office of the Government of the District of Columbia, "Drug Control Policy—Overview of Operations," 1989, p. 1.

45. Associates for Renewal in Education, *City of Magnificent Intentions,* Intac, Washington, D.C., 1983, pp. 479-480.

46. Dennis Desmond interview with the District of Columbia Office of Drug Control Policy, 12 August 1990.

47. Sterling Tucker, "Statement on Behalf of the People of the District of Columbia," Washington, D.C., District of Columbia Drug Policy Office, 13 April 1990.

48. Courtland Milloy, "Fancy Cars Show No Dent in Drug Trade," *Washington Post* , 17 May 1990.

49. Adam Gelb, "Drug War Needs a General, Critics Say," *Atlanta Constitution* , 9 July 1990, p. B1.

50. Karen R. Taylor, "Community Patrol Finds Success Closing Doors on Crack Houses," *The Capital Spotlight* , 26 April 1990, p. 1.

51. Dennis Desmond interview with Jackie Davison, Director of the Strategy Teams, Office of District of Columbia Drug Control Policy, 24 July 1990.

52. Dennis Desmond interview with Kwesi Rollins, District of Columbia ADASA, 9 October 1990.

53. Ibid.

54. Ibid; Office of Criminal Justice Plans and Analysis, *Drug Abuse and Crime* , p. 17.

55. Ibid.

56. "The Muslims to the Rescue," *Ebony* , August 1989, p. 136.

57. Ibid.

58. DeNeen L. Brown "Residents Have Drug Sellers on the Run," *Washington Post* , 4 June 1989, p. C1.

59. Ibid.

60. DeNeen L. Brown, "Crime-Fighting Groups Find It's Not as Simple as Dialing 911," *Washington Post* , 13 August 1989, p. A18.

61. Benjamin L. Hooks, "The Broader Issue of the Barry Case," *Washington Post* , 22 July 1990, p. C7.

62. Roger Wilkins, "Getting to the Business of Blackness," *Washington Post* , 15 July 1990, p. B7.

63. Clara Germani, "Barry Trial Shows City's Divisions," *Christian Science Monitor* , 4 June 1990, p. 6.

64. Elsa Walsh, "Prosecutor Denies FBI Targeted Blacks," *Washington Post* , 28 July 1990, p. A11.

65. Editorial, "The Message of Marion Barry," *Washington Post* , 12 August 1990, p. C6.

66. Chris Booker, "No Winners Seen as Barry Trial Sows Divisions," *Guardian* , 1 August 1990, p. 8.

67. Richard Morin, "Most Residents Oppose Retrial, Barry Candidacy," *Washington Post* , 12 August 1990, p. A1.

68. Douglas Farah, "Verdict in Bogota Is Assailed," *Washington Post*, 12 August 1990, p. A15.

69. Ibid; Booker.

70. Nathan McCall and Mary Ann French, "The Trial in Black and White," *Washington Post*, 22 July 1990, p. C1.

71. Rene Sanchez, "Wilson Elevated to Chairman; Cropp, Mason Beat Barry," *Washington Post*, 7 November 1990, p. A31.

72. Editorial, "The Verdict," *The Metro Chronicle*, 10 August 1990, p. 2.

73. Ibid; Desmond and Lusane interview with Reggie Walton.

74. Ron Harris, "Blacks Take Brunt of War on Drugs," *Los Angeles Times*, 22 April 1990, p. A1.

75. Ibid; Gelb.

76. Andrea Ford, "Los Angeles Hopes to Qualify for Special Drug War Aid," *Los Angeles Times*, 7 September 1989, p. 18.

77. John K. Watters, "A Street-Based Model of AIDS Prevention for Intravenous Drug Users: Preliminary Evaluation," *Contemporary Drug Problems*, Fall 1987, p. 411.

78. Ibid; D.C. Committee on Public Education, p. 124.

79. Walter E. Fauntroy, "Addressing the Fiscal Crisis in the District of Columbia," campaign position paper, 1990, p. 9.

80. Service Employees International Union, Commercial Office Buildings in Washington, D.C.: Underassessed, May 1989, p. 6.

Chapter 10

1. William Raspberry, "Why Not Buy Up Peru's Coca Crop?" *Washington Post,* 29 September 1989.

2. *Beyond Law Enforcement: Narcotics and Development,* The Panos Institute, Alexandria, VA. February 1990, pp. 6-7.

3. Edward Jay Epstein, *Agency of Fear,* G.P. Putnam's Sons, New York, 1977, pp. 124-125.

4. Ibid.

5. Ibid.

6. "Bolivia, Peru Reject Use of Bugs in Cocaine Fight," *Los Angeles Times,* 22 February 1990.

7. Rhetoric vs. Resources: "Just Say No" to Funds for Anti-Drug Efforts During the Reagan-Bush Administration, Democratic Study Group Special Report 101-16, U.S. House of Representatives, 2 September 1989, p. 16.

8. Peter Reuter, "Can the Borders Be Sealed?" *The Public Interest,* Summer 1988, No. 92, p. 52.

9. Pete Stark, "Pete Stark's Drug Test," *Washington Post,* 4 October 1989, p. A25.

10. Ibid.

11. "Drugs & Our Communities: A Plan of Action," *The Progressive Review,* June 1989, p. 7.

12. Ibid, Reuter, p. 54.

13. Ibid, p. 55.

14. Carleton R. Bryant, "Price of Getting High is Getting Higher in D.C. Area, *Washington Times,* 20 September 1990, p. B4.

15. Daniel Klaidman, "Taking a Different Tack Against Drug Scrounge," *Legal Times,* 19 March 1990, p. 14.

16. Ibid; "Drugs & Our Communities: A Plan of Action," p. 7.

17. For a more complete listing of groups see Deborah Prothrow-Stith *Deadly Consequences,* Harper Collins Publishers, New York, 1991.

18. Clarence Lusane interview with Elsie Scott, 7 October 1990.

19. Ibid.

20. Intermediate Sancitons, GAO Report, September 1990, p. 46.

21. George L. Church, "Fighting Back," *Time,* 11 September 1989, p. 13.

22. Clarence Lusane interview with Karen Bass.

23. Jim Rua, *Treatment Works,* National Association of State Alcohol and Drug Abuse Directors, Washington, D.C., March 1990, pp. vi-vii.

24. Clarence Lusane interview with Ron Clark.

25. Vivian Rouson Gossett, *Alcohol and Drug Abuse in Black America,* Institute on Black Chemical Abuse, Minneapolis, MN, 1988.

26. *Methadone Maintenance,* GAO Report to the Chairman, Select Committee on Narcotics Abuse and Control, House of Representatives, March 1990.

27. Ibid; Rua, pp. vi-vii.

28. Ibid, pp. v-vi.

29. Ibid; Epstein, p. 248.

30. Ibid, p. 249.

31. Timothy Kirn, "Methadone Maintenance Treatment Remains Controversial Even After 23 Years of Experience," *JAMA,* 25 November 1988, p. 2971.

32. Stanton Peele, "Control Yourself," *Reason,* February 1990, pp. 23-25.

33. Michael Isikoff, "Drug Abuse Treatment Experts Warn Against Seeking a Panacea for Addiction," *Washington Post,* 20 August 1990, p. A5.

34. William Bennett, *Understanding Drug Treatment,* An Office of National Drug Control Policy White Paper, June 1990.

35. Ibid.

36. Ibid.

37. Karen Ann Coburn, "Treating Drug Addicts with Needles," *Governing,* March 1990, p. 18.

38. Ibid.

39. Ibid; Klaidman, p. 14.

40. Martin Tolchin, "2 Bush Aides at Odds on Giving Needles to Addicts," *New York Times,* 11 March 1989.

41. "New York City," *Public Employee,* January 1990, p. 9.

42. Ibid.

43. Ibid.

44. Maia Szalavitz, "Clean Needle Programs Flourishing in Northwest," *High Times,* September 1990, p. 26.

45. Ibid.

46. Ibid.

47. Ibid.

48. "AIDS Plagues New York Hookers," *Washington Times,* 7 April 1990, p. A3.

49. Jonathan Kozol, *Illiterate America,* Anchor Press/Doubleday, Garden City, NY, 1985, p. 4.

50. William Bennett, "Mopping Up After the Legalizers," *Washington Times,* 15 December 1989, p. F1.

51. "Voices for Legalization," *High Times,* March 1990, p. 35.

52. Dale Gieringer, "The Health Hazards of Marijuana," *Sinsemilla Tips,* Spring 1990, pp. 25-27.

53. "State-by-State Comparison of the Marijuana Laws," *High Times,* September 1990, p. 16.

54. Morton Mintz, "No Ifs, Ands, or Butts," *The Washington Monthly,* July/August 1990, p. 35.

55. Jason DeParle, "Warning: Sports Stars May Be Hazardous to Your Health," *The Washington Monthly,* September 1989, p. 36.

56. Ibid; Mintz.

57. "How Your Tax Dollars Are Spent," *Jobs With Peace Campaign Fact Sheet 1,* Jobs With Peace Campaign.

58. "Winners & Losers," *Jobs With Peace Campaign Fact Sheet 3,* Jobs With Peace Campaign.

59. "We Need Homes Not Bombs," *Jobs With Peace Campaign Fact Sheet 6,* Jobs With Peace Campaign.

60. *CBC The Quality of Life FY'90 Alternative Budget,* Executive Summary, Congressional Black Caucus, U.S. Congress, p. ii.

61. Ibid, p. ix.

62. Effective Tax Rates for Rich Plummet Under Bush Capitol Gains Plan, DSG Special Report 101-36, Democratic Study Group, U.S. House of Representatives, 25 September 1990.

63. Spencer Rich, "Capital Gains and the Widening Income Gap," *Washington Post,* 24 July 1990, p. A21.

64. Ibid.

65. Michele L. Norris, "Growing Up in a World of Crack," *Washington Post National Weekly Edition,* 11 to 17 September 1990, p. 9.

RESOURCE LISTINGS

Where to go for Help With a Drug Problem or for Information About Drugs

There are thousands of organizations that assist people in the United States with a problem or a question related to drugs. Some of these are federal, state, or local government organizations and some are private. In the case of the federal government, for example, many federal agencies have a drug program. This Appendix is a list of the main government and private groups, i.e., groups where information or referrals are made that incorporate all of the other agencies or groups. With respect to both the government and the private groups, an effort is made to identify those treatment groups, resource groups, and activist organizations which are culturally specific, and which philosophically view the drug crisis as a health issue rather than a criminal or moral deficiency. The reader should keep in mind that these groups are fairly fluid, transitory by nature, and represent a wide range of views about legalization, drug law enforcement, treatment, education, and prevention.

Federal Government

The United States Department of Health and Human Services (HHS) has a conglomerate of drug-issue organizations under its name. These are grouped under the Alcohol, Drug Abuse, and Health Administration component of DHS. They are:

The National Institute on Drug Abuse (NIDA)
5600 Fishers Lane
10A-54 Parklawn Building
Rockville, MD 20857
(800) 662-HELP (800) 662-4357

NIDA is the leading federal agency for drug abuse research. It sponsors and conducts research and disseminates its findings through various means. It operates a toll-free Drug Abuse Information and

Drug-Free Workplace (both listed above). See Chapter 5 for more discussion about NIDA.

The Office for Substance Abuse Prevention (OSAP)
5600 Fishers Lane
Rockwall II Building
Rockville, MD 20857
(301) 443-0373

OSAP is the leading federal agency for drug abuse prevention. It places special emphasis on programs and resources for groups, such as young people, considered to be at high risk for alcohol and other drug problems. It funds, supports, and monitors grants to various anti-drug efforts around the nation. This office also sends out materials and advisors. It also operates the:

National Clearinghouse for Alcohol and Drug Information
P.O. Box 2345
Rockville, MD 20852
(301) 468-2600

The National Clearinghouse is the federal resource center for information about alcohol and drug problems. Specific target groups for its services include community leaders, people working with youth, parents, health and human service providers, and individuals with substance abuse problems. Among other activities, the Clearinghouse prepares and distributes publications, provides reference and referral services, conducts literature searches, and lends films and videotapes to people. In addition, it supports and assists a network of more than 110 national organizations and state-level "Regional Alcohol and Drug Awareness Resource Centers," which are the leading centers of state information (and are listed by state in this appendix).

Drug Enforcement Administration (DEA)
Washington, D.C. 20537
(202) 307-7936

The DEA, which is part of the Department of Justice, is the main law enforcement agency for federal drug policies. It has a "demand reduction section" that works in cooperation with various groups, such as athletic coaches, and makes available a variety of publications and videos on the prevention of drug abuse.

Office of National Drug Policy
Executive Office of the President
Washington, D.C. 20500
(202) 673-2520

This is the office headed by the Director of National Drug Control Policy, known popularly as the "Drug Czar." It was formerly headed by William Bennett, who was appointed by the President and approved by the U.S. Senate. This office is responsible for establishing policies and direction for the nation's drug-fighting efforts. Former Florida Governor Robert Martinez is the current director.

Indian Health Service
Alcoholism and Substance Abuse Branch
Room 6A-53
5600 Fishers Lane
Rockville, MD 20857
(301) 443-4297

This organization states that it provides a "comprehensive health services delivery system for American Indians and Alaskan Natives with opportunity for maximum tribal involvement." The Service has identified alcohol and other drug use as the most significant health problem affecting Native American communities.

State Organizations

District of Columbia
Office of Criminal Justice Plans and Analysis
D.C. Center for Drug Information
717 14th Street, N.W.
Suite 500
Washington, D.C. 20005
(202) 727-6551

Disseminates data and information, and publishes drug-related special reports. The Office works to increase communication between District agencies and the public, and provides technical assistance and information to community groups and other agencies.

Pennsylvania
Multicultural Prevention Work Group
c/o Alleghany County MHMR
429 Forest Avenue
9th floor
Pittsburgh, PA 15219
(412) 355-4457

State agency with a multicultural-educational approach to drug abuse prevention.

Toll-Free Telephone Numbers
1-800-COCAINE
National Cocaine Hot Line
Refers the caller to treatment and rehabilitation clinics around the nation for people with substance abuse problems. Operated by the Psychiatric Institute of America.

1-800-662-HELP
National Institute on Drug Abuse hotline; refers to treatment and support centers around the nation.

1-800-843-4971
National Institute on Drug Abuse Workplace Helpline for employers establishing workplace drug abuse programs.

1-800-622-2255
National Council on Alcoholism referral and counseling.

1-800-223-0179
National Hepatitis Hot Line
Sponsored by the American Liver Foundation, this line gives referrals and will mail information.

1-800-444-6472
U.S. Department of Health and Human Services
Shares information and publications on chemical dependence issues for Black, Latino, Asian, and Native American populations.

1-800-333-1069
Tough Love
Makes referrals to local chapters of this organization of parents with children having a substance abuse problem.

State Agencies

Alabama
Division of Mental Illness and Substance
Abuse Community Programs
Department of Mental Health
P.O. Box 3710
Montgomery 36193
(205) 271-9209

Alaska
Office of Alcoholism and Drug Abuse

Department of Health and Social Services
Pouch H-05-F
Juneau 99811
(907) 586-6201

Arizona
Office of Comm. Behav. Health
701 East Jefferson
Suite 400A
Phoenix 85034
(502) 255-1152

Arkansas
Office on Alcohol and Drug Abuse Prevention
Donaghey Plaza North
P.O. Box 1437
Little Rock 7220-1437
(501) 682-6650

California
Department of Alcohol and Drug Programs
111 Capitol Mall
Suite 450
Sacramento 95814
(916) 445-0834

Colorado
Alcohol and Drug Abuse Division
Department of Health
4210 East 11th Avenue
Denver 80220
(303) 331-8201

Connecticut
Alcohol and Drug Abuse Commission
999 Asylum Avenue
Hartford 06105
(203) 566-4145

Delaware
Bureau of Alcoholism and Drug Abuse
1901 North DuPont Highway
Newcastle 19720
(302) 421-6101

District of Columbia
Health Planning and Development
1875 Connecticut Avenue, N.W.
Suite 836
Washington 20009
(202) 673-7481

Florida
Alcohol and Drug Abuse Program
Department of Health and Rehabilitative Services
1317 Winewood Boulevard
Tallahassee 32301
(904) 428-0900

Georgia
Alcohol and Drug Services Section
878 Peachtree Street, N.E.
Suite 318
Atlanta 30309
(404) 894-6352

Hawaii
Alcohol and Drug Abuse Branch
Department of Health
P.O. Box 3378
Honolulu 96801
(308) 548-4280

Idaho
Bureau of Substance Abuse and Social Services
Department of Health and Recovery Welfare
450 West State Street
Boise 83720
(208) 334-5935

Illinois
Department of Alcoholism and Substance Abuse
100 West Randolph Street
Suite 5-600
Chicago 60601
(312) 917-3840

Indiana
Division of Addiction Services
Department of Mental Health

117 East Washington Street
Indianapolis 46204

Iowa
Department of Public Health
Division of Substance Abuse and Health Promotion
Lucas State Office Building
Des Moines 50319
(515) 281-3641

Kansas
Alcohol and Drug Abuse Services
2700 West Sixth Street
Biddle Building
Topeka 666606
(913) 296-3925

Kentucky
Branch Division of Substance Abuse
Department for Mental Health
Mental Retardation Services
275 East Main Street
Frankfort 40621
(502) 564-2880

Louisiana
Office of Prevention and Recovery from Alcohol and Drug Abuse
2744 B Woodale Boulevard
Baton Rouge 70805
(504) 922-0730

Maine
Office of Alcoholism and Drug Abuse Prevention
Bureau of Rehabilitation
State House Station #11
Augusta 04333
(207) 289-2781

Maryland
State Drug Abuse Administration
201 West Preston Street
Baltimore 21201
(301) 222-6926

Massachusetts
Division of Substance Abuse Services
150 Tremont Street
Boston 02111
(617) 727-8614

Michigan
Office of Substance Abuse Services
Department of Public Health
3423 North Logan Street
P.O. Box 30035
Lansing 48909
(517) 335-8809

Minnesota
Chemical Dependency Program Division
Department of Human Services
Centennial Building
658 Cedar Street
St. Paul 55155
(612) 296-4410

Mississippi
Division of Alcohol and Drug Abuse
Department of Mental Health
State Office Building
1500 Woolford
Jackson 39201
(601) 359-1297

Missouri
Division of Alcohol and Drug Abuse
Department of Mental Heath
1915 South Ridge Drive
P.O. Box 687
Jefferson City 65102
(314) 751-4942

Montana
Alcohol and Drug Abuse Division
Department of Institutions
Helena 59601
(406) 444-2827

Nebraska
Division of Alcoholism and Drug Abuse
Department of Public Institutions
P.O. Box 94728
Lincoln 68509
(402) 471-2851, Ext. 5583

Nevada
Bureau of Alcohol and Drug Abuse
Department of Human Resources
505 East King Street
Carson City 89710
(702) 885-4790

New Hampshire
Office of Alcohol and Drug Abuse Prevention
Health and Welfare Building
Hazen Drive
Concord 03301
(603) 271-4627

New Jersey
Division of Alcoholism
129 East Hanover Street
Trenton 08625
(609) 292-8947
Division of Narcotic and Drug Abuse Control
129 East Hanover Street
Trenton 08625
(609) 292-5760

New Mexico
Substance Abuse Bureau
Behavioral Health Services Division
P.O. Box 968
Santa Fe 87504
(505) 827-0117

New York
Division of Alcohol and Alcohol Abuse
194 Washington Avenue
Albany 12210
(518) 474-5417
Division of Substance Abuse Services
Executive Park South

P.O. Box 8200
Albany 12203
(518) 457-7629

North Carolina
Alcohol and Drug Abuse Section
Division of Mental Health and Mental Retardation Services
325 North Salisbury Street
Raleigh 27611
(919) 733-4670

North Dakota
Division of Alcoholism and Drug Abuse
Department of Human Services
State Capitol/Judicial Wing
Bismarck 58505
(701) 224-2769

Ohio
Bureau on Alcohol Abuse and Recovery
Department of Health
170 North High Street
Columbus 43266-0586
(614) 466-3445
Bureau on Drug Abuse
Department of Health
170 North High Street
Columbus 43266-0586
(614) 426-7893

Oklahoma
Alcohol and Drug Programs
Department of Mental Health
P.O. Box 53277
Capitol Station
Oklahoma City 73152
(405) 271-7474

Oregon
Office of Alcohol and Drug Abuse Programs
301 Public Service Building
Salem 97310
(504 378-1163

Pennsylvania
Deputy Secretary for Drug and Alcohol Programs
Department of Health
P.O. Box 90
Harrisburg 17108
(717) 787-9857

Rhode Island
Division of Substance Abuse
Substance Abuse Administrations Building
Cranston 02920
(401) 464-2091

South Carolina
Commission on Alcohol and Drug Abuse
3700 Forest Drive
Columbia 29204
(303) 734-9520

South Dakota
Division of Alcohol and Drug Abuse
523 East Capitol
Pierre 57501
(605) 773-3123

Tennessee
Alcohol and Drug Abuse Services
Department of Mental Health and Mental Retardation
706 Church Street
Nashville 37219
(615) 741-1921

Texas
Commission on Alcohol and Drug Abuse
1705 Guadalupe Street
Austin 78701
(512) 463-5510

Utah
Division of Alcoholism and Drugs
150 West North Temple Suite 350
P.O. Box 2500
Salt Lake City 84110
(801) 538-3939

Vermont
Office of Alcohol and Drug Abuse Programs
103 South Maine Street
Waterberry 05676
(802) 241-2170, 241-1000

Virginia
Office of Substance Abuse Services
Department of Mental Health and Mental Retardation
P.O. Box 1797
109 Governor Street
Richmond 23214
(804) 786-3906

Washington
Bureau of Alcoholism and Substance Abuse
Department of Social and Health Services
Mail Stop OB-44W
Olympia 98504
(206) 753-5866

West Virginia
Division of Alcohol and Drug Abuse
State Capitol
Room 451
1800 Washington Street, East
Charleston 25305
(304) 348-2276

Wisconsin
Office of Alcohol and Other Drug Abuse
1 West Wilson Street
P.O. Box 7851
Madison 53707
(608) 266-3442

Wyoming
Alcohol and Drug Abuse Programs
Hathaway Building
Cheyenne 82002
(307) 777-7115, Ext. 7118

Guam
Department of Mental Health and Substance Abuse
P.O. Box 8896

Tamuning 96911
(671) 477-9704

Puerto Rico
Department of Anti-Addiction Services
Box B-Y, Rio Piedras Station
Rio Piedras 00928
(809) 764-3795

Virgin Islands
Division of Mental Health, Alcoholism and Drug Dependency
P.O. Box 520
St. Croix 00820
(809) 773-1992

American Samoa
Human Services Clinic
Public Health Services
Alcohol and Drug Programs
LBJ Tropical Medical Center
Pago Pago 96799
Trust Territories
Health Services
Office of the High Commissioner
Saipan 96950

National Private Organizations, Civic and Activist Groups, and Religious Organizations

This category encompasses private nonprofit organizations, as well as activist groups. Some of these are resource centers, some provide treatment and counseling, and some conduct political work. The intent of this list is not to list every such group in the nation, of which there are thousands, but rather to highlight the main centers.

American Civil Liberties Union (ACLU)
122 Maryland Avenue, NE
Washington, D.C. 20002
(202) 544-1681
ACLU is involved in numerous cases around the country protecting citizens from civil rights violations emanating from the administration's drug war.

American Council on Drug Education
204 Monroe Street, Suite 110
Rockville, MD 20850

(301) 294-0600
The Council is a national nonprofit membership organization whose mission is to discourage drug use through public education. It produces materials for various groups, such as teachers and health workers.

Business Alliance for Commerce in Hemp (BACH)
P.O. Box 71093
Los Angeles, CA 90071-0093
BACH's goal is to develop hemp-based enterprises, such as clothes-making, with legalized hemp (marijuana). It provides information and samples of products produced from legalized hemp.

Campuses Without Drugs, Inc.
National Office
2530 Holly Drive
Pittsburgh, PA 15235
(412) 731-8019
A national nonprofit organization devoted to drug problem prevention through education; it conducts training in counseling and produces materials for college campuses.

Christic Institute
1324 North Capitol Street
Washington, D.C. 20002
(202) 797-8106
The Institute is a nonprofit law and policy center with a focus on the larger social issues. It has done some excellent research on the connection between the intelligence community and drug trafficking.

Clergy for Enlightened Drug Policy (CEDP)
St. Luke's Methodist Church
Wisconsin Avenue and Calvert Street, NW
Washington, D.C. 20007
CEDP does drug education work within the church community. It views current drug policies as harmful and seeks reform.

COALESCE
131 Ponce de Leon, Suite 125
Atlanta, GA 30308
(404) 874-2273
This is a new, for-profit organization dedicated to the treatment of substance abuse problems from an African-American culturally specific perspective.

Coalition of DC Citizens for HEALTH
P.O. Box 1519
Washington, D.C. 20013-1519
This group advocates for a more humane drug policy.

Community Coalition for Substance
Abuse Prevention and Treatment
8500 South Broadway
Los Angeles, CA 90003
(213) 750-9087
The goal of the Community Coalition is to transform the crisis of substance abuse that characterize parts of the South Los Angeles community into effective action and community building by bringing together as many of sectors of the community as possible.

Cork Institute on Black Alcohol and Other Drug Abuse
Morehouse School of Medicine
720 Westview Drive, S.W.
Atlanta, GA 30310-1495
(404) 753-1780
Focuses on prevention and treatment of substance abuse among African-Americans. Educates heath workers, promotes culturally appropriate prevention and treatment models for black populations.

Drug Policy Foundation
4801 Massachusetts Avenue
Suite 400
Washington, D.C. 20016
(202) 895-1634
Outstanding source of information from an anti-drug-war perspective. Favors legalization in some instances.

Drug Reform Coalition
225 Lafayette Street, Suite 911
New York, N.Y. 10012
New York-based coalition of groups representing concerns associated with drugs, such as AIDS, urban violence, and "safe drugs," aimed at changing drug policy.

The Family Council on Drug Awareness
P.O. Box 71093
Los Angeles, CA 90071-0093
The Council works with families affected by the drug crisis. Its main objective is to provide accurate and reliable information.

The Fanon Institute
1621 East 120th Street
Los Angeles, CA 90059
(213) 563-5910
Conducts research and writes studies on the impact of substance abuse on minority groups.

HIV Center for Clinical and Behavioral Studies
722 W. 168th Street
New York, N.Y. 10032
(212) 740-7296
The Center is involved in developing progressive approaches to helping drug addicts who have contracted HIV/AIDS. It produces resource materials and is involved in community education about AIDS and drugs.

Institute for Advanced Study of Black Family Life
155 Philbert Street
Suite 202
Oakland, CA 94607
(415) 826-3245
Contact: Dr. Wade Nobles
Leading research center on the social impact of substance abuse on the African-American community.

Institute on Black Chemical Abuse
2616 Nicollet Avenue
Minneapolis, MN 55408
(612) 871-7878
Leading center providing information, referral, and treatment geared in particular to the African-American community. Sponsors occasional conferences.

Lincoln Hospital Acupuncture Program
349 East 140th Street
Bronx, NY 10454
(212) 993-3100
Substance abuse counseling for all ages. Provides acupuncture and herbs for detoxification on an outpatient basis.

Links Foundation, Inc.
1200 Massachusetts Avenue, N.W.
Washington, D.C. 20005
(202) 842-0123

The Links is a nonprofit, cultural, educational, and civic national organization of professional women dedicated to, among other civic goals, the prevention of drug abuse through value clarification and enhanced self-esteem. The Links has built strong ties among Black fraternal groups.

Multicultural Training Resource Center
1540 Market Street, Suite 320
San Francisco, CA 94120
(415) 861-2142

This multicultural nonprofit organization produces educational materials about the relation between drug use and AIDS, and other aspects of substance abuse.

Nation of Islam
"Dopebusters" Program
3784 Hayes Street, N.E.
Washington, D.C. 20019
(202) 388-6668

Sponsors anti-drug patrol and other services in a number of urban centers.

National Asian-Pacific American Families
Against Substance Abuse, Inc.
(headquarters)
6303 Friendship Court
Bethesda, MD 20817
301-530-0945
(west coast office)
2678 17th Avenue
San Francisco, CA 94116

Disseminates information, sponsors workshops, and provides prevention education services. Its major focus is in the Asian Pacific communities.

National Association of Black Substance Abuse Workers
Hamilton Grange Station
P.O. Box 201
New York, N.Y. 10031
(212) 234-1660

Provides a forum through which black alcohol and other drug abuse workers can influence policy in the field, whether at the state or national level. It targets the adult and the at-risk population.

National Association for Native American Children of Alcoholics
c/o Seattle Indian Health Board
P.O. Box 3364
Seattle, WA 98114
(206) 324-9360

Facilitates positive change in Native American communities; integrates effects of alcoholism with analysis of cultural oppression. Prevention education and training are provided.

National Black Organizations Against Alcohol and Drug Use
22 Chapel Street
Brooklyn, N.Y. 11201

Provides information and referral. Write for information.

National Coalition of Hispanic Health and Human
Services Organizations (COSSMHO)
1030 15th Street, N.W.
Suite 1053
Washington, D.C. 20005
(202) 371-2100

COSSMHO is the only national public health agency for Latinos. Its Alcohol and Substance Abuse Department provides research and demonstration projects geared to the nation's Latino community, but it does not provide direct services to individuals.

National Crime Prevention Council (NCPC)
1700 K Street, NW, 2nd floor
Washington, D.C. 20005
(202)393-7141

This private, non-profit receives most of its funding from the federal government. The symbol for its national anti-crime campaign is "take a bite out of crime." Drug prevention is seen as an integral part of its work. It produces educational kits geared to such populations as teenagers, teachers, and parents.

National Drug Information Center of Families in Action
2296 Henderson Mill Road, Suite 204
Atlanta, Georgia 30345
(404) 934-6364

The mission of the Center is to educate society about the dangers of drug abuse by disseminating accurate and timely information. It produces an abstract which summarizes recent articles from the medical profession and the news media on drug abuse topics.

National Drug Strategy Network
2000 L Street, NW
Washington, D.C. 20036
(202) 835-9075
The Network is a coalition of progressive drug education and reform groups. It produces publications, critiques of drug policy, and organizes in opposition to the punititve approaches of the drug war.

National Organization for the Reform
of Marijuana Laws (NORML)
1636 R Street, NW
Washington, D.C. 20009
(202) 483-5500
NORML is the major national organization fighting for the legalization of marijuana. It sponsors conferences, lobbies, and produces resource materials.

National Training Information Center
810 North Milwaukee
Chicago, IL 60622
(312) 243-3035
Supervises federal grants to communities fighting drugs, and helps in the organization of these communities.

Neighborhood Anti-Crime Center
Citizens Committee for New York City
3 West 29th Street
New York, N.Y. 10001
(212) 684-6767
Supports community movements against drugs and crime in city neighborhoods.

Oakland Community Organizations
3914 East 14th Street
Oakland, CA 93707
(415) 261-6440
A federation of organizations, principally low-income, focusing on drug prevention.

The Rand Corporation
1700 Main Street
Santa Monica, CA 90406-2138
(213) 393-0411

The Rand Corporation produces a number of well-researched studies of drug trafficking and usage, for example, in the District of Columbia.

Rap, Inc.
3451 Holmead Place, NW
Washington, D.C. 20010
(301) 490-9995
Rap is one of the oldest, therapuetic treatment centers/halfway houses on the East Coast. It's program is prinicpally geared towards blacks.

Self-Help for African People
Through Education Community Center
3815 Live Oak
Houston, TX 77004
(713) 521-0629
Develops a holistic, culturally-relevant, community-building program aimed at eliminating or reducing crime and drug abuse.

Washington Area Council on Alcoholism
and Drug Abuse, Inc. (WACADA)
1232 M Street, N.W.
Washington, D.C. 20005
(202) 682-1703
A voluntary citizens group focusing public attention and education and prevention of substance abuse.

INDEX

D

F

G

286

"narco terrorist"
  see drug dealer

N

Narcotics and Drug Research, Inc., 94

Narcotics Addiction Rehabilitation Center (NARC), 160

Narcotics Treatment Administration (NTA), 106, 160

Nation of Islam (NOI), 39, 40, 182-184

National Acupuncture Detoxification Association, 211

National Agrarian University (Peru), 99

National Association for the Advancement of Colored People (NAACP), 51, 103, 167

National Association for Hospital Development, 64

National Association for Perinatal Addiction Research and Education (NAPARE), 57, 62

National Black Political Assembly (1972) Gary, Indiana, 162

National Capital Area Civil Liberties Union, 159

National Commission on the Causes and Prevention of Violence, 27

"National Drug Control Strategy," 67, 116

National Drug Control Strategy Implementation Act of 1990, 70

National Drug Law Enforcement Agency (Nigeria), 133

National Drug Policy Board, 77, 79

National Endowment for the Humanities, 75

National Institute on Drug Abuse (NIDA), 45, 80, 81, 101, 106

National Narcotics Border Interdiction System (1983), 79

National Opinion Research Center, Chicago, Illinois, 15

National Organization for the Reform of Marijuana Laws (NORML), 77, 215

National Organization of Black Law Enforcement Executives (NOBLE), 206

national sovereignty, 4

National Urban League, 4, 51, 104, 179, 218

National Youth Survey (1976-1980), 23

National War College, 72

Naples, Florida, 97

nationalism, 111

Native Americans, 6, 21, 30, 103, 104

Nauru, 95

Nazis, 17

Navy (United States), 78

Nebraska, 206

Neighborhood Judicial Councils, 205

neighborhood watch, 185

Neonatal Abstinence Syndrome (NAS), 63

Netherlands, 137, 138

Nevada, 81

New Horizons
  see Coors

New Orleans, 95

Newark, 206

Newport News, Virginia, 206

New York City, 49, 50, 61, 81, 84, 90, 132, 141, 144, 157, 206

New York State, 60, 72

Nicaragua contras, 96, 97, 116, 121, 122, 123, 125, 128, 129

Niemann, Albert, 32

Niger, 132

Nigeria, 132, 133

Niggers With Attitude (NWA), 23

Nixon, Richard M., 71, 77, 153, 162, 203

Non-Smokers Rights Act (Canada), 216

NORAD, 72

Noriega, Manuel, 82, 116, 123, 124, 125, 126, 127, 128, 134

North Caucusus, 130

North America, 121

North, Oliver (Lt. Col.), 119, 120, 121, 122, 128

Norton, Eleanor Holmes, 151, 194

Norwich Eaton, 101

"Not On My Block," 179-180, 211

Novoflupan, 101

Q

R

About South End Press

South End Press is a nonprofit, collectively-run book publisher with over 150 titles in print. Since our founding in 1977, we have tried to meet the needs of readers who are exploring, or are already committed to, the politics of radical social change.

Our goal is to publish books that encourage critical thinking and constructive action on the key political, cultural, social, economic, and ecological issues shaping life in the United States and in the world. In this way, we hope to give expression to a wide diversity of democratic social movements and to provide an alternative to the products of corporate publishing.

Through the Institute for Social and Cultural Change, South End Press works with other political media projects—*Z Magazine;* Speak Out!, a speakers bureau; the Publishers Support Project, and the New Liberation News Service—to expand access to information and critical analysis. If you would like a free catalog of South End Press books or information about our membership program—which offers two free books and a 40% discount on all titles—please write to us at South End Press, 116 Saint Botolph Street, Boston, MA 02115.

Other titles of interest from South End Press:

Breaking Bread
Insurgent Black Intellectual Life
bell hooks and Cornel West

Yearning
Race, Gender, and Cultural Politics
bell hooks

Race, Gender, and Work
A Multi-cultural Economic History of Women in the United States
Teresa Amott and Julie Matthaei

State of Native America
Genocide, Colonization, and Resistance
edited by Annette Jaimes